The Verbum Book of Electronic Page Design

Prentice Hall

New York London Toronto Sydney Tokyo Singapore

First published in 1990 in North America by M&T Publishing, Inc., 501 Galveston Drive, Redwood City, CA 94063-4728, USA, and co-published for sale outside North America by Prentice Hall International (UK) Limited, 66 Wood Lane End, Hemel Hempstead, Hertfordshire, HP2 4RG, England, a division of Simon & Schuster International Group.

British Library Cataloging-in-Publication Data available from Prentice Hall International

Library of Congress Cataloging-in-Publication Data
Gosney, Michael
    Electronic page design / by Michael Gosney, Linnea Dayton
    p. cm.
Includes bibliographical references and index.
ISBN 0-13-248279-7: $29.95
    1. Electronic publishing. 2. Printing, Practical — Layout — Data Processing. 3. Desktop publishing.
    I. Dayton, Linnea, 1944–
    II. Title.
    Z286.E43G67 1990
    686.2'2544- -dc20   90-7565
                                                              CIP

93 92 91 90   4 3 2 1

Produced by The Gosney Company, Inc. and Verbum Magazine
670 Seventh Avenue, Second Floor
San Diego, CA 92101
(619) 233-9977

Book and cover design: John Odam
Production Manager: Martha Siebert
Production Assistants: Doug Moore, Jonathan Parker
Administrative Manager: Jeanne Lear
Technical Graphics Consultant: Jack Davis
Proofreading, research: Audrey Nimura, Valerie Bayla

The Verbum Book of
Electronic Page Design

Michael Gosney ▪ Linnea Dayton

Prentice Hall

Also by Linnea Dayton and Michael Gosney
The Verbum Book of PostScript Illustration
(with Janet Ashford)
M&T Books/Prentice Hall, 1990

**This book
is dedicated to those visionaries
who build bridges between the Arts and Sciences.**

Contents

Welcome to the *Verbum Book of Electronic Page Design.* We hope you'll enjoy using this book as much as we enjoyed putting it together. Not that it wasn't a lot of hard work. Electronic page design is a big subject, and developing an instructional graphic design book that covers the leading microcomputer platforms and page layout programs was no small task. It should pay off, though — by empowering you to make better use of these remarkable new tools.

The first two chapters of the book will give you an overview of electronic page design technology and the powerful products that make it all happen. The following chapters take you step-by-step through the development of real-world design projects by talented designers. Each chapter introduces the artist and project, and re-creates both the artist's creative thought processes and the technical steps. At the end of each chapter is a "Portfolio" of other page design examples by the artist, with brief descriptions of each.

You'll find sidebars and tips throughout the book. The sidebars provide additional information on topics treated in the chapters. ▮ *Tips are introduced by this vertical symbol, and they appear in italics. They provide the kind of specific, practical tricks and techniques you can put to work right away.*

An extensive "Gallery" of exemplary electronic page design samples follows the project chapters. These samples are from leading designers who have had extensive experience with the new design systems. We've chosen works that represent not only excellent design, but effective and innovative use of the electronic tools. At the end of the book, an "Appendix" lists useful products and services. The "Production Notes" section provides details on the development of the book itself.

Origins of the electronic design revolution

Where did the electronic design world of the '90s come from? We could go back to the late 1970s and the emergence of mainframe- or minicomputer-based electronic page production systems. But why bother? Those systems, optimized for production of large, standardized publications — automobile repair instruction manuals and corporate employee handbooks, for instance — had little to do with *design*. The real beginning of the technology we're working with came in 1985. It was in that year that we witnessed the convergence of three amazing pieces of technology: the Apple Macintosh personal computer, the Apple LaserWriter laser printer and the Aldus PageMaker program. The combination of the Mac's graphic interface, the

LaserWriter's high-resolution output and PageMaker's powerful page design capabilities opened a new dimension. We could bring text and graphics files right into PageMaker, arrange them on the page, add design elements, and print out a perfect page with good-looking type, crisp lines and fine screens. The marketing people called it "desktop publishing." To those of us in the art and design fields, this system seemed to represent something more than publishing. It seemed like some kind of a revolution.

From our current vantage point, it's clear that it was the start of a new age. Since that time, we've seen the emergence of a major new market for personal computers, and the transformation of traditional graphic design, typesetting and color separation industries. Desktop publishing systems —and the sophisticated graphic design tools that come with them — have made their way into most major corporations, where they are now used to produce all manner of reports, manuals, newsletters and other publications that previously were handled by traditional typesetting and graphic production services. Small businesses are producing ad layouts and flyers.

Graphic designers, mostly independent designers initially, and then larger design firms and advertising agencies, have converted to the new tools. They're using the personal computer not only for design and camera-ready art production, but also for custom type design, illustration, photo retouching and related specialized tasks. Typesetters are now "imagesetters," delivering finished pages with illustrations and photos in place rather than the traditional type "galleys." Manufacturers of million-dollar color separation systems are adapting to the technology popularized by $8000 desktop publishing systems.

Creativity squared

After five years of rapid — sometimes exasperating — evolution, the field of electronic page design is firmly established. A plateau has been reached with hardware and software standards, services and support networks. During the next few years, we don't anticipate quantum leaps that will make the existing standards obsolete; rather, we expect steady refinements of existing tools, added speed and power in hardware platforms and progressive innovations in high-end processes such as color separation.

Now that the medium has established parameters, we can concentrate on using the tools for great design. Mastering the technical production aspects, obviously, is important. But perhaps the most significant benefit of electronic design systems is an enhancement of the creative process. When designers first encounter a pc system, they usually are most impressed by the amazing visualization capabilities: they can import text and manipulate type right on screen; scan in photos and then size and position them, even add special-effects screens; with the benefit of a color monitor, they can experiment with Pantone or process color, changing color combinations with the click of a mouse. Instant hardcopy proofs in black-and-white or full color take the process a step further, changing the definition of a "comp."

This ability to experiment with instant, tight visual feedback has allowed designers to spread their creative wings. It has also allowed many who have little design experience to become "design-literate" very quickly. But perhaps the most exciting result of designing on pc's is the new frontier that many of the artists featured in this book have helped pioneer — totally new design ideas that have been made possible by the computer's unique capabilities. In the world of electronic design — after all the technology, production and lifestyle changes are assimilated — we're back to the basic pursuit of doing good, creative work. It is our hope that this book will provide both information and inspiration to help you achieve that goal.

What is *Verbum*?

Verbum, the Journal of Personal Computer Aesthetics, is a magazine dedicated to exploring the aesthetic and human aspects of using microcomputers. Founded in 1986 by a group of artists and writers who had the good fortune to be involved with the early electronic design tools, the journal has tracked the evolution of electronic design and illustration tools, contributing the artist's perspective (and conscience) to an industry that has at times been unbalanced in its commercial and technical emphasis.

Each issue of *Verbum* has served as an example of the latest desktop publishing tools, beginning with the early issues' laser-printed camera-ready art on up to today's digital four-color separations. Through the development of the magazine, we've helped to galvanize the community of advanced artists, programmers and industry visionaries who have pushed the new frontier forward. As an ongoing experiment, *Verbum* has covered not only electronic design, but illustration, fine art, typography, digitized imaging, 3D graphics, animation, music and even the new realm of interactive multimedia. The Verbum Electronic Art and Design Series was conceived as a way to bring *Verbum's* accumulated resources into a practical, instructional context.

A few acknowledgments

The Verbum Book of Electronic Page Design and the entire *Verbum* book series have involved the helpful efforts of many people, too many to mention here. But we would like to give special thanks to the contributing artists who committed that most precious resource to the project — time. Also, we would like to thank our literary agent, William Gladstone; our patient editor at M&T Books, Brenda McLaughlin; our service bureau here in San Diego, Central Graphics; and the many software and hardware companies who helped keep us up-to-date on products. Lastly, we'd like to thank our *Verbum* readers, who keep inspiring us to push the envelope just a little further.

C H A P T E R   1

An Overview

Figure 1. Designing pages. This full-color brochure for a California antismoking campaign aimed at sixth graders was produced (from concept to press) in 10 days. Designer Scott Leyes of QuickType and Design of Anaheim, California used QuarkXPress 2.12 on the Macintosh. Each page was produced as a single piece of film, with illustrations and photos in place and no stripping required. QuickType's bid for the project was less than one-fifth the next lowest (conventional design and production) bid. The client was pleased with the product, and the brochure was effective in getting the attention of sixth graders.

Any time you're called upon to arrange more than one block of text or one photo or one illustration in a two-dimensional space, you're looking at a page design task. Whether you set out to design a book, an ad, a brochure, a poster, a manual or even a layout for a three-dimensional package, your goal is to assemble the components into a pleasing, functional design and then fine-tune the relationships between them — spec'ing type, editing text, cropping and resizing illustrations, aligning all the elements — to produce comps and eventually, finished camera-ready art (Figure 1). *Page layout software* running on a microcomputer provides a way to free these tasks from the limitations imposed by the physical world of ruling pens, X-acto knives, waxers and tissue overlays, to experiment with page design and often to follow a concept all the

way through the *desktop publishing* (*DTP*) process. *WYSIWYG* (what-you-see-is-what-you-get) capabilities of the software-hardware combinations provide a good on-screen rendering of what the final printed piece will look like. Proofs and even final film for making printing plates can be generated without having to wait for type to be set, stats to be made or film to be stripped together. Page layout programs let the graphic designer:

- Create pages in a variety of sizes
- Assemble documents of various lengths, in black-and-white or in color
- Work with an accurate on-screen view (more and more accurate lately) of what the finished document will look like
- Work on a single page at a time, or view an entire spread
- Set up master elements such as margins, column guides, folios (page numbers) and running heads, to appear automatically on every page of a publication
- Automatically lay out evenly spaced columns
- Choose from a vast library of typefaces, sizes and styles to establish a set of type specifications that can be quickly applied to paragraphs within the document, with the potential for professional typeset quality
- Set the starting point for a block of text, which then flows automatically from column to column or page to page throughout the document, jumping over, wrapping around or overprinting graphic elements according to the designer's specification

Figure 2. Putting the pieces together. Text from word processors, graphics from illustration programs, and scanned photographs can be combined within a page layout program, where more graphic elements and display type can be added. After fine tuning of the design, proof prints can be produced, final corrections made, and the file output on separated film for making printing plates.

- Edit text, which then reflows automatically, to seamlessly incorporate the editing changes
- Integrate drawings, scanned photos and blocks of text created in other programs
- Crop, enlarge or reduce photos and illustrations placed on the page
- Draw simple graphics, borders and rules with the native graphics tools
- Fill drawn objects with patterns and tints
- Manually or automatically align text and graphics
- Print documents at full size or magnified or reduced, with imported illustrations in place, or as quickly printed proofs with markers to indicate where the graphics will go
- Print a set of thumbnail sketches of the publication
- Print entire page layouts, with type and graphics in place, directly to camera-ready paper or plate-ready film, in many cases as spot color or process color separations

Putting the pieces together

Page layout programs were designed as the master graphics environment for electronic design — the programs that can identify, read and accept files in many other formats for arrangement and finally for output. Page layout programs let you import and manage text (from word processing programs) and illustrations — typically bitmaps, PICTs, EPS files (including illustrations and special-effects type produced in PostScript drawing programs) and TIFFs (Figure 2). (See "Graphics formats" on page 11.) Page layout programs have always provided typesetting advantages over word processing software, with greater control over the type (Figure 3). Most have also allowed you to embellish the page design with graphics tools for drawing rules, rectangles

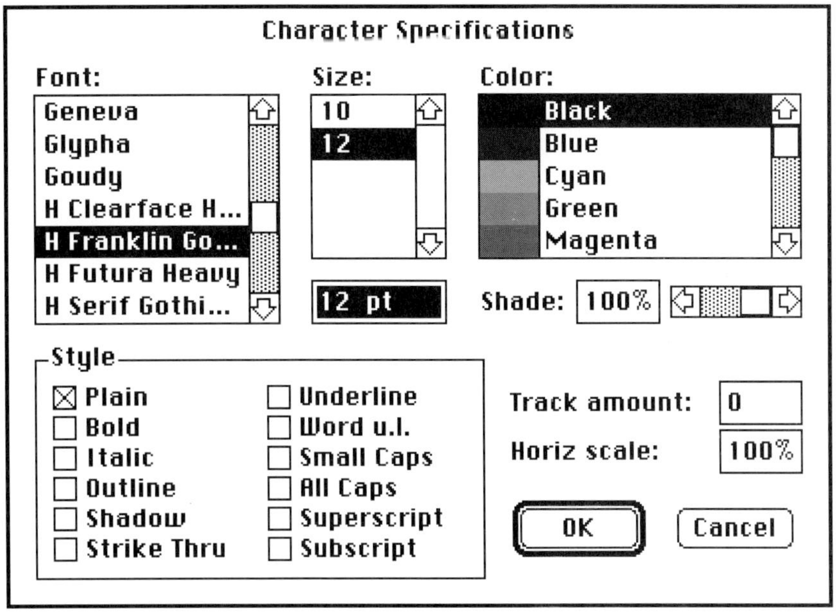

Figure 3. Spec'ing type. Within Quark-XProcc'o Character Specifications dialog box, the designer is able to control the Font, Size, Color, Style, Tracking and Horizontal Scale. Other dialog boxes allow adjustment of leading, paragraph format, hyphenation, justification and tabs.

and ellipses that could be filled with solid colors or patterns (Figure 4). As desktop publishing grew in popularity and sophistication, page layout applications evolved. They maintained their typographic and graphics advantages over word processors, adding more sophisticated type effects, and took on more of the efficient entry and editing features found in word processors, so that now it's quite easy and efficient to type and edit text directly in many page layout programs, bypassing word processing altogether (Figure 5).

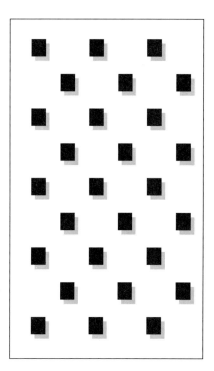

Figure 4. Creating graphic elements.
PageMaker's graphics tools are typically used for drawing rules, borders and keylines, or windows for illustrations to be stripped in mechanically. But they can also be used for making drop shadows, background patterns and other graphic features. These patterns from issue number 13 of David Doty's *ThePage* newsletter were made by repeating elements created with the drawing tools. Horizontal and vertical guidelines were set up at distances measured with PageMaker's rulers, and copies of graphic elements were pasted at intersections of the guidelines. Patterns can also be assembled from the pictures provided as part of the Zapf Dingbats and Symbol fonts. Drop shadows can be added to patterns by sending a screened copy of the element to the back and offsetting it slightly.

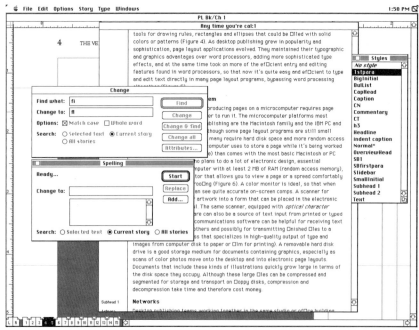

Figure 5. Typing onto the page.
PageMaker 4.0's new Story Editor provides a full range of word processing functions, making it efficient to enter and edit text right in the page layout program.

Figure 6. Assembling a DTP system. A microcomputer with sufficient RAM, a monitor and a hard disk drive are essential for producing page layouts electronically. A laser printer allows proofing of pages.

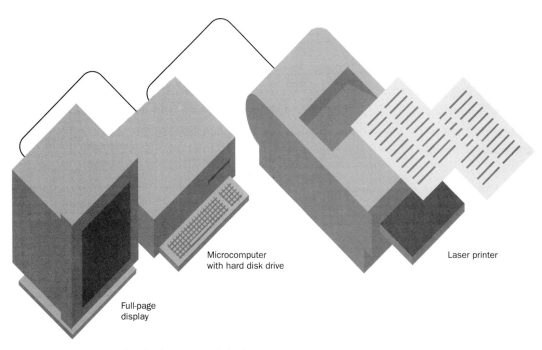

Full-page display

Microcomputer with hard disk drive

Laser printer

A desktop publishing system

At a minimum, designing and producing pages on a microcomputer requires page layout software and a computer to run it. The microcomputer platforms most commonly used for desktop publishing are the Macintosh family and the IBM PC and its imitations (PC clones).

Although some page layout programs are still small enough to fit on a floppy disk, many require hard disk space and more *random access memory* (*RAM*, the memory a computer uses to store a page while it's being worked on by the page layout software) than comes with the most basic Macintosh or PC systems. For someone who plans to do a lot of electronic design, essential equipment includes a computer with at least 2 MB of RAM, a hard disk drive, a monitor that allows you to view a page or a spread comfortably and a laser printer for proofing (Figure 6). A color monitor is ideal, so that when you design in color you can see accurate on-screen comps. A scanner for copying photos and other artwork into a form that can be placed in the electronic page layout is also useful. The same scanner, equipped with *optical character recognition* (*OCR*) software can also be a source of text input from printed or typed pages. And a modem and communications software can be helpful for receiving text and graphics files from others and possibly for transmitting finished files to a service bureau (a business that specializes in high-quality output of type and images from computer disk to paper or film for printing).

A removable hard disk drive is a good storage medium for documents containing graphics, especially as scans of color photos move onto the desktop and into electronic page layouts. Documents that include these kinds of illustrations quickly grow large. Although these large files can be compressed and segmented for storage and transport on floppy disks, compression and decompression take time and therefore cost money.

Networks

Desktop publishing teams working together in the same office building or studio can benefit from *local area networks,* or *LANs* — computers and their *peripherals* (related hardware) linked together electronically and managed by networking software (Figure 7). Networks allow transfer of files from one computer to another and sharing of hard disks, printers, scanners, modems and other peripherals.

Networking begins with the cable that carries signals from one piece of hardware in a network to another, and the connectors that attach the network cabling. Once the connections are made, networking software allows the members of a network to make parts of their hard disks available to other members. Networks can link Macintoshes to Macintoshes, PCs to PCs or Macs to PCs. They can be programmed to allow access from any computer on the network to any file at any time, or to allow only one person to open and work on a file at a time, or to restrict access even more.

Metaphors

Each page layout program uses as its operating "environment" some representation of the traditional physical-mechanical world of the graphic designer. In all page layout applications, this environment begins with a representation of the physical page. Some programs extend the workspace metaphor with a drafting table, or pasteboard. Others use a frame metaphor, requiring that

Figure 7. Implementing a network. In addition to the DTP basics shown in Figure 6, a scanner can provide a way to input photos for position only or in some cases, after treatment with image-processing software, as final art. Equipped with an optical character recognition program, the scanner can also read in printed text. A modem and communication software can bring input from a remote member of the DTP team or send files to a service bureau for output. A removable hard disk drive can store several megabytes, not an unusual requirement for page layout files incorporating complex illustrations and scanned photos. Cabling and networking software can link several work-stations together so that colleagues can share peripherals and can also access files on one another's hard disks. Unlike the local area network (LAN) shown here, some LANs have a single microcomputer that acts as a *file server,* to control network access and distribute files among network users.

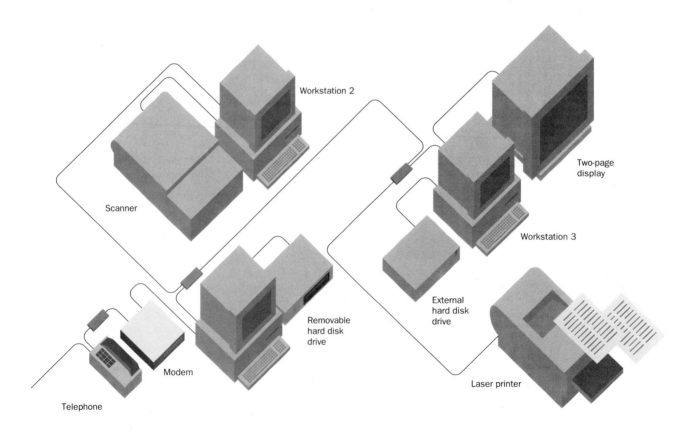

Workstation 2

Two-page display

Scanner

Workstation 3

Removable hard disk drive

External hard disk drive

Modem

Laser printer

Telephone

spaces be defined to hold graphics and text before these elements can be placed on the page (Figure 8).

Bringing in the pieces

Most page design and layout programs can import text and graphics more directly and easily than by electronically cutting and pasting from one application to another (see "Getting text in shape" on page 9). Some page layout programs require that editing changes to text or graphics be made

Figure 8. Choosing a working environment. Aldus PageMaker (top) originated the "pasteboard" metaphor for electronic page design, with space outside the page for storing elements to be used in the document. Type is stored on "windowshade" galleys, which are positioned and "pulled down" to place text in the document. Graphics are placed directly onto the page. QuarkXPress (shown here, bottom), Ready,Set,Go/ DesignStudio and Ventura Publisher use frames that must be positioned on the page before text and graphics can be placed.

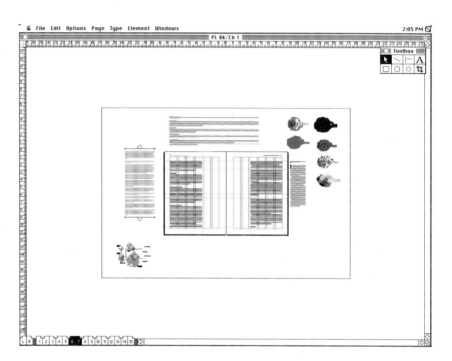

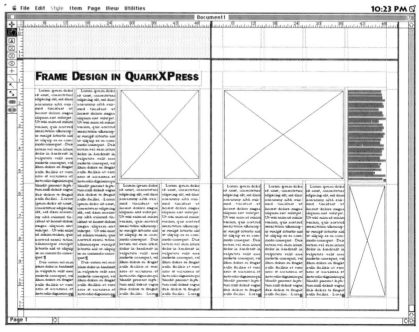

within the program; or if changes are made to the original word processing or graphics programs, the updated files must be re-placed on the page. Other programs use document-linking facilities that allow the text or graphics to remain outside the page layout program and available to their originating applications for updating; the updated versions are then automatically drawn into the page layout program via the link.

Putting out the pages

No matter how well-designed they are, pages need to be output before they can be of much use — for proofing and for final production of mechanicals, negative film or printing plates. Electronic comprehensive "sketches" of layouts are typically output on printers with a resolution of 300 or more *dots per inch* (*dpi*). At this resolution, the pages look good enough to accurately represent how the final printed piece will look, to act as the basis for making decisions about what changes must be made before printing. In some cases, 300 dpi output may be acceptable for final mechanicals. Black-and-white printers with 300 dpi resolution are typically laser printers, such as the Apple LaserWriter II series or the Hewlett-Packard LaserJet Plus, which electrostatically apply and thermally fuse dots of dry ink (toner) to plain paper pages (Figure 9).

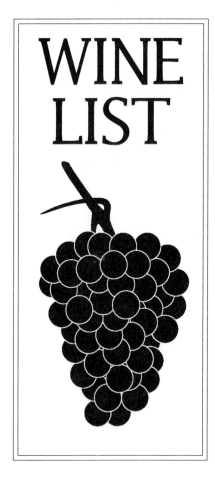

Figure 9. Using 300 dpi output. Page layouts that consist of simple line art and type can sometimes be reproduced effectively from 300 dpi laser-printed masters. Choosing a typeface specifically designed to look good at this resolution, such as Adobe's Lucida (shown here) can optimize the look of the page. Also, producing laser prints larger than finished page size, even if they have to be printed as partial pages and pasted up on boards as camera-ready art, boosts the effective resolution. For example, the type and line art shown here was laser-printed at finished size (left) and at 200 percent and reduced photographically to produce smoother curves (right).

It would be ideal if your clients (whether outside or in-house) always delivered their text files complete, fully edited and in a word processor that's entirely compatible with your computer system and your page layout program. If you can exercise control early in the process, you may be able to get the original text in exactly the form you want. But if you're working with clients outside your own department or studio, the chances are that at some point you'll be receiving text in a format that isn't directly compatible with your word processor or page layout program, let alone fully edited.

Translation
It's likely that sooner or later you'll get your client's input in one of these less-than-optimal forms:

1. A complete text file on disk in the right computer system format but in a word processor you're not familiar with
2. A complete text file on disk in an incompatible computer format
3. A text file received by modem
4. A typed or handwritten manuscript
5. Notes jotted on a yellow pad or on the back of an envelope
6. An idea in the client's head ("We haven't written it down yet, but we know what we want to say.")

Your first task in each of these cases will be to get the text into a form your page layout program can read, so you can avail yourself of the spell-checking and search-and-replace features that can help you do the clean-up necessary for producing typeset copy.

In case **1** or **3** you can try to place the file in your page layout program and proceed with clean-up activities (below). If the file isn't listed on your computer as one eligible to be placed, you can convert it to the appropriate format first, as you would in case **2** or **4**:

• By using a professional disk-conversion service that specializes in transferring files from one format or system to another,
• By using conversion/networking hardware and software that employs some of the same conversion processes in-house,
• By using optical character recognition software with a scanner to read in the text from a printout (presumably the client can produce a printed copy of the disk file if asked),
• Or by having someone type the text in a compatible form.

In cases **5** and **6,** you and your client will need some writing expertise, and in any of

the cases (**1** through **6**) you may need copy-editing help. Freelance copy editors typically charge from $20 to $30 an hour and can usually edit six to nine double-spaced typed pages per hour, depending on the difficulty of the material and the skill of the writer. It's certainly worth $40, for example, to ensure that the well-designed and beautifully produced brochure you send to the printer isn't riddled with errors in grammar or usage. If you don't know a good copy editor, you might telephone a publishing company (even a small, specialized one) near you and ask whether they can recommend someone.

Clean-up
There's a difference in styles between the type*written* look and the type*set* look you're aiming for in electronic page layout. So it's important to be able to quickly and efficiently clean up text files produced by someone with die-hard typewriter habits (or sent in ASCII format over a modem, which introduces many of the same typewriter treatments of the text).

Once the text file has been loaded into your page layout program, you can go to work with the spelling checker and the search-and-replace function:

Spelling   Check spelling first. Introducing ligatures (the typeset fi and fl combinations, for example), which you might do later, can interfere with the spell-checking function. Have a dictionary on hand to look up any word your page layout program doesn't recognize but can't suggest a replacement for.

Returns   Strip out end-of-line carriage returns. Text sent by modem often has a Return character at the end of each transmitted line, and usually two Returns between paragraphs. These characters will interfere with text wrap in your page layout, so they have to go. Here's a strategy for getting rid of the end-of-line Returns without wiping out the paragraph breaks:

^p^p   Search for the double Returns between paragraphs and replace them with an unusual combination of characters that won't occur anywhere in the text, such as "&&." (On the Mac, you can find the double Returns by searching for "^p^p.") Most page layout programs offer a global search-and-replace option, so you don't have to stop and approve each change.

^p   Next, search for the single Returns at the ends of the lines (^p) and replace each with a space (spacebar).

&&   At this point you should have a single "paragraph" of text punctuated with

an occasional "&&." Search for the "&&" combination and replace it with "^p." Now you'll have individual paragraphs again, without the end-of-line Returns.

Spaces   Get rid of double spaces purposely typed after punctuation or inadvertently introduced elsewhere. Search for "spacebar spacebar" and replace it with "spacebar." Since some typists and ASCII conversion processes substitute spaces for tabs, you may want to repeat this step until a search of the text turns up no instances of double space. (If a standard number of spaces has been used to indicate a Tab — say five spaces — you can start the space-hunt by replacing "spacebar spacebar spacebar spacebar spacebar" with "^t" before searching for double spaces.)

fi, fl   Introduce the "fi" and "fl" ligatures if the typeface you're using has them. Unless you're doing some fairly fancy kerning of type, these ligatures will improve the appearance of the text. On the Macintosh, the "fi" ligature is typed as Option-Shift-5, and the "fl" ligature is Option-Shift-6. Be sure to choose the option in the search-and-replace function that lets you specify lowercase only. Otherwise, you'll end up replacing "Fi" and "Fl" with the lowercase ligatures too.

"   If your page layout program doesn't automatically change the straight "typewriter quotes" to the "curly" ones used in typesetting, you can replace those also. On the Mac, use Option-[(for "), Option-Shift-[(for "), Option-] (for ') and Option-Shift-] (for ').

—   Replace typed dashes (--) with typeset em dashes (—). On the Mac the em dash is typed as Option-Shift-hyphen, with or without a space at each side of it.

Help!
Although it's worth knowing how to do these clean-up tasks yourself in your page layout program, you'll find that, at least on the Macintosh platform, many of them can be accomplished with programs written especially for that purpose (such as Overwood, shown in Figure 2 of Chapter 3.) Another option is to use a program like QuickKeys (also for the Mac), which helps you automate repetitive tasks, to set up your own miniprogram within the page layout program to routinely perform the checks and replacements you find you need.

Adapted from "Word-to-PageMaker: Flexibility and Style" by Linnea Dayton, Step-By-Step Electronic Design, *Volume 1, Number 5.*

For pages that include only type and line art, resolutions of 600 to 1270 dpi provide output that looks as good to the naked eye as higher-resolution output. Laser printers such as the Varityper VT-600, with a resolution of 600 dpi, print with toner on paper, while imagesetters such as Linotype's L-300 use photographic processes to print on resin-coated paper or on film.

The improvement in resolution from medium to high (1270 dpi versus 2540 dpi on a Linotronic L-300 imagesetter, for example) becomes important when pages include artwork with screen tints or halftone photographic images. Fine screens of black or colored dots on a white background are used to make grays or tints of other colors by patterning dots to fill halftone cells to greater or lesser degrees (Figure 10). Many EPS illustrations (see "Graphics formats" on page 11) include graduated fills or blends from one halftone screen density to another, and TIFF images are typically printed with halftoning to produce grays. Typically, screen patterns produced at less than high resolution are too coarse to be acceptable as pleasing representations of tints when printed.

High-resolution output is often made to negative film rather than to resin-coated paper in order to maintain the sharpness of the high-res image through the process of making printing plates. Negative film output from an imagesetter can be used directly to make printing plates by a contact process. But positive output on paper is two steps away from the final printing plate — the negative has to be produced by a contact exposure process before the plate can be made. At each step in the process, the dots that make up an image can shrink or spread, degrading the quality of the halftone screen.

Figure 10. Halftone screening. In both traditional and electronic halftone screens, dots of various sizes represent various dark and light tones. An area of large black dots makes a dark gray. An area of small dots, with large amounts of white space around them, makes a light gray. In computer-generated halftone screens, the halftone dots are themselves made up of smaller square dots.

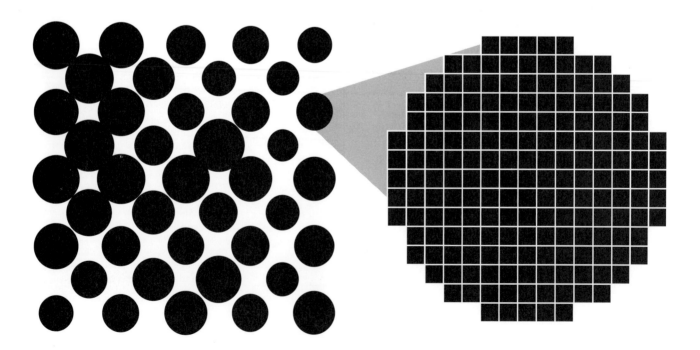

Page layout programs can import illustrations produced in a number of electronic formats and can incorporate them into pages. Among the most common of these formats are paint (black-and-white bitmapped), PICT, color PICT, encapsulated PostScript (EPS), TIFF, and color TIFF.

Bitmapped images

Programs like MacPaint, SuperPaint, Canvas and DeskPaint produce bitmapped images. Usually keyed to the computer's screen resolution (72 or 75 dots per inch for Macintosh computers, for example), these images are made up of small rectangular pixels, or on-screen dots. When these files are printed, their resolution stays the same as it was on the screen, regardless of how high a resolution the printer is capable of producing. On curved or slanted lines, the rectangular dots in the prints are quite apparent to the observer. Paint illustrations can be used in page layouts when the designer wants to achieve a "bitmapped look." They can also be reduced on the page, which in effect increases their resolution. PageMaker has a facility for producing a stepped series of reductions to get the best quality from the printer on which the page will be output. Black-and-white bitmaps store only 1 bit of information for each pixel, enough to tell whether the dot is black or white. But this information must be stored for each individual dot in the image, so bitmapped files tend to be relatively large.

PICT and PICT2

The PICT format is Apple's original interprogram-transferrable object-oriented file format. Object-oriented means that elements such as lines and shapes are defined by mathematical relationships — that is, they are described by a series of equations rather than a collection of dot descriptions. Interprogram-transferrable means that the format was established as a standard to be exported and imported, so that graphics created in this format can be passed from one program to another. The PICT format also has the capacity to combine objects and bitmaps. PICT 2 is a related file format that, in addition to its object-oriented descriptions, provides a way of defining color bitmaps with 8, 24 or 32 bits of information per dot, to describe color and brightness. Color bitmaps are several times larger than black-and-white.

Encapsulated PostScript

When you draw something in a PostScript illustration program such as Illustrator 88, FreeHand or Corel Draw, and you want to store it in a form that can be imported into a page layout, you can save it as pure PostScript code (see page 15), which tells the printer how to print the image, or as an encapsulated PostScript (EPS) file. Encapsulated PostScript includes the PostScript code for the printer *plus* a screen image of the graphic, so that when you place the illustration on a page, you can see it on your screen.

TIFFs and Color TIFFs

TIFF stands for tagged image file format, a widely accepted format used for storing the image information produced by grayscale and color scanners and certain graphics programs. Like EPS files, TIFF files have two parts. One is a low-resolution representation of the image (a PICT, in fact) that acts as a placeholder for the graphic in the page layout file. The other part includes all the information stored in the file; it's used to generate the best print the output device is capable of. To print the complete grayscale or color information, the TIFF file must be "linked" to the PICT that serves as its placeholder. That means it has to be where the page layout program can find it at printing time.

TIFF images are like bitmapped images in that the file stores a description of each dot in the image. But whereas bitmapped files store only one piece of information per dot, TIFF files typically store more information — up to 32 bits — precisely describing the brightness of each gray dot or the brightness and hue of each dot of color.

Bitmapped

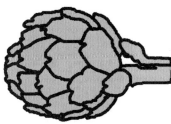

PICT

EPS

Bitmapped, 1-bit scan

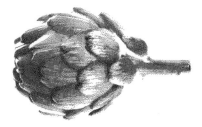

PICT, scanned image

TIFF

Color output

Low-resolution (300 dpi) color thermal transfer printers, such as those in the QMS ColorScript series, use a matrix of heated pins to apply dots of colored waxlike material to form an image on paper. The waxlike material comes in four colors, from which other colors are blended by *dithering,* a process of mixing dots of two colors to form the appearance of a third (Figure 11). A second 300 dpi color technology, employed by the Dupont 4Cast printer, for example, is dye sublimation. The dye is activated by heat, with the amount of spreading of each dot determined by the amount of heat applied. Although the resolution is 300 dpi, the color produced is continuous, because the dots of dye spread out to meet each other (Figure 12).

High-resoultion color output is achieved by producing separated film — a separate negative for each of the colors to be printed — either for spot colors, which will be applied on-press by using specially premixed inks (such as the Pantone series produced by Letraset), or for process colors (applied as fine, overlapping screens of dots of the four process ink colors, cyan, magenta, yellow and black)(Figure 13). The overlapping dot screens form tiny rosettes that are perceived by the eye as blended colors.

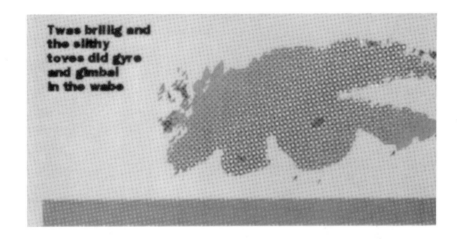

Figure 11. Dithering. Thermal transfer printers use patterns of dots of two colors to create the illusion of a third color. This 200 percent enlargement of a print from a QMS ColorScript printer shows this dot mixing at 300 dpi.

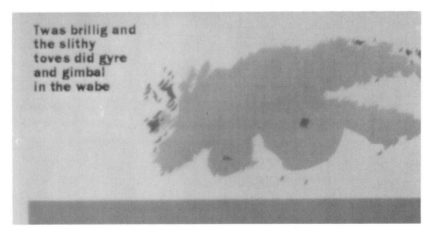

Figure 12. Dye sublimation. This 200 percent enlargement of a Dupont 4Cast print shows the continuous tone formed when the 300 dpi color is spread by applying heat. Up to four colors per dot (cyan, magenta, yellow and black) are mixed by this heating process.

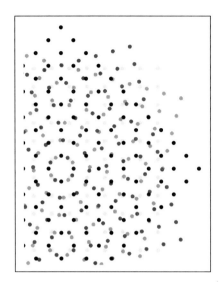

Figure 13. Printing with process color. The cover of this book was printed from separated film, with dot screens of four colors printed at four different angles, as shown here. On the press, the four colors were printed as fine dot screens, which overlay one another to produce the illusion of blended colors.

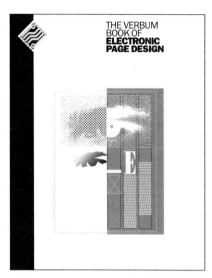

Cyan at –105˚

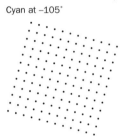

Magenta at –75˚

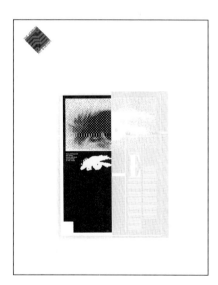

Yellow at –90˚

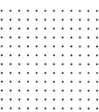

Black at –45˚

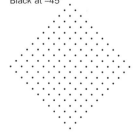

PostScript

The "brain" of a laser printer or imagesetter is the *raster image processor,* or RIP. In some cases — the Apple LaserWriter printers, for example — the RIP is located inside the printer. In other cases, such as the Linotronic imagesetters, it's located in an add-on piece of hardware (Figure 14). In still other cases, such as some laser printers run with PCs and their clones, it's on a circuit board located inside the microcomputer itself. The RIP uses a *page description language,* a computer programming language that provides a way to represent the lines, curves and solid areas that make up the text and graphic images on an electronically designed page, and to tell the printer where on the output medium (paper, film, monitor screen or 35mm slide generator, for example) to put the minute dots of ink, toner or light than make up the image.

In laser printers and imagesetters, PostScript is the most widely implemented of the page description languages (Figure 15). PostScript has the advantage of being *device-independent;* that is, the PostScript code created in designing a page can be interpreted by the RIP of the output device to produce the best (smoothest, highest-resolution) image possible with that device. In a sense, PostScript achieves device independence by telling the

Figure 14. Using a RIP. The raster image processor (or RIP) is the interpreter that translates the program code that describes a page into the dot pattern used by the printer or imagesetter to output that page. The RIP may reside in the computer, in the printer or in a separate piece of hardware. The number of dot positions on the output page depends on the resolution of the device that produced it. Numbers shown here are approximations for an 8 x 10-inch page at 300 dpi and at 2540 dpi.

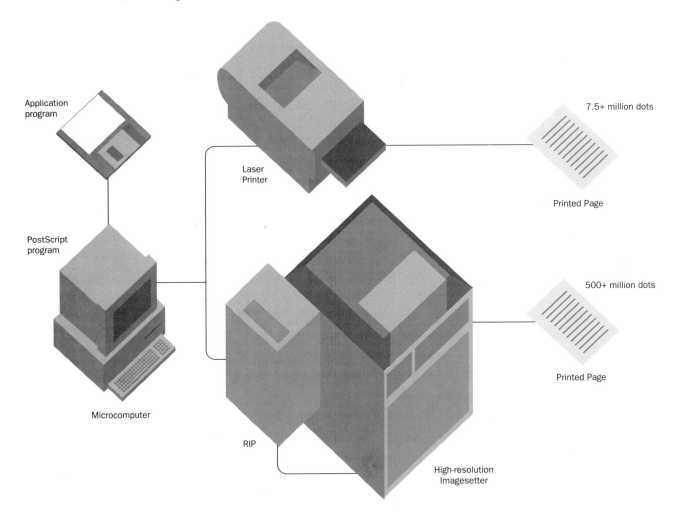

Application program

Laser Printer

7.5+ million dots

Printed Page

PostScript program

Microcomputer

RIP

500+ million dots

Printed Page

High-resolution Imagesetter

output device what the goal is and leaving it to the RIP to determine how best to achieve that goal.

You can look at this process as being like giving each of three builders the same assignment: to make a wall 5 feet high and 1 foot thick around a garden of a particular shape and size with the smallest building units available. One builder may have railroad ties available, another, concrete blocks, and the third, bricks. Specifying the finished dimensions and path of the wall will save you a lot of time over computing for each builder the number and arrangement of the particular materials to be used to build the wall. Let each builder (or RIP) figure out the details of completing the task, while you (or the computer) go on to other projects. PostScript provides equations for the paths that outline type and graphics, and specifications for the appearance of the fill for enclosed spaces, and the RIP for each particular output device figures out how many dots it has to arrange, and in what patterns, to make up the characters and graphics described for the page.

Changing roles

Using microcomputers and their associated page layout software changes the way graphic designers work, putting into their hands the tools to experiment with techniques such as wrapping type and using special type effects that were too time-consuming or costly to try very often in the past. The ability to arrange and rearrange elements on-screen, to set and reset type without sending out for typesetting, to design with photos in place on the screen and in proofs provides a freedom that encourages creativity.

Besides expanding their creative roles, designers also find themselves taking on production chores. Much of the work they do in the design process requires little modification to become final art, and the same page layout tools that make electronic design possible also make it easy to extend the process right through to the production of camera-ready art or final film. But along with the opportunity to set type, for example, comes the responsibility to see that it's set correctly. A professional typesetter no longer takes care of kerning display type; the typesetter's proofreader no longer sits in the back room catching typos introduced by the typesetter or grammatical errors missed by the writer or copy editor. Along with the opportunity to create or place color graphics on the page for electronic separation and output to plate-ready film comes the responsibility for producing knockouts and trapping color. A stripper no longer makes chokes and spreads to provide just the right amount of trap for the paper and press being used to print the job.

Many designers enjoy the direct, hands-on control that all the capabilities of electronic page design and production offer. Others are reluctant to do all the work required to fill in the gaps in their knowledge, preferring to provide computer-generated line art on art boards with tissue overlays and to leave the screen tints, stripping and trapping to the specialists. It's important to remember that the DTP process allows a whole range of ways for the designer

```
%!PS-Adobe-2.0
%%Title: PL Bk/Ch 1
%%Creator: PageMaker 4.0 rocky
%%CreationDate: 6-27-1990, 11:5:34
%%For: Martha
%%BoundingBox: 0 0 612 792
%%Pages: 1 0
%%DocumentPrinterRequired: "" ""
%%DocumentFonts: (atend)
%%DocumentSuppliedFonts: (atend)
%%DocumentNeededFonts: (atend)
%%DocumentNeededProcSets:
%%DocumentSuppliedProcSets: AldusDict2
209  55
%%DocumentPaperSizes: Letter
%%EndComments
%%BeginFile: PatchFile
userdict /AldusDict known {(A previous
version PageMaker header is loaded.) =
flush} if
%%EndFile
%%BeginProcSet: AldusDict2  209  55
% 209      55       AldusVersion/
AldRevision: This record must be first!!
% Copyright (C) 1987 Aldus Corporation. All
rights reserved.

/AldusDict2 325 dict def
AldusDict2
begin


/AldusVersion        209         def

/AldusRev            55          def

/bdef { bind def } bind def
systemdict /currentpacking known
{/AD_OldPacking currentpacking def
true setpacking
} if
/AD_PrevMatrix       matrix      def

/AD_SomethingOnPagefalse         def

/AD_OutlineWidth     30          def

/AD_ShadOffset       0.06        def

/AD_OLShadOffset     0.06        def

/AD_OLSmearFact      0.03        def

/AD_BoldSmearFact    0.03        def

/AD_ObliqueAngle     -0.21       def

/AD_TrueSetscreen /setscreen load def
/AD_NestedMirror false def

/AD_TextCutout false def
/BEGJOB
```

Figure 15. Describing a page. PostScript is a computer programming language that describes an image to be printed on a page. Shown here is part of the PostScript code used to describe this page to the Linotype L-300 that output it to film for printing. PostScript is a device-independent page description language, which means that the same code that was sent to the L-300 could also be sent to a laser printer for proofing. Both output devices were able to interpret the code, and each rendered the page using the smoothest type outlines it could produce.

to work — from the power designer, who maintains hands-on control of every aspect of design and production, to those electronic designers who, after the initial infatuation with the new medium, assemble their own groups with more traditional roles — designer, illustrator, production artist — and continue to maintain the same working relationships they have always had with film strippers and printers.

Finding allies

Besides hardware, software and their own closely associated colleagues, desktop publishers also need technical support provided by hardware and software companies to registered owners of their products and a good working relationship with a service bureau that keeps up-to-date on the software they use. Membership in a DTP users group or an on-line group (see "DTP on-line" below) can also make a big difference. Printed publications can help, too — books for background and tutorial help, and periodicals for news of updates, "bugs" and electronic solutions (see the "Appendix" for a list of helpful publications).

Future directions

To date, the short history of DTP shows several clear trends in the development of electronic page design software. WYSIWYG is getting more so, with better and better representation of type on-screen and the ability to

DTP on-line

Besides manuals, vendors' technical support phone lines, newsletters and magazines, and users groups, there's a source of support for desktop publishers available through on-line services. These services, which can be reached via modem and communications software, provide a way of keeping up with the fast pace of changes in this field. Several of the large services provide "conferences" (also variously called forums or roundtables) where desktop designers can "meet" to ask and answer questions. Desktop publishers aren't the only ones who participate in the exchange of information that takes place in these messaging services. Graphic designers, typesetters, copy writers and representatives of hardware and software vendors of the programs all participate with valuable insights and information — sometimes with early warnings of bugs or with workarounds for deficiencies in current versions of software. More experienced participants are generally very willing to share their knowledge, not only about hardware and software, but also about the business aspects of electronic design — for example, how to charge for the new way design and production services are provided.

Among on-line services that could prove useful are CompuServe (with forums for DTP, Adobe and Aldus software), GEnie (with roundtables on designing for print, image processing, and Letraset, Cricket and SuperMac hardware and software) and America On-line (with forums for desktop publishing, graphics, HyperCard and various vendors including Farallon and Microsoft, as well as magazine on-line). These services typically charge a small monthly fee and an additional amount for "connect" time. Most on-line services have introductory offers that give new users free connect time to explore. And although the software that provides the interface isn't as intuitive as a Macintosh paint program, for example, it gets easier to use with every new version issued.

display imported color graphics of all varieties. Programs have become more and more comprehensive in both text treatment and graphics capabilities, with spell-checking and search-and-replace features. Another trend is the development of features that help with the management of long documents, such as indexing, automatic generation of table of contents and the ability to tie graphics to a particular place in the text, so that as text is edited, associated figures move along with it (Figure 16). The ability to manipulate type and graphics — to kern type (tighten letter spacing) in finer and finer increments and to rotate type and text elements on the page — is improving. As programs become more capable, they also tend to become bigger, occupying more and more storage space on the hard disk and more and more memory in the computer. To keep them from taking on even more features and getting too big, more use is being made of dynamic linking, whereby changes made to a file in the originating word processing or graphics program automatically update the page layout file. All in all, electronic page layout is a great medium to work in when you're faced with a page design task — and it's likely to keep on getting better.

Figure 16. Looking ahead. Page layout programs are improving in the areas of easier handling of long documents, more precise control of type, broader range of type and graphics manipulation, better color separation facilities and greater similarity between on-screen display and printed output.

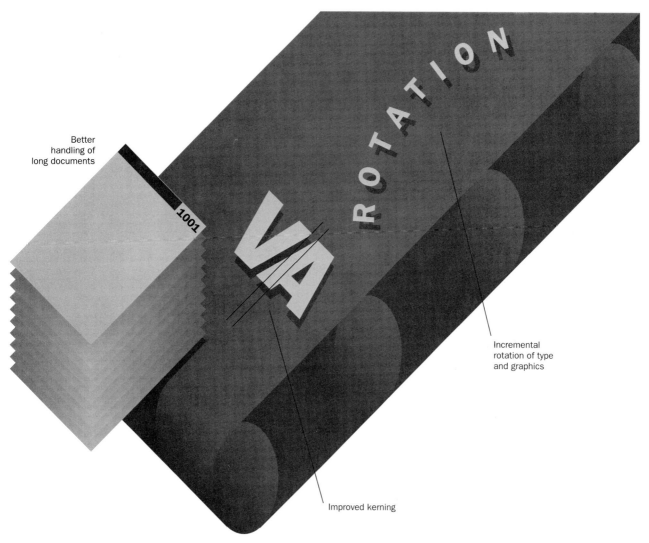

Better handling of long documents

Incremental rotation of type and graphics

Improved kerning

CHAPTER 2

Applications

Page layout programs started out being more distinctive and different from each other than they are now. As the technology has evolved, most of the programs have improved their own strong features and have also adopted the outstanding capabilities of their competitors. Although each page layout program still has a characteristic "look and feel," most of the major programs have many features in common:

- Text and graphics can be imported from word processing and illustration programs (Figure 1).
- Text can be typed in, edited, checked for spelling and altered by automatic search-and-replace functions.
- Text blocks can be linked, so that when you change the length of a column or delete or add text, the line changes caused by these edits automatically flow through the rest of the document.
- Imported graphics can be resized and cropped.
- For at least some kinds of imported graphics, contrast and brightness can be adjusted and halftone line screens can be specified.
- Typographic controls include adjustment of type size, style (bold, italic and so on), leading and letter and word spacing.
- Graphics tools draw rules and relatively simple geometric shapes.
- Styles can be defined and assigned to paragraphs, so that a whole set of type specifications can be assigned to text with one click of the mouse. (See "Using styles in PageMaker" on page 24.)
- Text columns (and gutters between them) can be automatically sized and positioned.
- Horizontal rulers, column guidelines and other nonprinting guides can be used to manually or automatically align elements on the page.

Figure 1. Importing text and graphics. These "Place" icons from PageMaker indicate the diversity of options available for importing files into page layout programs. Left to right, top: Text (manual flow), Text (autoflow), EPS; bottom: Paint, PICT, TIFF, Scrapbook. To place objects from the Scrapbook, click on Place, open the System folder, double-click the Scrapbook and then click on the PageMaker page. The number in the Place icon tells what page of the Scrapbook is being placed.

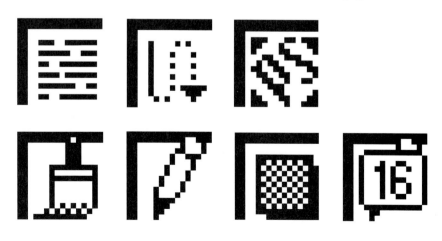

- Repeating type and graphic elements can be set on master pages, so that they'll automatically appear on each page of the document.
- Graphic elements can be permanently linked to a place in the text, so that they move along with the text as it's edited.
- Text can be made to wrap around or to overprint graphic elements (and in some cases other blocks of type).
- Close-up views in several degrees of magnification make it easy to work at various levels of detail.
- Thumbnails (reduced images) of all the pages in a document can be printed to give an overview of the full file (Figure 2).
- Pages can be saved as PostScript code, which can then be processed to output color separations.
- Oversized pages can be *tiled,* or printed in sections, in order to print proofs on a printer that can't handle the larger page size.
- Publication designs can be saved as *templates,* documents that retain their format and styles so that their page design can easily be applied to future issues of a publication series or, with modifications, to an entirely new publication. (Predesigned templates are available for many of the popular page layout programs; see "Designs on disk" on page 26.)

Aldus PageMaker

From its beginnings, Aldus PageMaker has provided an environment designed to make a graphic designer feel right at home. In its pasteboard-like environment, the pages are like mechanical boards on which you can position illustrations and galleyed text, picking them up and moving them as you desire. Tabletop (or pasteboard) space is available to store elements that you want to have at hand but aren't ready to put in place yet (see Figure 8 in Chapter 1). ■ *Fit In World can be accessed by holding down the Shift key while selecting Fit In Window from the Page menu. (Using the Shift key with the Command-W shortcut doesn't work.)*

Originally developed for the Macintosh, PageMaker was later released for the IBM PC and compatibles. On that platform, running in conjunction with Microsoft's Windows application, it provides much the same working environment as it does on the Macintosh.

PageMaker's combination of features and its ease of use help to make it the most popular of page layout programs. Text wrap around graphics can be specified numerically or adjusted by hand for custom wrap (see "Wrapping type" on page 57). The program's image control features allow you to manipulate the contrast and brightness of imported scanned images in TIFF and Paint formats and to control halftone screen frequency and angle (Figure 3). To reduce the disk space needed to store document files, PageMaker can compress imported TIFF images (usually grayscale or color scans) to a fraction of their original size.

Figure 2. Getting an overview. The thumbnails feature of page layout software lets you print out small thumbnail "sketches" of the pages in a file.

171

172   173

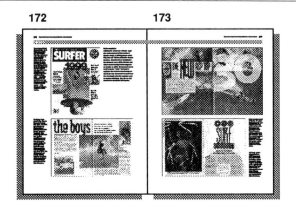

174   175

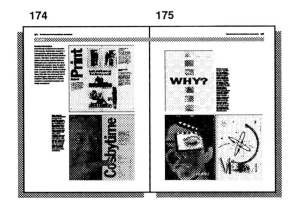

176   177

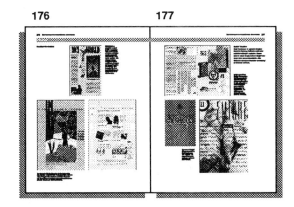

178   179

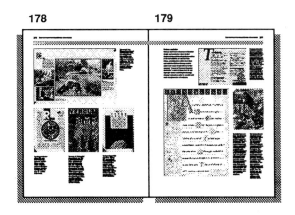

180   181

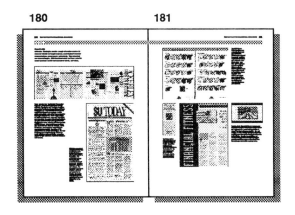

Figure 3. Using image control. The image control feature found in many page layout programs lets you control brightness, contrast, line screen density and angle and other aspects of bitmapped and gray-scale images. Shown from PageMaker: no adjustment (a), optimized contrast and brightness levels (b), setting of line screen (c), and remapping of histogram for special effect (d).

Version 4.0 of PageMaker for the Mac added features that users of the program had requested, such as finer typographic controls (kerning — tightening or loosening of space between pairs of letters — can now be controlled to within $1/100$ of an em space) and graphic control of type (type can now be condensed, expanded, rotated in 90-degree increments or force-justified to spread letters over a given width). ∎ *To tighten space between letters, press Command-Delete for large ($1/25$ em) increments or Option-Delete for small ($1/100$ em) increments. To loosen space, add the Shift key to either of these combinations.*

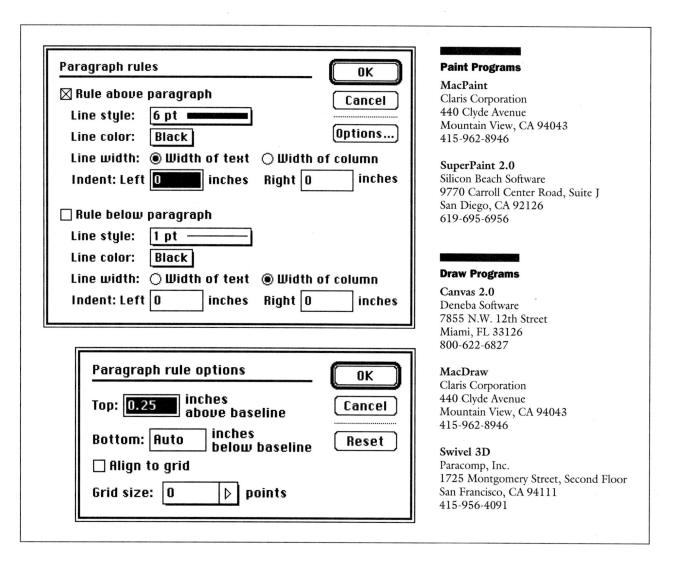

Figure 4. Using paragraph rules. PageMaker's paragraph rules make it practical to use rules with headings, for example, because the rules travel along with the type when editing the text. These dialog boxes indicate the specifications for the text, excerpted from the Appendix of this book (see page 197).

PageMaker can place rules and graphics within the text so that they stay attached when the text is edited (Figure 4). This feature makes it reasonable to use a rule as part of a heading style in a book, for example, or an imported illustration as an end mark at the close of a magazine story.

PageMaker's Story Editor allows quick and easy editing of text in a word processor environment complete with a spelling checker and a search-and-replace function that can search for styles of individual characters (bold, italic and so forth) or of paragraphs (full sets of type specifications assigned through the Styles menu) (see Figure 5 in Chapter 1). A linking feature makes it possible to automatically update text or graphics in PageMaker if you make a change in the original external file.

The program can handle documents of up to 1000 pages, or better yet, can keep track of several sections of a long document — chapters, for example — so they can be printed in order. Indexing and table of contents functions are especially useful for working with long documents; an index or table of contents can be generated for an entire book of linked chapters.

To keep the page layout program from getting ever larger and therefore less manageable, Aldus has chosen to add some features as separate applications. For example, the Table Editor, a spreadsheetlike utility for setting up tabular material, is supplied with PageMaker as a separate program.

Likewise, PageMaker's process color separation facility is not built in. Although PageMaker has always provided for spot color separation through the Print menu, process color separations are done through Aldus PrePrint, a separate color separation program that produces cyan, magenta, yellow and black plates from PageMaker files saved as PostScript code. ■ *When the PostScript file for separations from PageMaker is output, the cyan negatives for all the pages in the file are output first, then all the magenta negatives, and so on. That means that for a 10-page 8½ x 11-inch document, the negatives for the separations of each page will span a distance of about 30 feet. With this much leeway for physical factors to stretch the film or shift the alignment of the imagesetter, registration problems are much more likely to occur than if the files are broken down into smaller numbers of pages.*

**▌ Using styles in
PageMaker**

I n PageMaker, text styles are controlled primarily by assignment of type specifications to paragraphs. Styles are defined and edited through a series of dialog boxes that are made available by choosing Define Styles from the Type menu. Once a style is defined, it appears in the Styles menu. Then inserting the text cursor anywhere in the paragraph and clicking on a style choice from the Style menu assigns that style to the paragraph.

Since the unit of assignment is the paragraph, to change type specifications for only a portion of a paragraph, you must drag to select the desired words or lines, and then change the type specifications via other dialog boxes available through the Type menu. Clicking on a choice from the Styles menu would change the entire paragraph, not just the selected portion.

When a publication contains many type styles, it's sometimes helpful to choose style names so that styles that are often used together will appear close to each other in the Styles menu's alphabetical listing. For example, if body text includes an indent in each paragraph except the opening one, these style might be named "body text" and "body text, 1st" so that they will appear together. Another way to make the most often-used styles appear together (and at the top of the Styles menu) is to precede each of those style names with a hyphen.

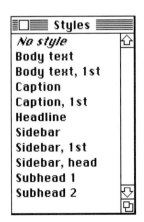

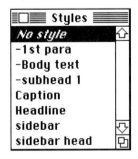

QuarkXPress

QuarkXPress has been unique among page layout programs in its hierarchical management of text and graphic elements. Child blocks are created inside parent blocks, and whenever the outer block is moved, its inner ones go along (Figure 5). The only way to separate a child from its parent in QuarkXPress is to select the child and cut it to the clipboard. While many users have been enthusiastic about QuarkXPress's ability to maintain complex layout blocks that can be moved around without being internally disrupted, others have found the parent-child link to be counterintuitive and awkward. In response, Quark designed version 3.0 of the program to operate with or without the parent-child relationship, at the user's option. Another advance in the direction of the popular PageMaker metaphor is the addition of a pasteboard for storage of text and graphic elements. And QuarkXPress is a leader among popular Macintosh page layout programs in its ability to define more than one master page.

Long the leader in typographic controls, QuarkXPress allows the broadest range of type sizes — from 2 to 720 points and increments of $\frac{1}{1000}$ point — and the ability to set leading in increments of $\frac{1}{1000}$ point. Kerning and tracking (overall control of letter spacing) can be done to within $\frac{1}{1000}$ em space. QuarkXPress also allows rotation of both text and graphics in increments of $\frac{1}{1000}$ degree. A vertical justification feature aligns both tops and bottoms of text columns, automatically distributing any extra space through the length of the column. This feature is used in formatting book pages, for example.

Figure 5. Nesting boxes. In Quark-XPress all objects (text and graphics) must be placed in pre-established boxes. "Child" boxes can be set inside a "parent" box; if the parent is moved, the children go along, maintaining their preset positions within the parent.

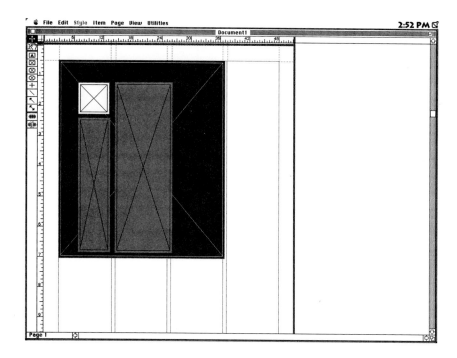

We sometimes think of them as "strictly for beginners," but electronic page layout templates can prove helpful to both nondesigners and designers:

• Novices (those with little or no experience in publication design or production) can probably benefit most. Using a template, becoming aware of its structure, and experimenting with placement and changes, the novice learns how to work with a page layout grid, how to see through to the underlying structure of all printed pieces, and how to vary template designs and generate original layouts.

• Experienced production artists who find their roles expanding into design now that they're using the electronic medium can derive some of the same benefits as novices from using templates.

• Experienced designers new to the electronic medium or to a particular software package can use a template as on-the-job training — learning the ins and outs of the program while generating an effective, useful product.

• Experienced electronic designers who haven't tackled a particular kind of format before (an invoice or order form, for example) can find useful models in templates. And until a designer has accumulated a library of original electronic formats, a commercial template package can provide an occasional quick design and production solution to meet a tight deadline or a restrictive budget.

A Variety of Packages

Template packages vary in strength of design, types of publications, variety of templates for a particular publication type and ease of use. Here are some of the packages available:

• **PageMaker Portfolios** Aldus, makers of PageMaker, have produced a series of design models in three packages for newsletters, business communications and manuals. The Newsletters package includes seven models in three versions each (primary, easy and sophisticated) for letter-size pages, in two- to five-column formats. The Manuals package includes 10 vertical and 10 horizontal designs in three page sizes, in one- to three-column formats. The Business Communications package provides two designs each for memos, reports, business plans, proposals, handbooks and overheads. Each of the template designs comes in "easy" and "sophisticated" versions. The designs are attractive, with extensive use of white space and bold black elements.

Each Portfolio includes the templates, a practice tutorial, very clear instruction on how to use the templates, and excellent guidelines on publication production and design principles in general.

• **PDQ Page Designs Quick** (PC and Mac) The PDQ series consists of 120 newsletter page templates, sixty in 3-column format and 60 in 4-column format. The pages are organized by the width and number of pictures to be included on a page. Pages use a flow-line design, rather

than greeking a full text block. Pages are in the same design format and each can function as a page in the same publication. The PDQ 5 series includes 225 page templates for 11 x 17-inch tabloid format. A booklet with an illustration of each template is included. Packages are available for both Macintosh and PC versions of PageMaker.

• **QuarkStyle** (Mac) QuarkStyle includes templates for a variety of publications, from simple memos and business cards to books, catalogs and newsletters. The package includes a version of QuarkXPress minus some of its high-end functions. Users may enter their own text, but text-formatting (horizontal scaling, kerning and so on) is fixed. For these kinds of modifications and for color separations, a QuarkStyle document must be opened in QuarkXPress. QuarkStyle is a less expensive, less difficult stand-alone page design package, for users who may not want to commit to a full-featured page layout program. Buyers receive a credit toward the purchase of QuarkXPress, and QuarkXPress owners can buy QuarkStyle at a discount.

Designers Ken Kendrick, Ronn Campisi, Stephen Doyle, Doug May, Paula Scher, Marjorie Spiegelman and John Van Hamersveld have contributed a series of templates for coordinated business forms to serve as a corporate identity package, ads, announcements, brochures, memos, overheads, reports, books, catalogs, newsletters and a magazine. The templates are simple and elegant. All templates are de-

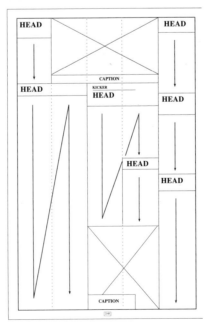

PageMaker Portfolios

QuarkStyle, above
PDQ Page Designs Quick, left

signed with resident LaserWriter fonts; some also include "Designer fonts" versions that use additional typefaces.

• **Document Gallery Style Sheets** (PC) From the developers of many of the style sheets that Xerox includes with Ventura Publishers, this package includes 17 newsletters, 18 directories and catalogs, 17 technical documentation styles and six business forms. Forty-one of the documents are 8½ x 11-inch format (five of these are landscape [sideways] orientation), five are 4¼ x 11-inch, and 12 are 5½ x 8½-inch. The user's guide is very brief; it provides instructions for installing the style sheets on a hard disk and a small illustration of each document's layout.

• **Desktop Manager Style Sheets** (PC) New Riders produces three Ventura Publisher template packages of two disks and a manual. Business Documents includes 30 templates for proposals, reports, marketing materials, brochures, ads and correspondence. Style Technical Documentation includes 25 templates for technical documents and books. Newsletters includes 25 templates, in 1- to 4-column formats. The templates are well-designed and simple to use.

• **Will-Harris Designer Disk 5** (PC) Designer Disk 5 provides a variety of style sheets for page layouts in WordPerfect. Document types include book, resume, proposal, flyer, price list, pamphlet, invoice, financial statement, lined form, outline, overhead transparency, sign, maga-

zine, advertisement, report cover, calendar, menu, invitation, storyboard, promotional pieces, letterhead stationery, two catalogs and technical documentation.

• **Layouts** (Mac) Layouts, designed by Jacqueline Fisher of Starburst Designs, is an extensive PageMaker template package covering the usual business publications plus many unusual items like 2-, 3- and 4-panel brochures, a variety of folded business card formats, business reply cards and flyers with graphics. Text blocks are indi-

cated by boxes with rules. This saves space on the template disks and requires the designer to specify type and leading. A 130-page manual provides hard copy of all designs, design tips, a booklist and a tutorial. The templates are well-designed and provide many choices in each category of publication.

From "Designs on Disk" by Janet Ashford, Step-By-Step Electronic Design, Volume 1, Number 11.

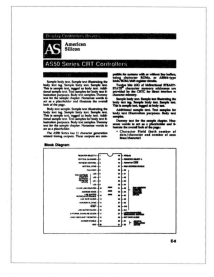

Desktop Manager Style Sheets

Will-Harris Designer Disk 5

Layouts, above
Document Gallery Style Sheets, left

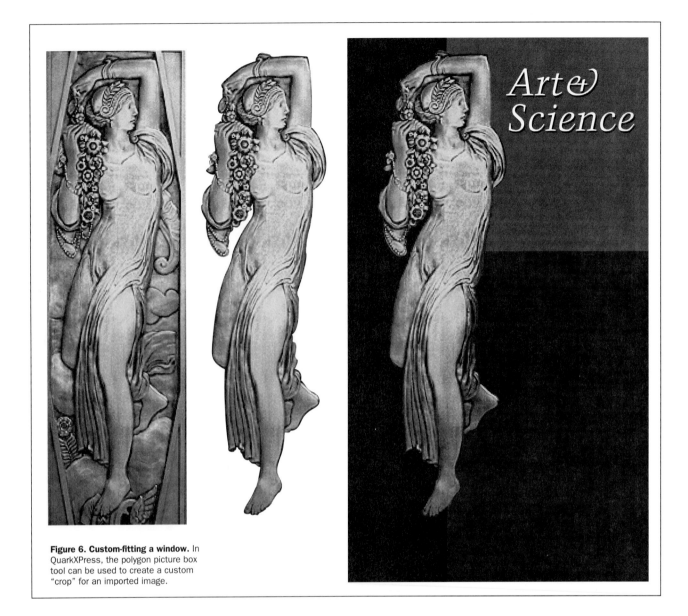

Figure 6. Custom-fitting a window. In QuarkXPress, the polygon picture box tool can be used to create a custom "crop" for an imported image.

Like PageMaker, QuarkXPress has a full-featured word processor. For example, the program can do a spelling check for a particular word, a story or an entire document.

QuarkXPress's graphics tools include a polygon picture box tool that essentially lets you create a geometric mask to frame one or more parts of a photo (Figure 6). The program also provides custom line widths and automatic arrowheads.

QuarkXPress allows you to group graphic and text elements, to slide graphics and text from one page or spread to another on-screen, and even to insert, delete or move document pages. Type runarounds are easy to create, both around graphics and around other type blocks (Figure 7).

The program can provide a complete list of type styles used in a document and of graphics imported from other programs, for convenience in sending

Figure 7. Wrapping text. Many page layout programs allow text to wrap around graphics. QuarkXPress can also wrap text around type elements.

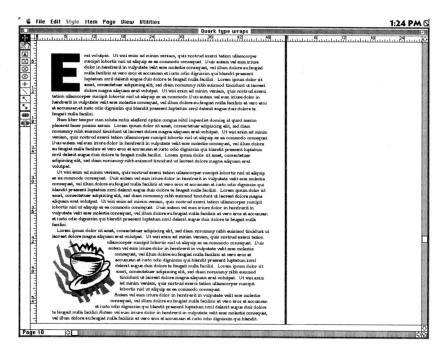

files to the service bureau. It can be very helpful to have a list of the fonts required for output of a file and a list of the linked graphics (picture name, file format and location) that have to be supplied with the file for it to print properly. The graphics files are linked so that changes to them are automatically reflected in updates to the QuarkXPress document.

Color separation facilities are built into the program. All separations for a single page are produced at the same time, so that all four negatives are produced as close together as possible. QuarkXPress can suppress printing of text, pictures, lines or groups.

DesignStudio/Ready,Set,Go!

Letraset's DesignStudio represents a major upgrade of its Ready,Set,Go!, (RSG) page layout software. Because the price took a major step up along with the program's capabilities, Letraset has also maintained RSG as an option for those who don't need the power of DesignStudio.

Although early versions were plagued with output problems, RSG developed a following among graphic artists and typesetters who especially liked its modular grid metaphor, which allowed them to organize information on the page both vertically (using columns) and horizontally (using rows) (Figure 8). In RSG each spread has its own pasteboard, so that when a user "turns the page," items on the pasteboard for the previous spread are no longer available. DesignStudio has expanded the pasteboard concept so that all spreads are served by a common pasteboard (Figure 9).

Type and leading can be specified to within $\frac{1}{100}$ of a point, and individual letter pairs, words, lines, paragraphs or entire documents can be kerned in increments of $\frac{1}{1000}$ em space. You can specify the size at which greeking (substitution of gray bars for lines of type) occurs, for ease of viewing a layout on-screen and for speeding up the screen redraw time when changes are made.

In DesignStudio, type styling specifications can be set through one dialog box (Figure 10). A name — and a keyboard shortcut — can be assigned to the type, so that the style can be applied to any selected text with a single keystroke combination. DesignStudio allows type and graphics rotation in 1-degree increments, as well as grouping of text and picture elements. And because

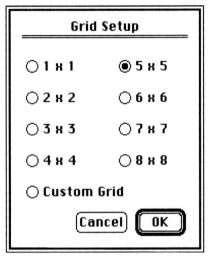

Figure 8. Designing with a grid.
DesignStudio and Ready,Set,Go let the user establish rows as well as columns for organizing elements on the page, as shown in this page spread from the *Continuum* newsletter designed by Laura Lamar.

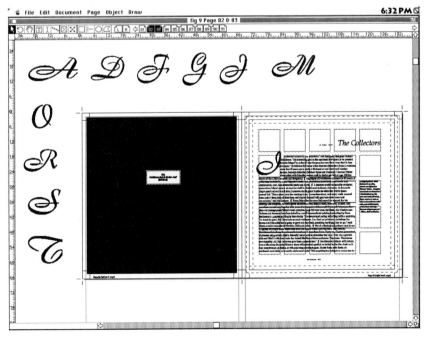

Figure 9. Combining the best elements.
DesignStudio retained Ready,Set,Go's grid organization but added PageMaker's common pasteboard; all elements stored on the pasteboard can be seen from any page of the document. Shown here is a working spread from *San Francisco Style* (see Chapter 8) with Max Seabaugh's initial caps on the pasteboard.

each text block, picture block or graphic element has its own specifications dialog box — with size, shape, placement on the page, percentage of reduction or enlargement and so on — the designer has precise control over every element on the page; and it's easy to determine how the elements were laid out and to apply the same layout specifications to other elements in the document (Figure 11).

In designer/collector Robert Hutchinson's city office, favorites are displayed on "floating" shelves. Among his international cast of characters: a Columbian burial jar, Thai terra-cotta heads, coil vessels, Mayan creatures in stone, an Indian seed vessel with a coiled snake, a carved African mask, an Ivory Coast tribal bed, a Korean carved granite pot, and a 200 B.C. Greek road marker.

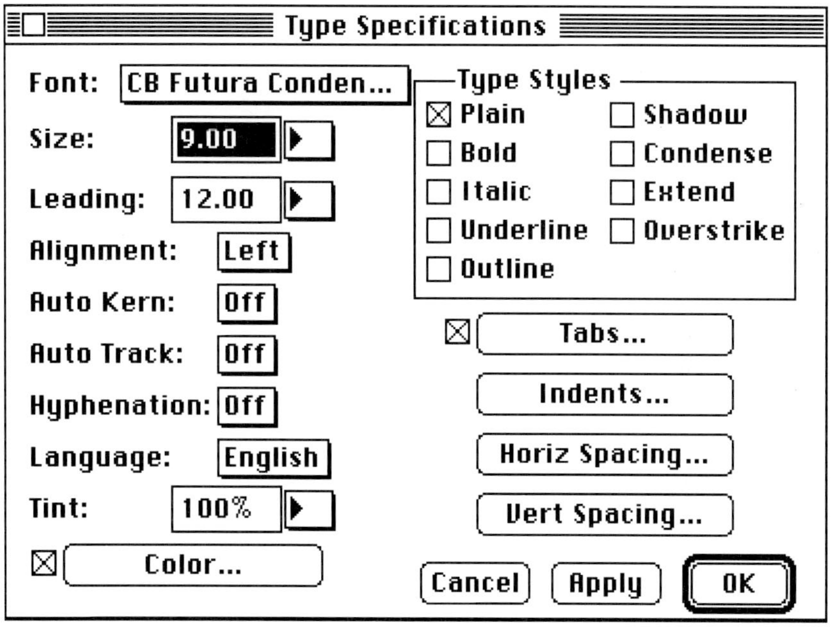

Figure 10. Specifying type in DesignStudio. The Type Specifications dialog box provides access to all the parameters of the type. Shown here are the spec's for this excerpt from *San Francisco Style*.

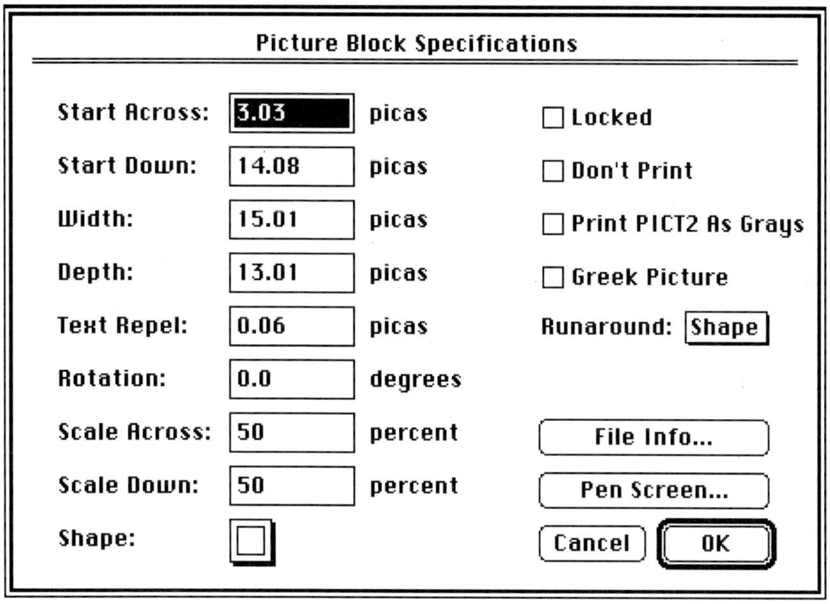

Figure 11. Recalling how it was done. The specifications box for graphics in Design-Studio provides information about how the graphic was treated to arrive at its final form and placement.

Type Specifications

Font: CB Futura Conden...

Size: 9.00 ▶

Leading: 12.00 ▶

Alignment: Left

Auto Kern: Off

Auto Track: Off

Hyphenation: Off

Language: English

Tint: 100% ▶

☒ Color...

Type Styles
☒ Plain   ☐ Shadow
☐ Bold   ☐ Condense
☐ Italic   ☐ Extend
☐ Underline   ☐ Overstrike
☐ Outline

☒ Tabs...
Indents...
Horiz Spacing...
Vert Spacing...

Cancel   Apply   OK

Picture Block Specifications

Start Across: 3.03   picas   ☐ Locked
Start Down: 14.08   picas   ☐ Don't Print
Width: 15.01   picas   ☐ Print PICT2 As Grays
Depth: 13.01   picas   ☐ Greek Picture
Text Repel: 0.06   picas   Runaround: Shape
Rotation: 0.0   degrees
Scale Across: 50   percent   File Info...
Scale Down: 50   percent   Pen Screen...
Shape: ☐   Cancel   OK

Ventura Publisher

Originally created for the IBM PC, Ventura Publisher (especially when combined with Ventura Publisher Professional Extension) is known for its ability to handle long documents with ease. For instance, besides automatic indexing and table of contents features, Ventura can also provide automatic footnotes. The program also lets you anchor graphics to specific positions in the text so that they are moved along as text is edited, and it automates the updating process for page references — for example, if editing changes cause cross-referenced text or illustrations to move to a different page, the page number in the cross-reference changes automatically.

Characteristic of Ventura Publisher documents are the style sheets that define everything from page size and numbering scheme to tab settings and type styles (Figure 12). Style sheets can be typed as lists of specifications in a word processor or text editor, or they can be entered on-screen in Ventura through menu choices and dialog boxes (Figure 13). Because several style sheets can be applied to the pages of one document, Ventura provides the equivalent of multiple master pages.

Although text can be run around rectangular graphics frames, it can't be custom-fitted to the irregular outline of a picture (Figure 14). Ventura's approach has always been to *link* text and graphics documents to the Ventura file rather than to *place* or *import* them. This means that rather than having extensive text- or graphics-editing capabilities (such as word processing and image control functions), Ventura allows editing in the programs of origin and updates the Ventura document as changes are made to the linked files.

Besides an emphasis on functions for creating long documents, the Ventura software has features especially helpful for technical documentation. Through its Professional Extension (originally a separate package but included in versions 3.0 and above), Ventura provides powerful equation-building tools as well as a table-editing function.

Base Page Settings

Page Size & Layout

Orientation;	Portrait
Paper Type & Dimension:	Letter, 8.5 x 11 in.
Sides:	Double
Start On:	Right Side

Auto-Numbering

Level 1:	[*Body Text,1]

Margins & Columns

# of Columns:	1
Settings For Left Page	
Top:	03,00 picas & points
Bottom:	17,06 picas & points
Left:	05,00 picas & points
Right:	04,00 picas & points
Widths/Gutters—1:	42,00 picas & points
Settings For Right Page	
Top:	03,00 picas & points
Bottom:	17,06 picas & points
Left:	04,00 picas & points
Right:	05,00 picas & points
Widths/Gutters—1:	42,00 picas & points

Sizing & Scaling

Flow Text Around:	On
Upper Left X:	00,00 picas & points
Upper Left Y:	00,00 picas & points
Frame Width:	51,00 picas & points
Frame Height:	66,00 picas & points

Vertical Rules

Settings For Left Page	
Inter-Col. Rules:	Off
Rule 1 Position:	00,00 picas & points
Rule 1 Width:	00,00 picas & points
Rule 2 Position:	00,00 picas & points
Rule 2 Width:	00,00 picas & points
Settings For Right Page	
Inter-Col. Rules:	Off
Rule 1 Position:	00,00 picas & points
Rule 1 Width:	00,00 picas & points
Rule 2 Position:	00,00 picas & points
Rule 2 Width:	00,00 picas & points

Frame Background

Color:	White
Pattern:	Hollow

Figure 12. Using Ventura's style sheets. In Ventura Publisher, style sheets define all aspects of page formatting.

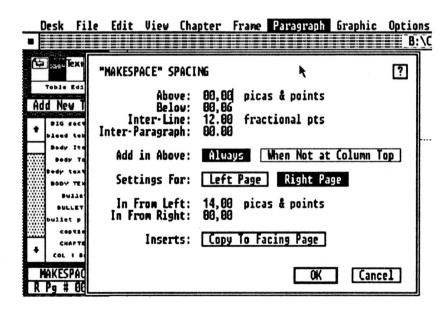

Figure 13. Using menus. Ventura Publisher's style sheets can be generated "on the fly" by making menu selections and filling in the dialog boxes that appear as a result of those choices.

FrameMaker

FrameMaker is the first publishing package for the NeXT computer (Figure 15). (NeXT is at the high end of the microcomputer range, based on the UNIX operating system with Display PostScript.) Before being released for the NeXT, and then for the Macintosh, it had been developed for higher-end networked systems. So it's not surprising that FrameMaker is strong in the features needed for streamlining production of long, complex documents and for *workgroup publishing* (document development by a group of artists, writers and editors, all working on different parts of the document at the same time).

Like QuarkXPress, FrameMaker organizes pages via boxes, or "frames," but it doesn't employ the parent-child nesting feature. The program's eight levels of magnification can be defined by the user, at any magnification

Figure 14. Wrapping text around a graphic. To achieve a custom wrap of type around this graphic, a series of graphics boxes had to be stacked to approximate the round curves of the watch.

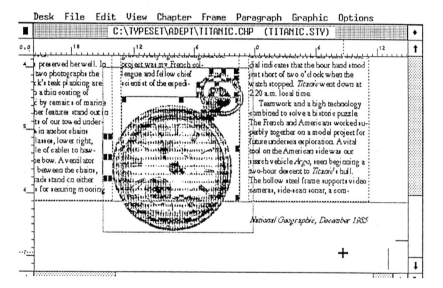

Figure 15. Display PostScript. Frame-Maker on the NeXT computer uses 92 dots per inch in its screen display, which is driven by Post-Script, so that what you see is very much like what you get when you print.

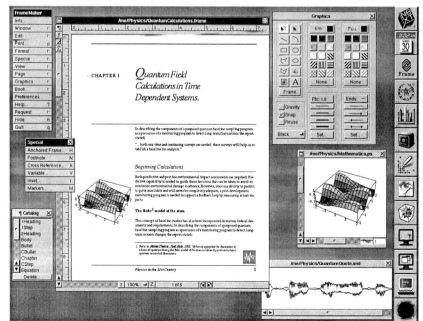

between 25 and 1600 percent. There can be up to 25 master pages, and it's possible to have both vertical and horizontal page formats in the same document. Type styles can be defined for single letters (initial capitals, for example), for words and even for bullets in bulleted lists as well as for paragraphs. Graphics can be rotated in 90-degree increments and can be anchored to text — either in the text column or in the margin next to a particular line of text — so they move along with the text as it's edited.

Along with its dictionaries, FrameMaker has a thesaurus. Also useful for editing text is the *change bar* feature, which highlights text that has been edited since the last saved version.

Other programs for page layout

Besides the "primary players" described so far in this chapter, there are other programs that can be very useful for page layout in certain situations. For example, at the same time page layout software has been evolving to provide more of the editing functions originally found only in word processors, word processing software has evolved to provide more page layout functions. Some advanced word processors such as the popular Microsoft Word and WordPerfect (Figure 16) for both Macintosh and PC-based systems, and Nisus for the Mac have many of the formatting features found in page layout programs. In general, these programs don't provide the typographic control or the graphics-handling capabilities of page layout programs. Typically, these programs are used for desktop publishing by those who need word processing capabilities and don't want to spend the extra money to add a page layout program. However, as the word processing functions of these programs have

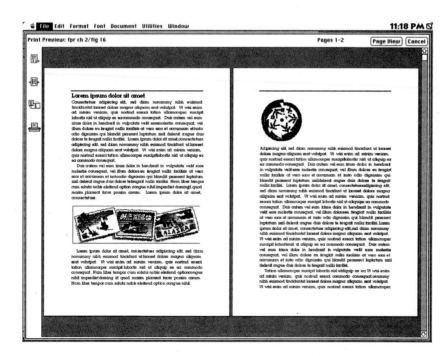

Figure 16. Formatting pages in word processing programs. Although Microsoft Word doesn't have the typographic controls typically found in page layout programs, it functions quite well for formatting certain kinds of documentation. It allows in-line placement of paint, draw and PostScript graphics and provides rules and boxes that travel along if the text configuration changes with editing.

advanced, it may make more sense to invest in a page layout program and use its text-editing functions, than the reverse.

In another example of convergent evolution of software packages, Post-Script illustration programs have been acquiring many of the typographic and design functions of page layout software while page layout programs add graphics capabilities. Designers find such programs as Aldus FreeHand, Adobe Illustrator and Corel Draw very useful for designing single-page layouts for flyers, posters and inserts for packaging of audiocassettes and compact disks, for example (Figure 17).

Finally, certain page design and production tasks are so specialized that software packages have been developed to deal specifically with them — for example, forms design, which can include links to spreadsheet programs to fill in the forms and presentation packages, designing for presenting information to be projected or viewed from a computer screen rather than printed and read from pages. The "Appendix" of this book lists programs of these types.

Figure 17. Formatting pages in Post-Script illustration programs. This real estate development project brochure cover was designed by Jack Davis in Adobe Illustrator 88. Many one-page layouts are designed in PostScript illustration programs because of the variety of type and illustration options they provide — for example, PostScript drawing tools, graduated and patterned fills, and special effects for type.

C H A P T E R   3

A Simple Brochure

Designer

Kathleen Tinkel writes and designs brochures, fact sheets, periodicals and reports for a variety of clients, from nonprofit organizations to small businesses. Her columns on graphic design and computers appear monthly in *Step-by-Step Electronic Design* and *Personal Publishing*. Tinkel Design, now located in Westport, Connecticut, has been in business for 21 years.

Project

This job was a direct mail brochure for a nonprofit organization that wanted to inform members about tax law changes and to encourage them to contribute funds to the association. The brochure was to be sent with a computer-printed letter and a business reply envelope. All had to fit in a #10 envelope. The client emphasized that he wanted the brochure to look as substantial as possible, but the budget for the piece was minimal.

The brochure was produced on a Macintosh SE with 2.5 MB of RAM, a Jasmine 70 MB hard disk drive, and a Radius two-page display. It was proofed on a LaserWriter Plus and output at 1270 dpi on a Linotronic L-300 at a service bureau. MicroPhone software was used for telecommunication, and Overwood was used to clean up the transmitted file; text was prepared in Microsoft Word, FreeHand and Illustrator were used for illustration, and PageMaker was used for page layout.

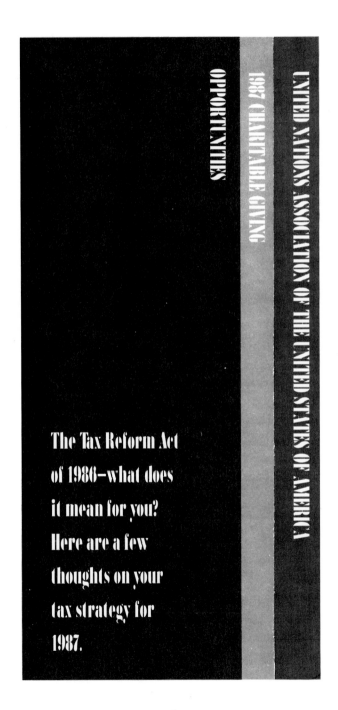

**PROJECT
OVERVIEW**

Design goals

The goal was to produce a brochure that cost a penny and a half but looked like it cost a dime. We couldn't use expensive paper — the design, layout and type were all we could afford to control. Random-length, open-looking column bottoms, extra leading, relatively wide margins and bleeds were all generous so it wouldn't look like we were squeezing the last drop out of the space we had. And we used Bodoni, a classy typeface, the banker's face.

The basic design — using stepped unequal folds — was not original. But the flaps provided an opportunity to present "stepped" information on the outside of the brochure. The folds made the piece look interesting, so people would be more likely to pick it up and read it. Likewise, the layering of gray shades helped make things look a little more intriguing.

Paper and ink

The paper was ordinary 60-pound offset, a little heavier than copier paper but with a similar texture. We used three screens to produce shades of gray. We could have used any color — a press wash-up doesn't cost much — but we couldn't think of a color that would be any more effective than black for this piece.

The finished flat size was 8½ x 14 inches. We printed a little larger all around to allow for trimming the bleeds.

The rotated labels on the flaps were graphic elements rather than information that had to be read. I used all caps and reversed them out of the gray, so the print would look like white stripes.

Minimizing Taxes

Remember the old adage about financial planning: "It's not what you earn but what you have left to spend that counts." And because 1987 is the special year of transition between the old tax structure and the new one, the role of charitable giving in your tax planning may be especially important this year.

We all hoped the Tax Reform Act of 1986 would simplify our taxes—and also reduce them. We now know that the law makes tax matters far from simple and that, while tax rates have been reduced, the loss of many deductions will counteract many of the benefits of lower rates. Middle income taxpayers, particularly in 1987, may find they owe more to Uncle Sam than in either 1986 or 1988.

New Tax Rates

In 1988 the dual tax rates of 15% and 28% will become fully operational. This means that 1987's top rate of 38.5% will drop to 28% (or 33% for some taxpayers) and that many taxpayers will be paying less in 1988 than in 1987. See for yourself how the marginal rates compare in your tax bracket:

Married, filing jointly

Taxable income		1987	1988
$ 0—	$ 3,000	11%	15%
$ 3,000—	$ 28,000	15%	15%
$ 28,000—	$ 29,750	28%	15%
$ 29,750—	$ 45,000	28%	28%
$ 45,000—	$ 71,900	35%	28%
$ 71,900—	$ 90,000	35%	33%
$ 90,000—	$149,250	38.5%	33%
Over—	$149,250	38.5%	28%

Single

Taxable income		1987	1988
$ 0—	$ 1,800	11%	15%
$ 1,800—	$ 16,800	15%	15%
$ 16,800—	$ 17,850	28%	15%
$ 17,850—	$ 27,000	28%	28%
$ 27,000—	$ 43,150	35%	28%
$ 43,150—	$ 54,000	35%	33%
$ 54,000—	$101,760	38.5%	33%
Over—	$101,760	38.5%	28%

1987 CHARITABLE GIVING

1987 Tax Strategy

Defer income

If your tax rate will fall in 1988, try to shift as much of your income as possible from 1987 to 1988. You will be taxed at a lower rate on that income, and you will have another year before paying those taxes. These are two very important reasons for deferring income.

Accelerate deductions

Deductions will not disappear entirely in 1988—and, undoubtedly, you will want to have as many as you can to reduce your taxes next year. However, because of the special transitional character of 1987, you may wish to consider taking some of your deductions in 1987.

Planning considerations

If your company sponsors a 401(k) plan, try to put the maximum ($7,000) into the plan. In this way you reduce your taxable income by the amount you contribute, and you can see your savings grow, tax-deferred, until retirement.

Here's another tip: try to bunch medical deductions and miscellaneous deductions (including employee expenses) into one year or the other. If you can bunch them in 1987, you may be better off. Since only those medical expenses exceeding 7.5% of adjusted gross income are deductible (in the case of miscellaneous expenses, only those exceeding 2% of adjusted

gross income), the more you can bunch such deductions, the more likely you are to be able to use them. Consider, for instance, paying off your child's monthly orthodontist payments for the next year or two by the end of this year. If this strategy were also to be followed with other large medical and dental expenses, the total might well exceed 7.5% of your adjusted gross income.

Consumer credit and loan interest is another important deduction. Keep in mind that 65% of consumer interest can still be used as a deduction in 1987, but only 40% will be available as a deduction in 1988. As a result, you may wish to take as much of that interest expense as you can this year.

You may also find 1987 a very good year for making the charitable contributions you have been contemplating. Although charitable deductions will be fully available to you in either year if you itemize, they may be worth more in tax savings in 1987.

Example: if you make a $1,000 gift to a charitable organization this year, and you are in the top 38.5% bracket, the gift will save you $385. Next year, since your top bracket will drop, that gift will save you less.

UNITED NATIONS ASSOCIATION OF THE UNITED STATES OF AMERICA

Working with the client

In the business of design, producing the document is only about a third of the task. Making the client feel satisfied is part of it; making something that can be printed is part of it. Staying within the budget and making the deadline are part of it as well.

To keep our timing under control, the client telecommunicated and faxed to me, and I faxed and FedEx'd to him. Normally I fax proofs (printouts from the LaserWriter), but in this case I used Federal Express because I wanted him to see the folds and get the overall feel of the brochure.

Because I do so much work for this organization, I scanned the logo and traced and filled it with Illustrator. It has saved me lots of time since, so I've more than regained the cost of the time it took to do the conversion.

Either you make a design fit the copy or you specify copy spaces for the writer. In this case, I got the copy at the same time the client approved the initial design. So I knew two things: the sheet size we could afford to print on and how much copy there was. My design job was to take the limitations and find a path between them. The path I found used wide columns, Bodoni type, open leading, a soft rag and uneven column bottoms. I could have used type much more economically if I'd had to, but the client agreed that to preserve the design he'd cut copy if necessary. As it turned out, he didn't need to.

Reversing the type was risky, because the black ink could have filled in the thin strokes of the Bodoni. I decided to try it, though, because black type on white paper can be humdrum.

The Alternative Minimum Tax reverse strategy

If you are one of the few taxpayers who will be subject to the more stringent alternative minimum tax (AMT), you may choose a planning strategy that is directly opposite the one employed by most taxpayers. That is, you may wish to defer your deductions until 1988 and accelerate your income into 1987. Since AMT rates are a flat 21%, you might do better to bring the income into a 21% year than to defer it to a 28% year. Likewise, because your rates may be higher in 1988, deferred deductions might be worth more to you next year. If AMT comes into your tax-planning picture, specific strategies should be worked out carefully with the help of a financial advisor.

The capital gains dilemma

Even with the recent downturn in the stock market, many stocks and mutual funds have appreciated in value since their acquisition. For many of us that means capital gain.

Any long-term capital gain will be taxed in both 1987 and 1988 at a minimum rate of 28% (or lower, if your tax rate is lower). Consequently, the timing of your decision to sell can be based upon market conditions instead of on a particular tax year. Whether you sell in 1987 or 1988, your tax on that

UNITED NATIONS ASSOCIATION OF THE UNITED STATES OF AMERICA

485 FIFTH AVENUE, NEW YORK, N.Y. 10017
(212) 697-3232

gain is going to be larger than it would have been a year ago. The impact of capital gains in boosting your taxes can be the worst shock of all.

Avoiding capital gain shock— partnership with charity

You can still take advantage of the higher value of your appreciated assets and avoid paying a capital gain tax by forming a partnership with a charity, such as the United Nations Association of the USA. If you intend to make a contribution to the Association this year, consider using appreciated assets instead of cash. Your out-of-pocket cost will be much lower when you donate appreciated property.

In the "old days," investments were often tax-driven and tax planning was pretty much restricted to those in the upper brackets. Now, despite a fall in tax rates, more of us find ourselves in high-income brackets. Tax and financial planning becomes important for many more people. Because charitable donations will continue to be "tax deductible," one of the best planning mechanisms remains a partnership with charity. Each partnership is unique and is based upon the donor's financial situation.

Tax planning may not enable you to avoid paying taxes in 1987, but it will certainly diminish the amount paid. At the very least, planning eliminates the element of surprise, and you can anticipate what you must pay in 1987 and what you can shift to 1988. Remember: It's what you have left that counts!

Please call or write

If you would like to find out more about some of the outright and deferred charitable-giving strategies that can help you save money, please check off the boxes on the back of the reply form for an immediate response. If time is of the essence, please contact:

Fred Tamalonis
Executive Director
United Nations Association Fund
485 Fifth Avenue
New York, N.Y. 10017

(212) 697-3232

Caution

Please keep in mind that all tax-planning and charitable-giving arrangements should be discussed with your financial-planning advisor.

UNA-USA will provide you with the most accurate information on charitable-giving opportunities that is now available. However, we must all wait for Congress to tie up some loose ends. Your lawyer, accountant, and financial planner are professional advisors who will be paying close attention to Congress and the Technical Corrections Bill of 1987 and will be able to offer up-to-the-minute information and advice on your year-end tax and gift-planning arrangements.

OPPORTUNITIES

The Tax Reform Act of 1986—what does it mean for you? Here are a few thoughts on your tax strategy for 1987.

When I started working on this project, I didn't have copy yet, but I knew appoximately what it would say. I started working on the design by playing with paper, folding it and cutting it at an angle and generally experimenting. I fiddled around, trying to see how large a piece of paper to use, how deep to make the folds and the protruding flaps, so it would be large enough for all the copy but would still fit in a #10 envelope. I found that an 8½ x 14 inch sheet would allow an interesting folding scheme with reasonably wide columns. Using this size in 60-pound offset paper, I could be sure that the brochure, a computer letter, and a #9 business reply envelope could be mailed in a #10 envelope for a single stamp. And I knew from previous experience that this client would want to keep paper and mailing costs as low as possible.

Layout

Side 1 and side 2 were mirror images of each other in the way the folds went. I set up PageMaker for double-sided spreads so I could work on both sides at once. (It helped to have the two-page display.) On the master pages I established where the folds would go, using wide columns that defined the eight panels for type (Figure 1).

Figure 1. Setting up the pages. Defining panels here was in a sense defining pages. This could have been done another way — eight pages could have been set up and then assembled later. If PageMaker had allowed marrying pages for output, using eight pages would have made sense. But it wouldn't have made sense for the client to pay for eight output pages instead of two.

Facing pages were set up with four columns each, and the gutters were defined as 5 picas. PageMaker provided equal-width columns (left page below), but because gutter width had been specified, column guides could be moved to set uneven column widths to match the folded paper model without changing the width of the gutters (right page below).

Dashed lines placed to mark the folds for the printer were covered with rectangles (with Lines set at None and Shades set at Paper), and guidelines were dragged into place from the vertical ruler.

Page setup — OK / Cancel

Page size: ○ Letter ● Legal ○ Tabloid ○ A4 ○ A3 ○ A5 ○ B5 ○ Custom: 84 by 51 picas

Orientation: ○ Tall ● Wide

Start page #: 1   # of pages: 2

Options: ☒ Double-sided ☒ Facing pages

Margin in picas: Inside 3 Outside 3 Top 2p6 Bottom 2p6

Column guides — OK / Cancel

Number of columns: 4

Space between columns: 5 picas

"Paper" rectangles mask fold lines so they won't print.

Guidelines mark the folds.

Default: Equal-width columns

Adjusted: Uneven columns

Narrowest column

Widest column

5-pica gutters

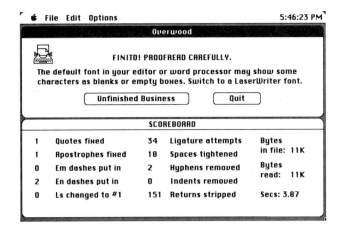

Figure 2. Cleaning up transmitted files. Telecommunicated files in word processor or ASCII text format can be prepared for placement in a page layout program with a utility like Overwood, which changes typed quotation marks and apostrophes to typeset marks, removes returns at the ends of lines, changes double spaces after punctuation to single spaces and so forth.

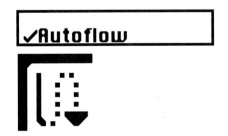

Newspapers can be set in really skinny columns, justified, with lots of small words, for an audience with an eighth-grade reading level. But the audience for this piece had a graduate school reading level. I knew that the words in the copy would be worth 75 cents apiece, so narrow columns and small type would be inappropriate. I also knew that this client wanted the type to be set in at least 10-point — he claims no one can read 9-point type. I know readability depends on the typeface as well as the audience, but I don't think it's usually worthwhile to argue with a client with such a strong opinion. This text would be set in 10-point type, so wide columns were essential. The gutters were 5 picas (almost an inch) wide.

I used a dashed hairline rule to mark each fold for the printer. I covered the hairlines with "Paper"-colored rectangles so they wouldn't show up on the printed pages. Then I placed a ruler guide over each fold line to serve as a reference while I worked on the screen.

Choosing a typeface

I took the text, which the client had transmitted by modem, and dumped it into Overwood, a shareware utility that takes out extra spaces and converts straight quotes to curly ones and double hyphens to em dashes (Figure 2). Then I dumped the modified file into Microsoft Word and printed it out.

I experimented with different typefaces and got a sense of how the words looked. At first I considered New Century Schoolbook, but when I printed it out, I saw that it was all wrong — very readable, but too bold and naive-looking. I also tried New Baskerville, but it just didn't sing to me. In the end I came to Bodoni (Figure 3). Actually, I think I chose Bodoni because the brochure was talking about money. Whenever I think about discussions of money, my mind turns to Bodoni, the banker's typeface. A few years ago all of Apple's advertising was done in Garamond, which is warm and accessible, and all of IBM's was done in Bodoni.

Even the running text is Bodoni. Some people think Bodoni shouldn't be used for text, but I think it looks fine. It's very elegant. Even though it's a broad face, the characters are vertical looking — not skinny, but vertical. It's like a rich person's house, upright, solid. A little hard to read, just a little, but that gives it a tone of high value.

Before I left Microsoft Word, I divided the text into three files — one for each of the two major body copy sections and one for the table. I also set the type size and face and formatted the table, putting in the bold column headings and setting tabs.

Placing text

Next I placed the text in my PageMaker file. ∎ *With column guides established, Autoflow makes the text flow automatically from one column to the next.*

In the end, I widened "Minimizing Taxes" beyond the righthand column guide. It looked better that way, and I kept it narrow enough so it didn't run into the fold.

Headings and subheads

I made the the subheads 1 point larger than the text. It's a little unusual to use italics for subheads, but Bodoni italic is beautiful and I like using it. In general, I avoid capitalizing words in subheads — it makes them harder to read and it's a bit old-fashioned.

For the main headings I used 30-point Bodoni Bold. I condensed it in FreeHand since the version of Page-Maker I was using did not allow type manipulation.

Leading

Leading, or line spacing, is influenced by the width of the column, the look you want, and the size and style of the type. I always lead Bodoni out (add space between the lines) to counterbalance the face's strong vertical emphasis. In that respect, it's like a sans serif typeface. The added leading creates bigger horizontal stripes of white to help guide the reader's eye across the column. The 10-point Bodoni was set on 14-point leading. It's generous, but we were trying to make this brochure look like more than it was, and leaded-out type has a generous feel. Tightly leaded type doesn't look generous.

Like many designers, I'm a little surprised by the standards the computer world tries to set. Somewhere in one of its PostScript books Adobe refers to "normal" leading as 120 percent of the type's point size. That astonishes me, because determining the right leading is a visual, not a mathematical process.

Rough bottoms

Some desktop publishers seem to go through contortions to make the column bottoms line up. Columnists in magazines about desktop publishing ask for vertical justification, but it's madness to force the bottoms of columns to line up, with different leading for different columns.

Books and newspapers use vertical justification because they have a tradition. If they can't make the vertical measure naturally, they add rules or space to make it work. The effort hardly shows in books, and newspapers have different graphic standards from other publications. But periodicals and brochures don't have a tradition of vertical justification, and it's a dreadful thing to do to the reader.

Flush-left paragraphs

Flush-left paragraphs contribute to the open, generous look needed for this brochure. A flush-left setting requires additional vertical spacing to separate

1987 Tax Strategy

Defer income

If your tax rate will fall in 1988, try to shift as much of your income as possible from 1987 to 1988. You will be taxed at a lower rate on that income, and you will have another year before paying those taxes. These are two very important reasons for deferring income.

Accelerate deductions

Deductions will not disappear entirely in 1988—and, undoubtedly, you will want to have as many as you can to reduce your taxes next year. However, because of the special transitional character of

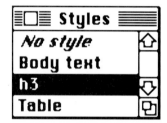

Figure 3. Defining styles. The brochure required defining only three styles. The Body Text paragraph style was defined as 10-point Bodoni flush left with 7 points (half the 14-point leading value) of space after. The h3 subheads were 1 point larger than Body text, with 6 points of space before. Headings were 30-point Bodoni Bold condensed to about 60 percent in FreeHand and placed as graphic elements.

An "as-needed" hyphen, typed Command-hyphen, will disappear if the word doesn't fall at the end of a line.

the paragraphs — I added half the leading value (or 7 points). ■ *Adding leading makes having an even, squared-up bottom (if that's what you're aiming for) very difficult, because you have a different number of paragraphs in each column and the extra spaces won't add up. For a formal, lined-up format, you have to use indented paragraphs.*

Many designs done by nondesigners have both first-line indents and additional line space after paragraphs. Not only does this not help the reader, it makes the pages look disjointed and amateurish. On the other hand, some arty designers will set the paragraphs flush left without adding space between. That's really hard to read.

Soft rag

With a rough rag, where no hyphenation is allowed, line length can differ by an inch or more. This is too much for almost any publication. For this brochure I used a soft rag, setting the hyphenation gutter for PageMaker's automatic hyphenation function to 1½ picas (the default is 2 picas), and then I went through and checked it visually. Occasionally I wanted different hyphenation than the program provided, so I fixed it manually. ■ *Typing Command-hyphen inserts an "as-needed" hyphen, which will disappear if the text is rearranged in later editing so that the word no longer falls at the end of a line.*

■ **Making grays**

A printer's screen (top panels) uses centered smooth-edged dots on a grid, with different sizes for different screen percentages. A PostScript screen (lower panels) uses square pixels to make the dots. At low resolutions, you can see the difference. At high resolutions the difference is not detectable. But problems can arise when the printer has to do a dot copy of a high-resolution computer-generated screen output on resin-coated paper.

It makes sense to have the printer put in the screens: A printer doesn't charge much to make a screen and accepts full responsibility for the way it prints. For this brochure, all of the gray areas were made solid black in the PageMaker file, and instructions were provided for the printer to strip in screens of the right densities.

Gray areas

The grays on the front and edges of the brochure were printer's screens, not PostScript screens defined in PageMaker and printed on the Linotronic (see "Making grays" on page 43). Lino screens can be problematic unless they output directly to film at high resolution, which I wasn't doing in this case. It seemed better to let the printer put in the screens. That way the printer had full control of the process and was accountable for the result.

Tabular material

The gray blocks above the headings in the table (to be put in by the printer) were for graphic interest (Figure 4), because the title was a little too arid otherwise. I used PageMaker's rectangle tool to form the gray bars and the .5-point rule around the table. I thought the client would agree to this degree of ornamentation but not much more.

Vertical labels

I used all caps on the rotated labels on the flaps (Figure 5). The type is reversed, a dangerous thing to do, but it's to further the impression of richness. I wanted

Figure 5. Setting vertical type. At the time this project was done, it was not possible to rotate type in PageMaker. So the Bodoni Poster labels (in white on a black background) were set and rotated in FreeHand before they were placed as graphic elements in PageMaker.

Married, filing jointly

Taxable income		1987	1988
$ 0— $ 3,000		11%	15%
$ 3,000— $ 28,000		15%	15%
$ 28,000— $ 29,750		28%	15%
$ 29,750— $ 45,000		28%	28%
$ 45,000— $ 71,900		35%	28%

Figure 4. Designing the tables. When the Word table file was placed, small adjustments were made to the positions of the two left-hand tabs (used for headings and dollar signs) and two right tabs (for columns of numbers). A half-point surrounding rule and gray bars added graphic interest (see page 38).

Stretching type

Not all type can be successfully stretched or condensed. In faces such as Helvetica, in which the difference between thick and thin strokes is minimal, condensing or extending the characters changes the relationship between the horizontal and vertical strokes, radically changing the character of the type. Faces such as Bodoni Poster already have extreme contrast between horizontal and vertical strokes, so they stand up better to condensing.

the labels to look like white stripes, so using uppercase and lowercase letters would have been distracting. It's not important, by the way, that this type be read. If it were important information, I wouldn't have reversed it from the panels, and I wouldn't have set it in all caps. Sometimes type is a graphic element, or an illustration, or an icon, and for those purposes readability is not the primary goal.

I set the type for the flaps in FreeHand 24-point Bodoni Poster condensed to 60 percent. Each label was set as a separate file and inserted on the PageMaker page with the Place function. Display text for the cover was set, imported and reversed in the same way.

Logo

The first step in converting the client's logo with Illustrator was to scan it in, making a paint file to use as a template for tracing with the pen tool. Putting in the stars was great fun (Figure 6). I drew a nonprinting circle slightly larger than the central circle and placed a single star (from the Adobe Collector's Edition, as I recall). Then I used the Rotate-Copy function (holding down the Option key while using the rotation tool) to place the next one; I clicked on the center of the circle (indicated by crossed nonprinting lines) as the center of rotation. Then I used Command-D to duplicate it 48 more times, all around the circle. ▌ *Using Illustrator in this way requires calculating the degree*

Figure 6. Converting the logo. With Illustrator 88, FreeHand or Streamline (an autotracing program), the autotrace function can be used to convert clients' logos to electronic format. But the results can be imprecise, and tracing with the drawing tools works better much of the time.

To make the 50-star border, a single star from Adobe's Collector's Edition was pasted into position on a nonprinting circle and then copied to a position 7.2 degrees farther around the circle using the rotation tool, with the center of the circle used as the center of rotation. (The minus sign before the angle size indicates clockwise rotation. Then this copy-and-move process was repeated (Command-D) 48 times.

of arc occupied by each character (degrees in a circle [360] divided by the number of items [50 stars in this case] equals degrees of rotation).

I converted the logo gratis so that I would have it when I needed it. It probably took about 10 hours to do, but every time I use it I can charge the client a small fee, and having it saves me lots of time. Now I can use it in any document in any size, which is fabulous. When I do roughs of a new job, I can show the client all the logos in size and position. I don't have a stat machine, so without the Illustrator file I would have to go out to get stats made if I needed them.

Bleeds

I used bleeds for the front of the brochure and the stepped edges. Bleeds are a fairly cheap thrill. You have to allow about ⅛ inch for the bleed on each edge, and then the printer charges so much per cut to trim off the excess. Since we were printing 150,000 brochures, we could afford to have the printer run the job on large sheets on a large press so that our final cut size could be 8½ x 14 inches. But if I had been doing 200 at the corner "quick print" shop, using standard legal paper would have saved a lot of money. In that case, I would have designed the sheet to be 8¼ x 13¾ inches, printed it on the legal paper, and then trimmed it.

Preparing the mechanical

The Linotronic L-300 can handle legal-size images with outside crop marks by outputting on a tabloid-sized page. PageMaker lets you print both full bleeds (extending off the nominal page) and outside crop marks for trimming (Figure 7).

I used the resin-coated paper output from the Linotronic to paste up a mechanical. ▌ *Even though the Linotronic output includes the bleeds and crop marks, it's a good idea to mount pages on boards for the printer. The output is fragile, and mounting protects it. Mounting the page also makes it easier to add cover tissues with production notes for the printer.*

All three of the gray panels were output as solid black with white type reversed out. My instructions on the tissue told the printer the screen percentage of each of the gray panels, where to bleed, and that the type knocks out of the gray and prints white. Even though I had reversed the type out of the black panels, I still repeated the instructions on the tissue, because it was important for the printer to know exactly what I wanted. I also sent a copy of the dummy, showing the folds.

Going to the printer

This client usually manages the printing process. The organization has a publications department that uses a competitive bidding system and has printers the department likes to work with. For this piece, the printer, who was also a mailing specialist, was in upstate New York. Once the client approved copies of the mechanical (via fax), I sent the artwork directly to the printer. It's not the classical arrangement. Ideally, at least for high-quality jobs or projects with more than two colors, the designer and client watch the job production. But that's not necessary for a little one-color job like this one. There wasn't even a blueline proof. The printer just ran the pieces off, folded and stacked them up, stuffed the envelopes and mailed them.

In retrospect

This project was not a dream design job, but it's a fairly typical one. There are immutable constraints — the budget is often one, the number of words, the size of the page and so on.

This brochure would be wonderful done on a paper like Curtis Flannel. The piece would feel deluxe from the beginning. But it's hard to sell paper to conservative, cost-conscious clients because they know the costs will go up. Typically, paper accounts for 30 or 40 percent of the cost of the print job. A really good paper can make up more than half the printing cost. Price depends on the size of the print run, since the paper costs keep going up as the quantity goes up, whereas some of the other costs don't go up proportionally. Paper is sold by poundage in case lots. You pay a 40 percent charge if you buy less than a case, but once you order at least one lot, the price stays the same until you get to really big volume, where discounts come into play.

Print to "LaserWriter Plus" OK

Copies: 3 ☐ Collate ☐ Reverse order Cancel

Page range: ○ All ◉ From 2 to 2

Paper source: ◉ Paper tray ○ Manual feed

Scaling: 100 percent ☐ Thumbnails, 16 per page

Options: ☐ Proof print ☐ Spot color overlays ☐ Cutouts
☐ Substitute fonts ☐ Smooth ☒ Crop marks
☐ Tile: ○ Manual ◉ Auto overlap 6 picas

Printer type: Linotronic 100/300 Driver: Aldus Change...
Paper: Tabloid Options: Wide

Figure 7. Setting up for Linotronic output. Printing each legal-size page on tabloid size repro paper allowed crop marks, fold lines and bleeds to show. The Linotronic output was pasted up and tissued for the printer.

PORTFOLIO

Kathleen Tinkel

"One of the reasons designers can be more adventurous than nondesigners is that we know we can slap the computer output down on a board, cut it up and remedy any problems with traditional paste-up. Knowing that I can always fix things gives me more freedom in the beginning — I don't have to be conservative while I'm laying out the pages. WYSIWYG (what you see is what you get) is one of the world's great lies, so being able to use traditional paste-up methods to fix the surprises in the output is very useful."

This cover for the **UNA-USA annual report** was laid out in FreeHand. FreeHand is ideal for single-page layouts, especially if the file has to be telecommunicated to the service bureau, because FreeHand files are typically so much smaller than PageMaker files. The document was output and provided to the printer on resin-coated paper at 2540 dpi. The printer then screened the logo at 133 lpi.

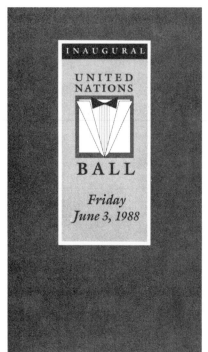

This **program** for the annual fundraiser for the United Nations Association of the United States of America was designed in PageMaker, along with a seating plan and menu card. The type is Adobe Garamond.

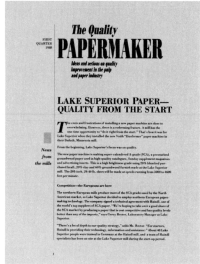

The Quality Papermaker is a newsletter published by a maker of heavy equipment for the paper industry. It was designed in PageMaker to be printed on a different deluxe paper every issue. The typeface is Bodoni. The wide left margin holds right-justified text that provides a very brief "executive summary" of each article.

The Commonwealth Fund Annual Report was a two-color 142-page book, which was produced as four PageMaker documents. (At the time it was done, PageMaker, with a 127-page limit, couldn't have handled the job as one file, and for storage and handling convenience, it seemed appropriate to break it into four parts.) On the cover and throughout the book, 75 dpi scans saved as TIFFs were used as placeholders for photos. The low-resolution TIFFs took less disk space than higher-res ones would have, but LaserWriter Plus printing was still very slow. When the Plus was replaced with a LaserWriter IINTX (even without a hard disk drive), printing time for one of the four sections of the job went from 2½ hours to 17 minutes.

Charts and graphs for the report were produced quickly in Cricket Graph, saved as PICT files and opened in Illustrator 88 as templates, where they were used as rough guides for tracing. Illustrator EPS files were imported into PageMaker, where type was added. Some very strange "bugs" occurred when the pages were output on a Linotronic L-300: First, on pages with charts, the type over the placed EPS files printed on both plates; second, also on pages with imported Illustrator files, all the apostrophes disappeared from the italic type in the text. These problems, which probably wouldn't have occurred with Linotronic's RIP3, were never solved electronically, and the cause remains a mystery; type on the color plate had to be opaqued out by hand, and the apostrophes were painstakingly fixed with a knife and waxed repro.

THE TREASURER'S REPORT

John E. Craig, Jr., Vice President and Treasurer

A review of a U.S. institutional endowment's performance over the twelve-month period beginning on July 1, 1987, and ending on June 30, 1988 (the Fund's 1987–88 fiscal year) must focus on the stock market "crash" of October 19, 1987, which signaled the end of the great bull stock market of 1982–87. This report has such a focus, because those who follow the Fund's activities are likely to be interested in both how its finances fared in the market downturn and whether the Fund has made significant changes in its investment and spending policies as a result of the crisis of the fall of 1987.

As indicated in Figure 1, the value of the Fund's endowment declined from $292.2 million on June 30, 1987, to $279.2 million on June 30, 1988—a reduction of $13 million, or 4.4 percent. The purchasing power of the Fund's endowment, measured in 1967 constant dollars, fell from $86.6 million to $79.5 million, or by 8.2 percent. The decline in the Fund's assets in a fiscal year when the U.S. stock market's return was −7.0 percent (as measured by the S&P 500 Index) was thus, relatively speaking, not exceptional. By example, in 1983–84, in the midst of the 1980s' bull market, the Fund experienced a 13.0 percent decline in its end-of-fiscal year assets, as a result of that year's market downturn.

THE END OF THE BULL MARKET IN STOCKS: 1982–1987

The 1982–87 bull market in stocks lasted a record 62 months, twice the post–World War II average for bull markets of 31 months. By the end of September 1987, U.S. stocks had achieved price/earnings ratios that exceeded all previous market records but still remained generally below those of foreign stocks. Corporate earnings were rising, providing hope that the prevailing price/earnings ratios might ultimately be justified by economic realities. Offsetting the positive economic news were concerns about the possibility of

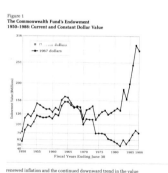

Figure 1
The Commonwealth Fund's Endowment 1950–1988: Current and Constant Dollar Value

renewed inflation and the continued downward trend in the value of the U.S. dollar—both of these negative factors leading to rising interest rates.

The issue of whether U.S. stocks were overvalued or headed to new record highs was settled in mid-October 1987, when the weight of the disturbing news from the financial markets overcame the encouraging news on the U.S. economy. The results were record declines in all stock market indices and unprecedented hourly and

74

75

THE SPORTS & HEALTH CENTER OF SCRIPPS CLINIC

*T*here will be plenty for you to do on Saturday, July 8.

The Torrey Pines Stride will set the pace for the day, starting at 7:30 a.m. You'll have two courses to choose from in this fun walking event: a five-miler through Torrey Pines Park or a three-mile course to the Glider Port.

Exercise your options at our

C H A P T E R   4

Metamorphosis of a Newspaper Ad

Designer

Tom Lewis, president of Tom Lewis, Inc. in Del Mar, California, writes and designs collateral and editorial pieces. Collectively, he and his staff represent over 50 years of experience in award-winning publication design for such clients as IBM, Stanford University and CBS Publications.

Project

This piece was an ad for Scripps Clinic of La Jolla, California, to be printed in a San Diego daily newspaper. It was an announcement for the grand opening of the clinic's new Sports & Health Center, encouraging participation in both their open house and a 5-mile or 3-mile walk.

The ad was produced with a Macintosh II with 2.5 MB of RAM and a 40 MB internal hard disk drive and a Radius two-page display. It was proofed on a LaserWriter Plus and output to a Linotronic L-300 at medium resolution (1270 dpi) at a service bureau. PageMaker was used for text input and for page layout. FreeHand was used for setting display type, which was imported into PageMaker for placement. The studio photocopier also played an important role in the page design and proofing processes.

PROJECT OVERVIEW

Design goal

Our goal for the Scripps Clinic Sports & Health Center grand opening ad was to produce a piece that was large, dynamic and very readable, to be published in the *San Diego Union*. We originally designed a tall, narrow ad, but later decided to reformat it to capture two pages of the local news section of the morning paper.

The ad had to include an invitation to tour the Center, a list of the facilities available there and an entry form for the Torrey Pines Stride, an outdoor walking event associated with the opening. Tying all three objectives together in a unified, attention-getting ad was a challenge.

Attention-getters for the piece included four eye-catching photos and the 136-point "Exercise your options" banner that jumped the gutter to tie the two pages of the ad together.

The Campanile italic type in the top bar echoes the headline. The second time the ad was run, the type was moved to the right side to balance the large type on the lower left.

■ ■ ■ ■ ■ ■ ■ ■ **ENTRY FORM** ■ ■ ■ ■ ■ ■ ■ ■
(ONE PER PERSON; PHOTOCOPIES ACCEPTED)

GREEN HOSPITAL
OF SCRIPPS CLINIC
An Affiliate of **HCA**. The Healthcare Company.

CHECK ONE:_____ 5 MILE_____3 MILE
I WON'T BE STRIDING, BUT I'LL JOIN YOU FOR THE OPEN
HOUSE AT 11:00 A.M._____
PLEASE PRINT

NAME:_____
LAST   FIRST   INITIAL
ADDRESS:_____

CITY:_____

STATE: _____ ZIP:_____

PHONE: WORK_____HOME:_____

ENTRY FEE (INCLUDES T-SHIRT) $15.00
LATE ENTRY FEE (AFTER 6-30-89)   20.00
    ADDITIONAL DONATION TO THE
    HEART, LUNG AND VASCULAR
    CENTER AND THE SPORTS AND
    HEALTH CENTER   _____

TOTAL ENCLOSED   _____

PLEASE MAKE CHECK PAYABLE TO:
TORREY PINES STRIDE
I'M A TEAM STRIDER_____
TEAM NAME EMPLOYER
MAIL ENTRIES TO:
TORRY PINES STRIDE
C/O SCRIPPS CLINIC AUXILIARY
10666 N. TORREY PINES ROAD, LA JOLLA, CA 92037
TO RECEIVE YOUR BIB BY RETURN MAIL, PLEASE INCLUDE A STAMPED,
SELF-ADDRESSED ENVELOPE.
WAIVER
I HEREBY RELEASE SCRIPPS CLINIC AND RESEARCH FOUN-
DATION, AND ANY OTHER ORGANIZATION(S) ASSOCIATED
WITH THIS STRIDE, THEIR AFFILIATES, DIRECTORS, OFFI-
CERS, EMPLOYEES, SUCCESSORS AND ASSIGNS, FROM
ANY AND ALL LIABILITY ARISING FROM OR IN ANY WAY
CONNECTED WITH MY PARTICIPATION IN THE SCRIPPS
CLINIC TORREY PINES STRIDE. I CERTIFY THAT I AM IN
GOOD CONDITION AND AM ABLE TO SAFELY PARTICIPATE
IN THIS EVENT. I WILL ADDITIONALLY PERMIT USE OF MY
NAME OR PICTURE IN BROADCASTS, VIDEO, PROMOTION
OR OTHER ACCOUNT OF THIS EVENT, AND I UNDERSTAND
THE ENTRY FEE IS NONREFUNDABLE. I HAVE READ THE
ENTRY INFORMATION PROVIDED AND CERTIFY MY COMPLI-
ANCE BY SIGNING BELOW.

X_____
SIGNATURE (PARENT/GUARDIAN SIGNATURE IF UNDER 18 YEARS OF AGE)
IF UNDER AGE 18: THIS IS TO CERTIFY THAT MY SON/
DAUGHTER HAS MY PERMISSION TO PARTICIPATE IN THE
SCRIPPS CLINIC TORREY PINES STRIDE, IS IN GOOD
CONDITION, AND THAT EVENT OFFICIALS HAVE MY PER-
MISSION TO AUTHORIZE EMERGENCY MEDICAL TREAT-
MENT IF NECESSARY.

Working with the client

We worked directly with a marketing representative from Scripps Clinic, just a few minutes from our office, which helped facilitate proofing, changes and approvals. We were given three weeks to complete the project, which was extended to six weeks when the opening date was changed. We considered three weeks to be a generous amount of time for a project of this nature, even with the photos that had to be shot, so six weeks was wonderful.

Putting motion on the page

The generous use of white space, the action photographs, extra leading with bold type for the body copy, the condensed and slightly italicized heads and the five-line-deep initial caps gave the main body of the ad its dynamic look and offset the volume of static copy required in the Entry Form.

A t 11:00 a.m., we'll be hosting the grand opening of our new Sports and Health Center—a 30,000 square-foot facility with our Sports Medicine Center, Health Resource Center, Health Risk Appraisal, and Fitness Center with gym, lap-pool, track, strength training, and *Choices*, a spa cuisine restaurant.

screenings to refreshments and prizes. *FIRM UP YOUR RESERVATION.*

We'll give you a run-through of the new Center, introduce you to the staff and provide you with everything from health

Will you be participating in the Stride or joining us at the Open House? Let us know by completing this entry form.

Setting type in 8-point sans serif caps isn't exactly standard procedure, but in this case it worked well. The drastic difference from the type of the body copy helped set off the Entry Form as an entity of its own. And for the "fine print" sort of material it needed to present, the type seemed quite appropriate and readable. Even the 5-point type in the entry fee copy is clear.

Body copy wrapped around rectangular and silhouetted photos. The Franklin Gothic Bold type was big and solid; generous leading and ragged right columns provided openness. The easy-to-read text was designed to tempt the person turning through the newspaper to stop and read. The initial caps tied the body copy to the headline type and provided obvious starting points for the reader.

Since PageMaker 3.0 didn't allow compressing and skewing of type, the Campanile display type was set in FreeHand, saved as encapsulated Post-Script, and Placed on the PageMaker page.

The Sports & Health Center grand opening ad was originally designed to run vertically on a single page of the newspaper (Figure 1). When we decided to change from a vertical to a horizontal format to capture two pages of the paper, it took far less effort and cost to convert our electronic layout than it would have conventionally. For example, it was easy to adjust column widths, type style and leading of the body copy, and layout of the entry form to fit the new format.

It took a little bit of coordinative effort to get the newspaper to run the ad to jump the gutter. Several telephone calls were required to (1) find someone at the paper who knew it could be done, (2) arrange to contract for the space and (3) find out exactly what the design constraints imposed by the gutter would be. In the meantime, we started redesigning the ad.

Layout

In PageMaker we set up a 21.75 x 7.75-inch page with .75-inch margins on the top, bottom and outside edges (Figure 2). We specified an underlying grid of 10 columns with 1-pica gutters. Our page layout included several graphic elements that served to define the ad as a whole and separate it from other items on the newspaper page: A ½-inch black bar at the top was formed with the rectangle tool to tie the two parts of the ad together, and a white borderless rectangle was used to mask the line where it jumped the gutter. A dotted-line border enclosed the ad elements.

Body copy

Because we had a limited amount of copy, we set the ad directly in PageMaker rather than importing it from a word processing program as we do for more substantial copy. ∎ *PageMaker 4.0's word processing functions, not available when this project was done, make it much easier to produce clean copy (with*

Figure 1. Designing the original ad. The Sports & Health Center ad was originally designed in a vertical format. Many elements of the design and format of the original ad were retained when the format was changed to horizontal to jump the gutter of the newspaper spread.

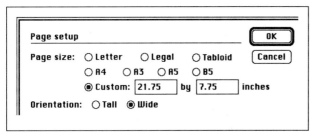

Figure 2. Establishing the horizontal format. A single Custom, Wide page was set up to design the ad. The solid bar and dotted border helped define the space, which would stretch across two newspaper pages, as a single unit.

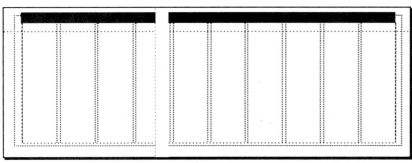

checked spelling, ligatures inserted with the search-and-replace function and no extra spaces after punctuation) right in the page layout program.

We split the body copy into two sections, each with its own initial cap (see pages 50 and 51). The single-column section on the left announced the Torrey Pines Stride, and the three-column section on the right gave the time for the Open House and listed Center facilities. We wanted a typeface that was really bold and readable for the body copy, so we chose sans serif Franklin Gothic Heavy, 12-point on 18-point leading.

We decided on the ragged-right paragraphs to help with the openness of the ad. With so little copy and open leading, secondary leading between paragraphs would only have confused the reader, so we went with healthy indents to identify paragraph changes.

Heads, subheads and drop caps

In contrast to the Franklin Gothic Heavy type, we chose Casady & Greene's Campanile Condensed Bold face for the heads and drop caps. We decided to run the large headline across the bottom of the ad to help support the bold rule at the top and the big action photo, and to balance the bold body copy of the ad. By jumping the gutter, the headline helped the top rule provide a sense of unity. The reversed type at the upper left and the drops caps also helped with the continuity.

Figure 3. Customizing type. Campanile Condensed Bold was condensed even further and italicized to produce a large, energetic banner.

We set the Campanile type in FreeHand, condensed it further, sheared it for the italic effect, saved the four elements (two heads and two drop caps) as separate EPS (encapsulated PostScript) files and placed them as graphic elements in the PageMaker document (Figure 3). Because this face is so condensed, we could set the heading very large (approximately 136 points) without running out of room for the copy.

By using the Text Wrap dialog box, we could adjust the way the body copy wrapped around the initial caps (Figure 4). (See "Wrapping type" on page 57 for hints on using the Text Wrap option.)

Entry form

We chose Franklin Gothic for the entry form for its clean readability at 6 points. By setting the type in caps, we eliminated ascenders and descenders, so that even on relatively tight leading (6.5 points) stripes of white space guided the eye across the 12.5-pica column. The type was justified as part of the businesslike, rectangular format of the form, and to set it apart from the body of the ad.

Like the border of the ad, the border of the entry form was made with the rectangle tool and choices from the Lines menu. Square dots were used for the form in contrast to the round ones of the overall border (Figure 5). Extending the entry form outside the boundary created by the larger rectangle helped identify the form as a separate element.

Images

Images for the ad consisted of four photos. We used snapshots, enlarged on the photocopy machine, to design the layout. Then we shot the real pictures as 35mm color slides on site at the Health Center. The largest picture was made up of several photos collaged together to produce the one image.

We used PageMaker's rectangle tool to place the traditional black boxes to indicate halftone placements (Figure 6). The largest photo sat between columns of type, so the gutters served to separare it from the text. The smaller rectangular photos were wrapped with a standoff of ⅛-inch on the right; no standoff was required on the left, top or bottom because of the ragged right margin and generous leading specified for the text (Figure 7).

We could have scanned in a copy of the silhouetted photo as a position-only shot for type wrapping, but it seemed like overkill — there were only three lines of type that required fitting, and it didn't seem to make sense to increase the size of the file and the screen-refresh time to accommodate a scanned

Figure 4. Wrapping type around type. Like the headlines, initial caps were generated in FreeHand, saved as encapsulated PostScript files, and placed in PageMaker 3.0 as graphic elements. Through Text Wrap, text was wrapped to fit the bold italic letters.

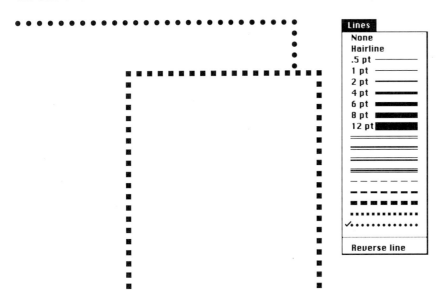

Figure 5. Making dotted borders. Two kinds of dotted lines were chosen from the Lines menu (found under the Element menu in PageMaker 4.0) to make borders for the ad. The border of the entry form was drawn with the rectangle tool, with Black chosen from the Colors palette and Paper chosen from the Shades menu (renamed Fill and found under the Element menu in PageMaker 4.0) to mask the outer border where the two overlapped.

image. So we estimated the type wrap, proofed the page on the laser printer and used a photocopy of our snapshot of the woman doing calisthenics to check the wrap. We got it right on the first try. ∎ *A TIFF or paint image can be "Image-Controlled" through the Option menu so that it doesn't print (see "FPO images" on page 58), but the image information is still stored in the PageMaker file, and this increases the document by the same amount as if the image were printed.*

Preparing the mechanical

The ad was output to a Linotronic L-300 at medium resolution — there was no need to go higher than 1270 dpi, since we chose not to incorporate the halftones in the file — and pasted up as a mechanical. Since our service bureau didn't have the Campanile font, we supplied both screen and printer versions. ∎ *Casady & Greene (the company that markets Campanile) and many other*

Figure 6. Using placeholders. To hold space for the photos, which would be halftoned and stripped in conventionally, solid black rectangles were placed in the layout.

∎ **Wrapping type**

Wrapping type around an object begins with selecting the object with the pointer tool and then choosing Text Wrap. Clicking the center Wrap option (full-wrap) puts a "repellent" border around the rectangle occupied by the object. A 1-pica standoff on all sides is the typical PageMaker default.

The standoff can be changed by typing new numbers into the four boundary boxes — lower numbers to bring the boundaries closer to the edges of the image, higher numbers to put more space between object and text. The wrap boundaries around a rectangular object can also be changed by dragging the dotted boundary line right or left (for vertical boundaries), or up or down (for horizontals).

To make a boundary for wrapping type around an irregular shape, you can drag existing handles. You can also create and move new handles to make smaller line segments that conform to the shape of the image. To create a new handle, click on the boundary line at a point where a handle is needed, release the mouse button to form the handle, and then drag the handle to a new position.

If you have text in place around the object while you're changing the boundary, PageMaker will refresh the screen, rewrapping the type, each time you move a handle. To save time, hold down the spacebar to prevent screen refresh until you've finished the boundary.

suppliers of non-Adobe fonts allow users to provide both screen and printer fonts to their service bureau for one-time use in outputting any project in which they are used. They do this to encourage graphic artists to incorporate their typefaces in illustrations and page designs — because you can "lend" the font to the service bureau, it's not necessary to find a shop that owns the font or is willing to buy it in order to get high-resolution output. ∎ One way to avoid font ID conflict when you have to

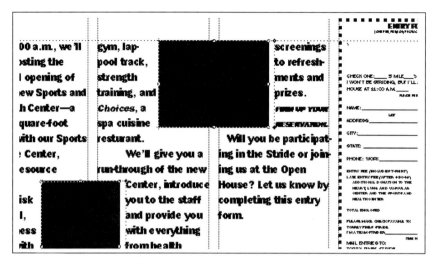

Figure 7. Balancing the text wrap. A relatively well-balanced border of space around the photographs was achieved by setting a ⅛-inch wrap on the right-hand side. The 18-point leading provided the space needed above and below the photos, and the ragged right text provided a natural standoff on the left sides.

supply a font to your service bureau, is to supply an entire System along with the project file. That way the service bureau can run your job without running into problems that can result if the font numbering or naming scheme on your System is different than theirs.

Photocopies of our original snapshots were pasted onto the board for position only. The strip of type to be reversed out of the top rule was cut from the PageMaker output and provided as a separate piece of art on an overlay, to be stripped in conventionally; this would give the printer more control in maintaining stroke weight of the reversed lettering. The logos for the Health Center (top right) and Green Hospital (at the top of the entry form) were also provided separately because they hadn't yet been converted to electronic form.

∎ FPO images

TIFF (tagged image file format) files made by scanning photos or hand-drawn line art, even at low resolution, are often used in electronic page layouts "for position only" (FPO) — as working substitutes for artwork to be pasted up or stripped in later. They're useful not only for holding a shape for type wrapping but also for proofing the pages.

To avoid having to cut up the final imagesetter output to remove a placeholder image, you can make these invisible by cropping the image down to nothing or setting Brightness to the maximum (or Contrast to the minimum) using Image Control. However, when cropping or Image Control is used, the graphic disappears from the screen as well as from the output. No matter which method is used to hide the image, the picture still adds just as much to the size of the PageMaker file as if it were fully visible.

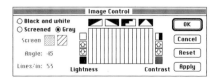

Also on the overlay were horizontal rules to be reversed out of the large central photo (see pages 50 and 51). These lines helped with the continuity of the piece, leading the reader from the copy on the left to the copy on the right. The rules were spaced 18 points apart and aligned with the baselines of the type.

The *Union* would have accepted negative film for the ad. But we chose to output on RC paper for this particular project so that our client could conveniently proof the final art that went to the newspaper.

Reusing the art

To coordinate the ad with the Sports & Health Center brochure, we used a similar design for both (Figure 8). The brochure was produced in color, and some of the display type was given a drop shadow of a second color by cloning the type, offsetting the clone slightly from the original, and assigning different colors to original and clone.

In retrospect

Electronic graphics technology continues to evolve. If I were doing this project today, I'd condense the type right in the page layout program.

I would probably also scan the photos and set them in place in the page file. In the early summer of 1989 when we did this project, we had only a 75 dpi scanner. But we've upgraded since, and we've had great success in outputting halftones and line art at high resolution. The L-300's faster RIP (raster image processor, the PostScript interpreter for the imagesetter) makes this an economical process.

Figure 8. Coordinating collateral materials. The Sports & Health Center brochure was coordinated with the ad. Many of the same elements were used in both pieces. At the time the ad was done, PageMaker did not separate process colors, so the shadowed lettering was done by making two overlays and specifying colors for the printer.

PORTFOLIO

Tom Lewis

"When I was a one-man design studio, I used X-acto knife and waxer to move blocks of copy and illustrations around on the board. When my studio expanded and my role became that of art director, I had to turn these tasks over to graphic designers. Like most other art directors I knew, I had lost control of the design subtleties of the job. Limited by time constraints or cost factors, I tended to go along with spacing changes pasted up by the designer. With the Mac, I can once again play with the elements of a design — placing them exactly where I want them, "crafting" the page to my liking. As an art director friend of mine said about designing on the Macintosh, 'I have my X-acto knife back!'

"But the art director isn't the only one who benefits from electronic design tools. I encourage each of my illustrators and graphic designers to explore, to become proficient with special-effects programs such as SmartArt, as well as the more standard applications. We're all in there pushing ourselves in terms of techniques, learning how to work with more programs and asking ourselves about each job, 'Is computer design and production feasible for this piece? What would be the best technique to execute this design?'"

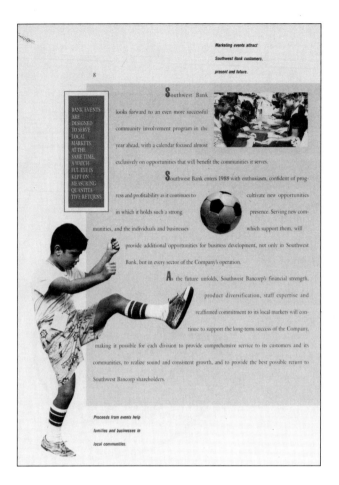

In designing the **Southwest Bank annual report,** solid PageMaker rectangles were used to hold space for some photos, while others were scanned and placed as TIFFs to allow type wrapping. Image Control was used to decrease contrast of the TIFFs to the point that they didn't appear on the L-300 output, but they still held the "wrap." This allowed pasteup of the actual photos without knife work to trim away placeholders.

LA Lawyer **magazine** was designed in PageMaker. The letters used in the logo were derived from Huxley by graphic designer John Odam using Fontographer. Later the entire font was completed for use in the magazine. In the spread shown here, Lewis was able to design the table of contents as he wanted it to appear and then vary the type size and spacing of the editor's letter (on the left page) and the advisory staff listing (on the right) to fit around this design.

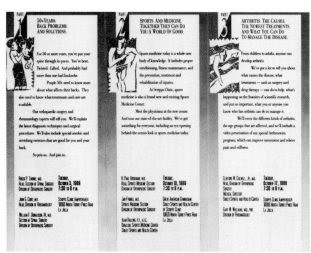

This **brochure** included hand-drawn illustrations, scanned and used as place-holders in the layout. (Illustrator Roger Chandler later began using the Macintosh and found that it suited his drawing style very well.) Once the brochure had been designed, individual panels provided the elements and design direction for a set of ads and flyers.

HeartCorps **magazine** is designed and produced in PageMaker. To design the subscription offer (far right), TIFF and encapsulated PostScript elements from past issues were picked up and reassembled into a page to promote the magazine. In an article about foods, the type wrap for the "Herbs" spread (shown at bottom) was done by scanning the Polaroid preliminary shot from the photo session and Placing it on the PageMaker page. Designers were given unusual editorial control in rearranging and recombining blocks of text to fit the information to the layout.

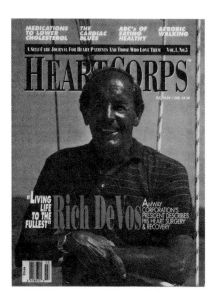

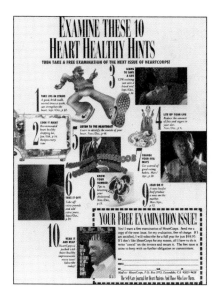

C H A P T E R 5

Designer to Client, Mac to IBM

Designer

Michael Waitsman is CEO of Synthesis Concepts, Inc., a Chicago design and consulting firm. He has written and lectured on a variety of topics about computers and desktop publishing, including articles in *Step-By-Step Electronic Design, Personal Publishing, ThePage* and *Publish.* As a pioneer in the use of computers for design and production, he founded the Association for the Development of Electronic Publishing Technique (A.D.E.P.T), a rapidly growing user group of desktop publishers.

Project

Our goal was to design a monthly newsletter to go to all offices of the national law firm of Wildman, Harrold, Allen & Dixon. We wanted to set it up so that the firm could then lay it out and produce it in-house. Like the Chicago office newsletter we had already designed for them, this one was to have a lively but respectable look, and it had to be easy to produce on their IBM PC–based desktop publishing system.

Our firm uses Macintoshes, but we'd had an IBM PC before the Mac came out, so we're comfortable with that system as well. Lisa Marks-Ellis designed the layout for the newsletter in PageMaker, which is very similar on both platforms, and we made an effort to use design elements that could be constructed in that program. When we had to go outside PageMaker to achieve the effect we wanted for some graphic element, we chose a program that we were sure would create a file suitable for conversion to an IBM format.

We designed the newsletter on a Macintosh II computer system with a LaserWriter Plus printer. Wildman Harrold had an IBM PS/2 Model 30 (at that time the computer system recommended by IBM for desktop publishing applications) equipped with PageMaker and an NEC

PostScript laser printer, one of the very few non-Apple PostScript printers then available for the IBM. Although we would have advised them to use a Macintosh-based system, their management information systems group had set an IBM standard and didn't want the company to depart from it. (Besides that, their firm was headquartered in the IBM building in

Chicago!) The restriction to the non-Mac platform was not an overwhelming handicap from our point of view because of the similarity of PageMaker on both systems. But we had strongly recommended a PostScript printer for proofing. Final output is produced on a Linotronic L-300 at 2540 dpi.

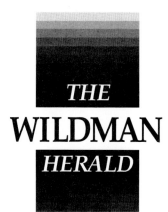

Volume 1, Number 2
June 1988

The National Newsletter of
Wildman, Harrold, Allen & Dixon

THE WILDMAN HERALD

IN THIS ISSUE

National Administrator Chosen

by Rod Heard

Paul Penning is an avid science fiction reader. That is fortunate for him because as Rod Serling might observe, he's about to walk into the Twilight Zone, that enigmatic region that exists on the edge of reality — the National Law Firm. The Iowa native who moved to Houston seven years ago will assume the dual role of National Administrator and Houston Office Manager.

"I'm excited about the challenge." Paul says. "It's going to require a team effort to stimulate and coordinate the ideas of others while hopefully initiating a few of my own in creating a national firm mechanism."

Paul is uniquely **qualified** to spearhead the national project. He received a B.A. in accounting from Creighton University in 1978 and is a CPA in Texas. For the last four years, Paul has been the controller for Greenwood, Koby, et al., a 12-person law firm in Houston. His initial responsibility was to automate the firm's manual timekeeping and financial systems. Soon, however, Paul was in charge of the entire administration of the firm — its operation policies, personnel and finances. In Paul's first year with Greenwood, Koby its gross revenues increased 100 percent. WHAD looks forward to a repeat performance.

Between 1981 and 1983, Paul was a Senior Financial Analyst with the Gray Tool Company in Houston. He was directly responsible for accounting procedures in not only Houston, but for several of its national and international subsidiaries.

Paul has also worked with Godfather's Pizza as an internal auditor in the company's franchise program in Omaha. "They made me an offer," Paul smirked, "and you know the rest." In his first job out of Creighton, Paul was an auditor for the Prudential Insurance Company in Minneapolis.

Paul and his wife, Carole, have been married for one year. They live in Houston, but enjoy jogging, *please turn to page 19*

**PROJECT
OVERVIEW**

Working with the client

Typically, our design firm follows its design work through the production process. But more and more, clients using desktop publishing ask that we take a different approach: We provide the design services and they handle the layout and production. That way we spend more of our time designing, and our clients can hold production costs down and exercise tighter control of their publication schedules.

Wildman, Harrold liked the newletter we had already designed for their Chicago office and wanted a design that was similar but not identical. For the previous newsletter (*The Wildman Reporter*) we had been commissioned to advise the firm on what electronic publishing equipment they should buy, to design a newsletter for them and to ease them into learning how to produce it. We had planned to produce the first two or three issues but actually

produced the first five, since their equipment took longer than expected to arrive. This gave Maureen McNair, a legal secretary with no prior desktop publishing experience, more time to get familiar with the process—and more examples to follow for differing article types and lengths. (Later we went to her office for key steps while she produced it. This two-stage training process was critical to the success of this cooperative project.) Our role after the first five issues of the *Reporter* (and after a single issue of the *Herald*) has been limited to checking the page proofs and offering corrections or suggestions.

With the exception of the banner, which was created in ImageStudio, all other elements were originated in PageMaker, to make the transition from Mac to IBM PC as easy as possible. Even the gavel in the "Practice Reports" heading was drawn with PageMaker's rectangle and line tools. Graphic elements used in the newsletter were stored on the pasteboard of the Master template.

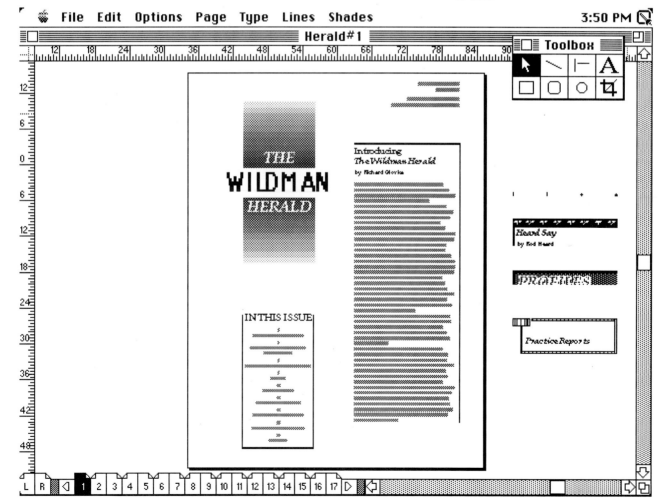

Folios (in 12-point bold type) were placed on the master pages, so that newsletter pages were numbered automatically: The type tool (the A from the tool palette) was chosen and clicked on one of the master pages; then the Command and Option keys were held down while a P was typed, placing a zero onto the page. This was dragged into place at the bottom of the page, between two rules created with the line tool. The entire footer was copied and pasted onto the other master page.

The headings for articles were given a graphic accent, with a 6-point rule above and a 1-point rule at the left edge of the column, extending down to the baseline of the last line of the title or the byline. This treatment echoed the treatment of the article that began on the first page, where the vertical rule (½-point in this case) extended the length of the type column and appeared on the right side rather than the left.

The masthead on page 2 included a modified banner, similar to the one used for the header on right-hand pages of the newsletter. Selecting the staff listing and choosing Align Right from Alignment under the Type menu aligned the names and created a ragged left margin.

Keylines were provided for photos, which were stripped in by the printer.

Ragged right column text and bouncing page bottoms contributed to an informal design that made layout easier for the clients, who were novice desktop publishers.

THE
WILDMAN
HERALD

December 1988

Michigan Graduates Establish Scholarship

The Michigan Law School graduates of the firm have pledged $100,000 to establish the Wildman, Harrold, Allen & Dixon Scholarship Fund at the law school. The fund will provide financial aid to needy law students serving as Senior Judges or Junior Clerks in the law School's Case Club program. This program provides training in legal research, writing and analysis, and an introduction to oral advocacy. The Michigan graduates felt this was a particularly appropriate purpose since Max Wildman was active in the Case Club program and served as a Senior Judge during his law school days. Max reminisced that "the Case Club program was my best practical experience in law school. It is where I really got my start as an advocate."

The firm's Michigan graduates, all of whom contributed to the fund, are Tom Allen, John Arado, Ed Butt, Stew Dixon, Doug Mielock, Ann Petersen, Dave Radelet, Jayne Rizzo, Tom Snyder, Max Wildman, and John Ybarra.

Carlson Organizes Lawyers' Association

Doug Carlson of the Chicago office was a co-founder of a recently organized association of lawyers who received undergraduate degrees from Monmouth College. Monmouth, a small liberal arts college in Monmouth, Illinois, has approximately 200 living graduates who have gone on to receive law degrees at law schools across the country. Some 30 lawyers filled out the application enclosed in the association's initial mailing, and 25 of those were dues-paying members. The first priority of the founders is to complete a comprehensive directory of Monmouth lawyers. "At a minimum, this directory will be distributed to association members," Carlson said. "Ultimately it would be great if the directory could have an even wider distribution among Monmouth alumni generally."

It is no secret that networking is an important factor in the referral of business. Carlson's innova-

tive concept may be one that should be considered by others in the firm. It may not be right for all undergraduate schools, but for small, close-knit institutions, it could pay benefits. As Carlson put it, "Monmouth is a school where people develop close bonds. All things being equal, I suspect many would prefer to do business with a fellow alumnus. Besides, even if there is no business benefit, it's great just to stay in touch."

Editor-in-Chief
Richard Glovka

Associate Editors
Eugene Holmes, Atlanta
Daniel Krohn, Houston
John Razulis, Toronto
Thomas Walsh, Memphis
Debra Wolf, New York

Reporters and Contributors
Louis Brett, Memphis
Paul Burgess, Toronto
Renee Castle, Memphis
A. J. Cook, Memphis
Dana Connell, Chicago
George Cottrelle, Toronto
Robert Crawford, Memphis
Jim Easto, Toronto
James Fiffer, Chicago
Susan Flieder, Chicago
John Goldsmith, Toronto
Jeffrey Gray, Chicago
Rod Heard, Chicago
Robert Keel, Toronto
Jack Kopald, Memphis
Anita Lotz, Memphis
Wendy L. Markee, Houston
Robert McLean, Memphis
David Rees, Chicago
Joseph Switzer, Chicago
Terri Turk, Houston

Production
Coordinator
Maureen McNair

Design Consultants
Lisa Marks-Ellis
Michael Waitsman
Synthesis Concepts Inc.

Printing
Rider Dickerson Inc.

THE
WILDMAN
HERALD

Volume 1, Number 4
December 1988

The Wildman Herald is published quarterly by Wildman, Harrold, Allen & Dixon. One IBM Plaza Chicago, Illinois 60611 Copyright © 1988. All rights reserved.

Year End Reflections
by Max Wildman

As the year draws to a close, I always find myself looking back at how far we've come. Invariably I am awed by our accomplishments and our good fortune. In a mere 21 years we have become one of the most successful law firms in this country. In addition to our professional accomplishments, we have a camaraderie the likes of which I've seen in no other firm.

I've had the good fortune to visit all of our offices on a number of occasions. I'm convinced that our lawyers and our staff are extra special. Just sit back for a minute and try to think of people you know who have as much fun in their work as those of us at WHAD. I'll bet you can't think of one. It's that special relationship we have with each other that sets us apart from the rest.

To me, 1988 has been a particularly exciting year. Our National Firm has taken off. The National Management Committee has made vast strides. We have a computerized system for detecting conflicts, a directory of all of our lawyers, a number of functioning national practice groups, and inter-office collaboration to a greater extent than ever before.

I know there are a few of you who have some gripes, and that's okay. The way to gain excellence is by always striving to be better. I just urge you to keep things in perspective. We should all work to improve this fine organization, but in a constructive, positive way. Be a builder, not a detractor.

In that spirit, which this season exemplifies, I urge you to take stock of your blessings. I believe you'll agree with me that we have so very much to be thankful for.

Best wishes to all for a Happy Holiday.

Allen Presentation in Argentina

Tom Allen of the Chicago office recently participated in a program at the 22nd Biennial Conference of the International Bar Association in Buenos Aires, Argentina. He was one of four speakers, from four different countries, who spoke to the Civil Practice Committee on the subject of "Procedures for Obtaining Summary Judgment." Tom described procedures in the United States while the other speakers, from Argentina, Switzerland, and India discussed procedures in their countries and on their continents. Two of the speakers were from civil law countries and two were from common law countries.

The speakers addressed nine topics concerning summary judgment procedure so that the audience could compare the procedures in the various countries. After the presentation on each topic, members of the audience asked questions and also commented on the procedures in their own countries. Those commenting included Norway, Belgium, Nigeria, Hong Kong and the United Kingdom.

Tom described the program as a "fascinating intellectual experience. Since summary judgment is a creature of statute or rules, the procedure does not necessarily depend on the legal system of the country." He felt that the Argentine procedure was closer to ours than that of India, the only other common law country on the panel. He went on to note that "in most countries summary judgment is a procedure by which the plaintiff can get a quick judgment in an allegedly uncontested case, usually for money owed. The audience was surprised to hear that in the United States the procedure is used principally by defendants."

The IBA meeting was attended by approximately 3,000 lawyers, spouses and guests from 79 different countries. In addition to an extensive professional program, very similar to an ABA meeting, the program included a concert at the Buenos Aires Opera House, a reception at the U.S. Ambassador's residence, and a black-tie dinner. Tom and his wife, Joyce, enjoyed hospitality at the home of, of all people, a partner in the Buenos Aires office of Baker & McKenzie. All and all they felt it was a most interesting and worthwhile experience. This was Tom's second IBA meeting, the first being in Montreux, Switzerland.

We made Wildman, Harrold's national newsletter similar to the home office version, *The Wildman Reporter* (Figure 1). Both for design reasons (consistency of look) and for production purposes, we decided to use the same 8½ x 11-inch format. Master pages included column guides, rules and large folios at the bottom of the pages. The right-hand master also included a running head with the newsletter's title and the date — a smaller, simpler version of the banner planned for the front page (Figure 2).

The master pages, empty of copy, were saved as a template. (This file would later be converted by our service bureau into IBM format for the client's computer.) ▋ *Selecting Template instead of Publication in PageMaker's Save As box provides a locked document for future use and prevents accidental change of the publication file. Opening the file brings up a copy, rather than the original. The first Save acts like a Save As, bringing up a dialog box that alerts you to name the new document.*

Type

The typefaces, all from the Palatino family, were also carried over from the first newsletter. We used Palatino plain, bold, italic and bold italic (Figure 3). Both designer and client liked these faces, all were resident in both laser printers, and, after we had worked out a few proofing problems, they had served well in the other newsletter.

The front page

On the first page of the newsletter, we "suspended" the master page elements by deselecting Display Master Items in the Page menu, because we didn't want the folio or rules to appear. For the banner design, we decided to use graduated bars extending vertically in both directions from the title (Figure 4). Generating these bars was the only departure from the PageMaker program. We produced the graphic in ImageStudio, using the graduated

Figure 1. *The Wildman Reporter.* Wildman Harrold's Chicago office newsletter used a three-column format — two text columns and a margin column for article and column titles, pull quotes and photos larger than the text column.

One-point rules marked the top of the margin column, the bottom of the page and the beginning of each article. The header appeared on each page, and a large folio aligned with the left edge of the right text column.

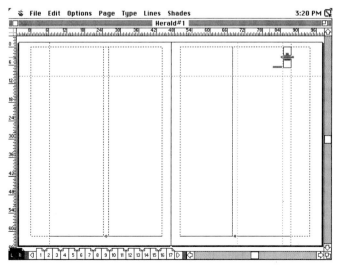

Figure 2. Setting up master pages. Master pages included column guides, bottom rules, folios and a modified banner drawn in PageMaker with the rectangle tool.

paint bucket feature. We saved it as a TIFF (tagged image file format, a format that we knew would transfer to the PC platform) and placed it on the front page of the newsletter. We expected to get a smooth fade in each direction, but it came out stepped because we forgot to link the TIFF image to the screen image embedded in the PageMaker file. However, we liked the stepped effect, so we left it unlinked. ∎ *When a TIFF is placed in a PageMaker file, a simpler, lower-resolution version of the image appears on-screen. The PageMaker file includes PostScript code that calls the TIFF file for printing. If the TIFF file is not in the same folder as the PageMaker file, it will not automatically be linked to the page, and the coarser screen image will print in its place.*

"The Wildman Herald" type for the banner was set and kerned as three separate pieces of text, and the word "Wildman" was condensed by exporting it as an encapsulated PostScript file, placing it back on the page and manipulating it like a graphic element (see "Encapsulating PageMaker elements" on page 70). Type for the table of contents was aligned using Alignment from the Type menu (Figure 5).

Built-in flexibility

The newsletter's modular format has consistent 1½-inch top margins with flexible column lengths. The folio and rule define the page bottom and a consistent ½-inch bottom margin. The two-column format includes two text columns, each 18 picas wide, flush left. Text columns were designed to be wide enough to accommodate photos and still leave a space wide enough for text to wrap around. Boxes for photos and other illustrations are made with

Introducing
The Wildman Herald
by Richard Glovka

The National Firm is on the move. The "other offices" are no longer just places to take a deposition. They are a resource and an opportunity. They have skills to offer and clients to serve.

The National Firm has been around for some time. Basically, however, it was a paper tiger. Only a few lawyers knew people in the other offices. A

Figure 3. Choosing type. The Palatino family of typefaces were the only fonts used in *The Wildman Herald*. Column text was set at 9 points on auto leading (120% of the type's point size in PageMaker).

Figure 4. Creating the banner. Graduated vertical bars created in ImageStudio appeared above and below the word "Wildman," which was kerned (tightened in spacing) by placing the text cursor between letters and holding down the Command key while pressing the Backspace/Delete key. The type was also condensed slightly.

PageMaker's rectangle tool, using a ½-point line. Illustration boxes can be "portrait size" (two-thirds of the text column width, with wrapped type), full-column width or even wider (extending into the margin column) (Figure 6). Halftones are inserted conventionally by the printer into keylined boxes provided within the columns. Other than the photos, the newsletter design requires no physical art or conventionally set type.

Graphic elements

Headings for articles are framed by a 1-point rule on the left and a 6-point rule above (Figure 7), clearly signaling the start of a new subject. The "Profiles" and "Practice Reports" sections, which appear in every issue, have their own logos (Figures 8 and 9). In the "Profiles" column, a small portrait sits where an initial cap might be expected, announcing each person who is the subject of a profile. Subheads in "Practice Reports" are lighter-weight versions of the article frames shown in Figure 7. Finally, Rod Heard's "Heard Say" column on the back page has a logo composed of a 6-point vertical rule and and a black horizontal bar drawn with PageMaker's rectangle tool, with punctuation marks reversed out of it (Figure 10). The back-cover position of the "Heard Say" column was important to the client, but that left a question of what to do in the fourth issue, when the column ran long. It was decided to run the continuation inside the back cover — a little unorthodox, but it seems to work.

All the graphic elements were stored on the PageMaker pasteboard (the area of the interface outside the pages themselves). From there they could be pulled into place on the pages as needed.

Refining the design

We knew from our previous experience with *The Wildman Reporter* how to deal with a series of little hitches that developed:

▮ *Programs like FontSizer, and now Adobe Type Manager, provide screen fonts that look more like their printed versions (see "What you see is getting better" on*

Figure 5. Setting up the table of contents. Center-aligned type, with page numbers in bold, created a pleasing design for the "In This Issue" listing. A 6-point rule formed the base for this element, and vertical rules defined its width to be the same as the banner's.

Figure 6. Using photos and pull quotes. Relatively wide (18-pica) columns allowed text to wrap around photos. Pictures could also extend into the margin if necessary. Pull quotes were column width, but offset slightly toward the margin.

page 71). They can be very useful in reducing the number of trial-and-error prints needed to arrive at proper placement and kerning of type.

▌ *Excess leading before the last line of a block of type in PageMaker can usually be corrected by pressing Return at the end of that last line. Other perplexing leading problems can often be corrected by selecting Type Specs from the Type menu and then clicking OK in the dialog box that appears on-screen (in essence simply reaffirming the type specs already set for that type block).*

▌ *Sometimes, for reasons unknown, a font substitution occurs during laser proofing of a PC PageMaker file, even though the correct font is resident in the printer. To correct the problem, choose Printer Setup from the File menu and select the printer again; then click OK. This reloads the fonts in the file.*

Establishing the production process

Each article and column for Volume 1, Number 1 of the newsletter was prepared at Wildman Harrold as a separate file in WordPerfect for the PC and supplied on a 5¼-inch diskette. The service bureau converted them into Macintosh text (ASCII) files, and we formatted them using Microsoft Word, stripping out extra spaces and search/replacing typewritten with typographical punctuation.

Next we Placed each text file into the PageMaker publication. Laser proofs were printed and submitted to the editor at Wildman Harrold. When he had finished marking the proofs with his copy changes, we went back to the computer to make the changes and perfect the layout. When everyone was satisfied, we sent the file to the service bureau for high-resolution output. In the meantime, we cropped and sized the photos, keying them (with letters) to the appropriate boxes on the laser proofs. The final output and original photos were sent to the printer.

Figure 7. Titling articles.
Headings for articles were set in 18-point bold type on 22-point leading and kerned. The byline was 12-point Palatino roman type.

Figure 8. Creating "Profiles."
The word "PROFILES" was typed and assigned a style of Reverse and Shadowed. Space was added between letters by "reverse kerning" — holding down the Command and Shift keys and pressing the Backspace/Delete key. A 60-percent black rectangle bounded by black rules (6-point on the top and 4-point on the left) provides definition for the white letters.

Figure 9. Drawing the "Practice Reports" heading. Rectangles and lines were used to draw the "gavel border" around the 18-point bold italic column title.

Figure 10. Making a thicker rule.
The punctuation marks were reversed out of a black background. Although the vertical rule is a 4-point line, the horizontal bar was too thick to be created with the Lines menu (under the Element menu in PageMaker 4.0). This was drawn instead as a filled rectangle.

Figure 7

Figure 8

Figure 9

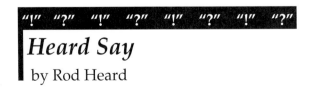

Figure 10

Making the transition

When the time came to convert the template from Mac to IBM format, we turned to our service bureau once again. The IBM version of PageMaker is, indeed, analogous to the Macintosh version, except for file access, which is provided through the typical DOS directories and subdirectories, and the fact that it runs more slowly, even on comparable equipment. The only other problem we ran into was the need for a lot of "tweaking" — the alignment of the elements that made up some of our PageMaker graphics went "off" when we made the transfer from Mac to IBM and had to be adjusted. This meant about an hour of my sitting at Wildman Harrold's computer fiddling with detail on the master layout.

Related projects

Wildman Harrold has been producing *The Wildman Reporter* for over two years now and *The Wildman Herald* for over a year. The efficiency of our arrangement has led to our doing other design projects for them, and their desktop publishing experience has led them to appreciate our expertise more rather than less. When deadlines are tight, it's tempting for them to do both design and production in-house in a hurry, but a few experiences of that sort have led Maureen to lobby actively — and successfully — for calling us in for design and proof-checking. ▮ *The role of the designer in checking proofs for inexperienced desktop publishers using templates should not be underestimated. Some of the things nondesigners typically miss are typewriter quotation marks, alignment and font substitution.*

▮ Encapsulating PageMaker elements

The encapsulated PostScript (EPS) file format provides a way to store a graphic image in a form that can be Placed in a page layout and both viewed on-screen and printed. For example, many illustrations used in page layouts are created in PostScript illustration programs, saved in EPS format, and then Placed.

You can also make an EPS file, which you can then treat as a graphic element, from any PageMaker page or from any section of a page.

Saving a page

To save an entire page as an EPS file using PageMaker 4.0:
(1) Choose Print from the File menu.
(2) Select a single page in the From and To boxes that indicate page range.
(3) Choose PostScript.
(4) Select the applicable options available in the dialog box.
(5) Choose Print PostScript To Disk, and click on EPS.

(6) Choose File Name and type in a name. (It's a good idea to use a name that indicates what the page is and also that it's an EPS file; for example, "book cover.eps.") Click OK.
(7) Click Print in the PostScript Print Options box.

Saving part of a page

To save an element from a page without saving the whole page, follow these steps:
(1) Use the pointer tool to select all parts of the element you want to save, either by Shift-clicking or by drawing a marquee around all the parts together.
(2) Copy the element to the clipboard by choosing Copy from the Edit menu or by pressing Command-C.
(3) Close the PageMaker file and open a new one by choosing New from the File menu.
(4) In the Page Setup dialog box that appears, specify a page just a little larger than the element in the clipboard, and click OK. (You don't need

to be concerned about the margin specifications, just the overall page dimensions.)
(5) Paste the element into the new page.
(6) Now save the entire new page according to the directions for "Saving a page." Extra white space around the element can be eliminated with the cropping tool.

This page was saved as an EPS file, imported into FreeHand, where it was rotated 30 degrees and resaved in EPS format, and then Placed on this page.

In some cases, we still do both design and production for Wildman Harrold. For instance, the firm asked us to design their corporate capabilities brochure. They wondered if they should produce that piece as well, but since it was a one-time project, we felt it would take less time to produce it ourselves than to oversee someone else. This was especially true since certain design subtleties would be settled during production. The firm accepted our advice. However, we designed the piece as a combination brochure and pocket folder, and we provided them with a template so they could produce the updatable pages that go into the pocket. This project, too, has been cost-effective.

In retrospect

We've found that working with clients who have their own production capabilities is mutually beneficial: The client can save money on outside production charges but still get professional publication design. And the designer can focus more energy on designing. However, both parties have to consider some important points in using this approach:

▌ *The client needs to choose a design firm that understands desktop publishing in general — and their system in particular — to avoid unforeseen pitfalls in the process.*

▌ *The design firm has to be able to afford the equipment and training needed to gain expertise on client systems, and then must be able to amortize those costs through design work without having to rely on billing a lot of production.*

▌ What you see is getting better

WYSIWYG is the acronym for "What you see is what you get," an important concept in the development of desktop publishing — the idea that you can see on the screen a faithful representation of what will eventually be printed on paper or on film emulsion. Adobe Type Manager (ATM) is a system software utility for the Macintosh that improves what you see when you view PostScript-based type on the screen.

A Macintosh PostScript typeface consists of two separate entities — a screen font, which is a bitmap with characters built of pixels (the square dots that make up the screen image), and a printer font, which is the set of PostScript instructions that tell the printer how to form the character outlines. In order to get as accurate as possible WYSIWYG representation of characters at all sizes and in all styles (bold, italic and so on), a separate alphabet of bitmaps must be stored in the System for each size and style. This occupies a lot of memory, and unusual sizes are not even available as screen fonts. If an appropriate bitmap is not available for a character that must be displayed on-screen, the bitmap for a smaller size is enlarged, which leads to enlargement of the square dots into square chunks, rather than a smooth enlargement of the character.

To solve the problem of large and odd-size screen fonts not looking like their printed counterparts, ATM builds on-screen type, as sharp and smooth as the monitor is capable of, at any size on the fly, from the same PostScript outline fonts used by the printer. ("On the fly" means "as needed"; screen representations of the letters are formed as they're called for, and therefore they don't occupy disk space for storage.) Accurate on-screen representations of type take much of the guesswork out of kerning and alignment of headlines. The on-screen outlines can also be scaled, skewed, rotated or filled with a pattern.

Palatino A's, set at 96 points, as they appear on the Macintosh screen with and without Adobe Type Manager. From left to right: 10-point screen font only, no ATM; 24-point screen font, no ATM; 10-point screen font, ATM; 10-point screen font, ATM, skewed in FreeHand.

PORTFOLIO

Michael Waitsman

"Desktop publishing provides a single environment in which a multitalented individual can write, edit, design, illustrate, typeset and assemble a complete publication on his or her own. However, today's publishing systems are so powerful that it can take a long time to learn how to use them professionally. And once the initial plunge is taken, keeping up with advances in the technology can be challenging as well. But the change is inevitable — electronic publishing is the path into the future."

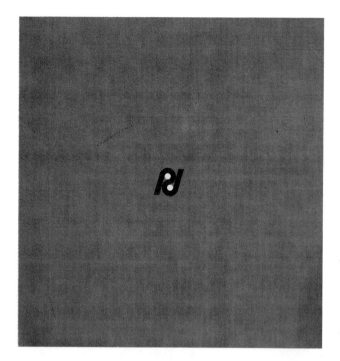

Michael Waitsman and designer Lisa Marks-Ellis, also of Synthesis Concepts, designed, wrote and produced this **promotional package** for a Chicago printing firm to market their printing services to desktop publishers. The cover has built-in pockets to hold technical publications and gauges. The cover of the four-page bound-in brochure was done in FreeHand. The rest of the brochure and the technical papers are PageMaker layouts. Gauges useful to electronic designers were also produced in FreeHand and printed on a transparent but not completely clear material that would not get lost on the literal desktop.

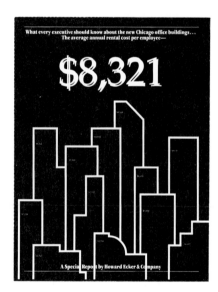

A special **report** on rental costs of Chicago office buildings for the Howard Ecker & Company brokerage was done in PageMaker and FreeHand. Reversed type and red boxes were produced in PageMaker, and building illustrations, along with their enclosed black type, were produced in FreeHand and placed on the PageMaker pages. The inside of the gatefold brochure was designed as a single (25½ x 11-inch) page.

The 32-page **recruitment brochure** for the law firm Jenner & Block was done using Page-Maker. All type is Adobe's ITC Galliard. The spectrum lines were executed as black lines in Page-Maker, and color was stripped in by the printer. Producing the piece electronically provided close control of text formatting, which was important to the design of the piece.

Litigation and **Litigation News,** both publications of the Section of Litigation of the American Bar Association, were designed as two-color pieces and separated using the Spot Color Overlays option from PageMaker's Print dialog box. In the newsletter, black initial caps overprinted rectangles made of stacked brown lines. In the banner for the journal, the dots above the i's were covered with white boxes.

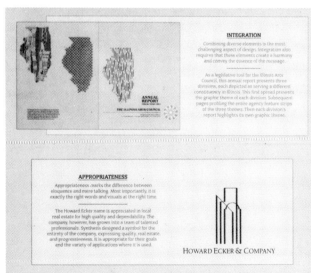

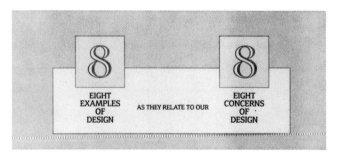

"Eight Examples of Design" is a **self-promotional brochure** for Synthesis Concepts. The pages were designed and the boxes drawn in PageMaker. The type was set conventionally, because it was an exclusive Compugraphic face. Since that time Compugraphic has made it, along with many of their other typefaces, available as a PostScript font. Some of the pieces shown in the brochure were desktop published, others conventionally produced.

CHAPTER 6

Power Production with Ventura

Design team

Michael Sullivan, art director, and Cynthia Delfino, designer, are well-acquainted with Ventura Publisher. Their Cambridge, Massachusetts firm, Imprimatur Design Systems, Inc. won second place in technical documentation design for the Xerox-sponsored Ventura Publisher design contest, and has won numerous other awards for design.

Project

Our goal was to design and produce a manual for MathCAD, a program for setting equations, computing their results and adding text and graphs. The book was to be "Macintosh-looking" — open, lively and obviously graphical. Yet we didn't just want the graphics sprinkled throughout the text. Instead, they had to become part of the text — they had to be integrated.

As is almost always the case with software packages, we had to be producing an accurate manual at the same time the product was being finalized. To achieve our goals, we had to work closely with the writer/client, Josh Bernoff. We also had to come up with the most efficient process and most powerful software tool for the job. We arrived at a design that provided an easy way for the writer to enter the necessary information and that also communicated its information effectively.

We used several PC clones and Macintoshes, as parts of the project were divided up among several people. The platforms we used most were an IBM PC/AT running Ventura Publisher and a Macintosh SE with the MathCAD software itself, Capture (a screen-capture program) and MacPaint. Proofing was done on a LaserWriter Plus, and final output was 600 dpi positives from a Varityper 600W imagesetter.

**PROJECT
OVERVIEW**

Choosing Ventura

The problem of building a Mac manual is one of managing text and graphics, of laying out both on a grid, and most importantly, of creating chapters that can survive revision after revision without constantly reshuffling dozens of frames. Our firm is completely "fluent" in both Mac and PC desktop publishing. We came to the conclusion that Ventura was the best all-around choice for the MathCAD manual, even though at that time it ran only on the PC! It was the only product that let you place and anchor graphical elements automatically on the same grid as textual ones. And revisions to illustrations were a snap — we could just copy the new graphic over the old version by the same name (on the right subdirectory) and Ventura placed it, sized it, scaled it and positioned it perfectly. Another advantage of Ventura's batch-oriented layout properties was that it allowed us to separate the design from the writing. The designer could be refining the style sheet while the writers were editing their text.

This portion of the text file was used to generate page 6 of the MathCAD manual (shown at bottom). Note the style tags (preceded by @ and followed by =) that determine the type size, style and position of each element, and the character formatting codes embedded in the text.

@SECTION = Numbers

@INDEX = <$Inumbers><$Svalues; numbers>

This section describes the various types of numbers that MathCAD uses and how to enter them into equations.

@SUBSECTION = Types of numbers

MathCAD uses the following types of numbers:

@DHEAD = Floating-point numbers

@DTEXT = For example, **<F1B>6**<F255D> or **<F1B>-3.14159**<F255D>. <$Inumbers; floating-point><$Ifloating-point numbers>

@DHEAD = Imaginary numbers

@DTEXT = To enter an imaginary number, follow it with **<F1B>i**<F255D> or **<F1B>j**<F255D>, for example, **<F1B>li**<F255D> or **<F1B>-2.5j**<F255D>. <$Inumbers; imaginary><$Iimaginary numbers><$Inumbers; complex>

@NOTE HEAD = Warning.

@NOTE TEXT = You cannot use **<F1B>i**<F255D> or **<F1B>j**<F255D> alone to represent the imaginary unit. You must always type **<F1B>li**<F255D> or **<F1B>1j**<F255D>. See the description under <169>Complex numbers and calculations<170> later in this chapter.

@SUBSECTION = Combining types of numbers

You can combine all types of numbers in various ways to create complex numbers, exponential notation, and dimensions, as shown in Figure 2.

@CAPTION = Figure 2: Combining different types of numbersasaf

@MAKESPACE = <$&local.mac[-]>

@INDEX =

The INDEX tag (shown above and highlighted at the top of the text file figure) identifies page references that don't print but that will provide subject information when Ventura compiles the index.

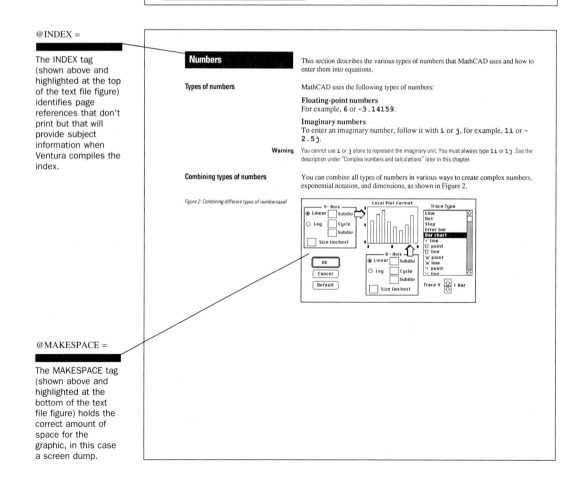

@MAKESPACE =

The MAKESPACE tag (shown above and highlighted at the bottom of the text file figure) holds the correct amount of space for the graphic, in this case a screen dump.

Working with the client

Cambridge-based Josh Bernoff enjoys the process of working closely with a professional designer. The process is an interactive one, with writer and designer each contributing in an iterative process. To start, Josh handed us early drafts of a few chapters, together with some graphics and an idea of what he was looking for. Then it was our problem for a while, until he saw the mockups of the pages, with the first ideas on grid, typefaces and the relationship between text and graphics. Because the client provided us with real text, we could develop a design "tuned" to the material.

This portion of the text file for page 7 of the MathCAD manual (shown at bottom) includes the definition of the table.

MathCAD has the following special functions and operators for dealing with complex numbers:

@TABLE BEGIN 5 =

@COL 2-2 BOLD = Re (z)

@COL 3-6 = Real part of number z.

@COL 2-2 BOLD = Im (z)

@COL 3-6 = Imaginary part of number z.

@COL 2-2 BOLD = arg (z)

@COL 3-6 = Angle in complex plane from real axis to z: between <F128M>-p<F255D> and <F128M>p<F255D>.

@COL 2-2 BOLD = I z I

@COL 3-6 = Magnitude of number z. To see this, press the vertical bar key followed by the argument:I **z.**

@COL 2-2 BOLD = **<BO>z<D>**

@COL 3-6 = Complex conjugate of z. To apply the conjugate operator to an expression, select the expression, then click on the conjugate (<MIO>x<D>) on the operators palette or type <F128M> [**<F1B>Option**<F128M>] **<F1B>**U<F255D>. The conjugate of the complex number $a+b$<F128M><183><F255M>i is a<F128M>-<F255MI>b<F128M><183>F255MI>i.

@TABLE END 5 =

You can apply the square root operator and all the standard trigonometric, hyperbolic, and inverse trigonometric and hyperbolic functions to complex arguments. Where a function is multivalued, MathCAD uses the principal value.

@TABLE BEGIN 5 =

The TABLE BEGIN 5 tag (shown above and highlighted at the top of the text file figure) provides a bold rule five grid columns wide to define the start of the table.

@COL 2-2 BOLD =

@COL 3-6 =

The COL tags (shown above and highlighted within the text file figure) define column widths. There are two column types used in this table: COL 2-2 BOLD is a single grid column wide, occurs in the second grid column position and is printed in bold type; COL 3-6 is four grid columns wide, starting with column 3.

Complex numbers and calculations

As described above in the section on "Numbers," MathCAD accepts complex numbers of the form $a+bi$, where a and b are ordinary floating-point numbers. You can use j instead of i if you prefer that notation.

Complex numbers can also arise if you enter an expression with a complex result. (Even a MathCAD expression that involves only real numbers can have a complex value. For example, if you try to compute $\sqrt{-1}$, MathCAD will calculate an answer of $1i$.)

Although you can enter imaginary numbers followed by either i or j, MathCAD normally shows them followed by i. To show imaginary numbers with j, change the setting for **Imaginary symbol** in the Global Equation Settings dialog box. (Select **Global Equation Settings** from the **Settings** menu to see this dialog box. See the previous chapter for a full description of this dialog box.)

Warning.   When entering complex numbers, you cannot use i or j alone to represent the imaginary unit. You must always type $1i$ or $1j$. When you move the cursor out of an equation that shows $1i$ or $1j$, MathCAD hides the superfluous 1.

Complex operators and functions

MathCAD has the following special functions and operators for dealing with complex numbers:

Re(z)	Real part of number z.
Im(z)	Imaginary part of number z.
arg(z)	Angle in complex plane from real axis to z: between $-\pi$ and π.
Izl	Magnitude of number z. To see this, press the vertical bar key followed by the argument: Iz.
z	Complex conjugate of z. To apply the conjugate operator to an expression, select the expression, the click on the conjugate (x) on the operators palette or type [**Option**]U. The conjugate of the complex number $a+b$ i is $a-b$ i.

You can apply the square root operator and all the standard trigonometric, hyperbolic, and inverse trigonometric and hyperbolic functions to complex arguments. Where a function is multivalued, MathCAD uses the principal value.

Chapter 8   Names, Numbers, and Imaginaries

7

To emphasize the mathematical nature of the MathCAD product, we chose a square format, with a trim size of 8½ inches on a side. The base we used for laying out text and graphics is a three-column grid 42 picas wide, with a subgrid of six columns to be used for tables (Figure 1). A 28-pica column on the right side of each page held text, and a 14-pica gutter margin on the left provided some white space, as well as a place for captions, heads, subheads and marginal notes. Margins of 4½ picas right and left provided space for the comb binding (inside) and the vertical "running heads" outside (see page 77).

Choosing typefaces

We wanted to use a Univers Condensed typeface, as Univers was the corporate identity font used for logos, collateral materials and packaging. I decided to use it for headlines, notes and tables (Figure 2). We wanted a serif face for the body text, to put more emphasis on the section heads (set in Univers 67) by contrast, and also to maximize readability. Because the client had only a LaserWriter Plus for proofing, we had to use one of the ROM fonts for the text face, since we were downloading the entire Univers family, which took up almost all available memory. Therefore, we chose Times Roman for body text; its clean, simple and elegant feel wouldn't overwhelm the delicate nature of the Univers (Figure 3).

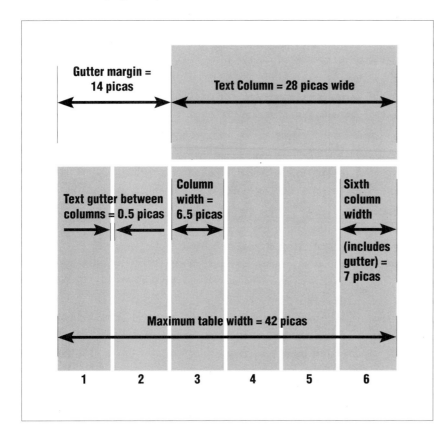

Figure 1. Designing a flexible grid. The text portions of the pages were set on a two-column format. A six-column format was set up so that tables could be designed to fit the information they presented: A table column could be anywhere from one grid column to six grid columns wide; any combination of table columns could be used to make up a table, as long as the total number of grid columns didn't exceed six.

We also had to design a special font for the writer so he could type the Command key symbol (the cloverleaf necessary for explaining the MathCAD commands) from within Ventura. We used Fontographer to create the font and then linked it into Ventura by building a new width table using the AFMTOVFM and VFMTOWID utility programs supplied with Ventura Publisher.

Fontographer comes with a demo font that has the cloverleaf character in it. So we first saved this file as a new font, calling it CLOVER. This font would then be downloaded to the LaserWriter before we printed a chapter. Creating the printer font also created an AFM (Adobe Font Metric) file, in this case named CLOVER.AFM. We copied this file to the PC subdirectory where the Ventura utility AFMTOVFM.EXE was. To run the conversion program, which creates a .VFM (Ventura Font Metric) file, we typed

AFMTOVFM CLOVER.AFM

This created a file called CLOVER.VFM on the hard disk. Then we created an ASCII text file called CLOVER.LST by using Microsoft Word to create a file with the following line in it: CLOVER.VFM. Then we ran the utility called VFMTOWID.EXE by typing

VFMTOWID CLOVER.LST

which created a new width table for that one font. Finally, we loaded Ventura and under the Options menu we chose Add/Remove Fonts. In that dialog

Figure 2. Using Univers Condensed. Univers 67 type was used for all headings throughout the manual, for any notes that appeared in the left-hand column (gutter margin) and for tabular material. Section heads and column heads for tables were set up as white type on a black rule.

Reading and writing structured files

Bessel function	MathCAD function
$J_0(x)$	J0(x)
$Y_0(x)$	Y0(x)
$J_1(x)$	J1(x)
$Y_1(x)$	Y1(x)
$J_2(x)$	Jn(2,x)
$Y_2(x)$	Yn(2,x)
$J_3(x)$	Jn(3,x)
$Y_3(x)$	Yn(3,x)
etc.	

Imaginary Numbers

To enter an imaginary number, follow it with **i** or **j**, for example, **1i** or **2.5j**. (You cannot use **i** or **j** alone to represent the imaginary unit. You must always type **1i** or **1j**. See "Complex numbers and calculations" later in this chapter.)

Dimensional values

Dimensional values are numbers associated with one of the MathCAD dimensions: *length, mass, time,* and *charge.* MathCAD uses these dimensions to keep track of units for dimensional analysis and unit conversions. To enter a dimensional value, type a number followed by an uppercase or lowercase **L** for length, **M** for mass, **T** for time, or **Q** for charge. For example, **4.5m** represents 4.5 mass units. For more detailed information on units and dimensions, see Chapter 9, "Units and Dimensions."

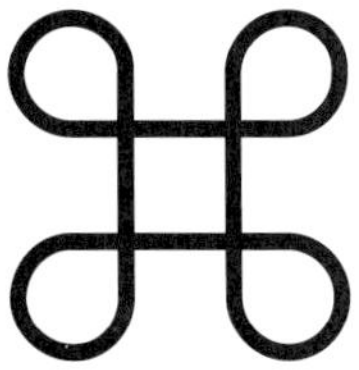

Figure 3. Selecting a serif face. Times Roman was chosen for the text face, as a LaserWriter-resident font that would contrast with the Univers in the headings. Univers was also used for numerals, variables, constants and formulas presented in the text column.
   The Macintosh Command key symbol was assigned to a special font accessible from Ventura Publisher.

box, we chose Merge Width Tables. To finish the process, we found CLOVER.WID on the hard disk and selected it.

Styling text

The writer was using Final Word, an ASCII text editor, to input the text. For words he wanted to emphasize, he entered character formatting (for bold, italic and so on) right in the text by using codes. These were later replaced with Ventura's formatting commands by using a search-and-replace function.

Meanwhile, we used a Ventura style sheet to set up almost 40 styles (and their associated tags, or names) for text elements, heads, subheads and space around graphics (Figure 4). In addition, we established almost 30 styles for table columns.

Tabular format

We designed a table format that was flexible in width; that is, each table column could occupy as many columns of the grid as needed (Figure 5). This format also allowed the vertical height for each "row" to be determined by the amount of text (or the size of the graphic element) that had to fit. We created a set of tag names for columns of various widths that would allow the writer to create the table right in the text file, defining column width as 1 to 6 columns, according to the requirements of the information to be presented. Rather than ask the writer or an editor to style boldface entries for columns, we set up style tags for column material to be set in bold. To help the writer remember which table format went with which style tag, we named the styles according to how many of the six columns they occupied. We set the style specification so that text wrapped automatically within columns and horizontal rules above the rows were automatically placed to accommodate the longest column entry in the previous row.

Many of the attributes for the table style tags remained the same regardless of column width. So once one column format was defined, it could be copied and adjusted for each new column format (Figure 6).

Figure 4. Defining styles. The Ventura style sheet for the MathCAD manual contained document-wide formatting rules (page size and elements defined in some page layout programs on "master pages") and tag formatting. The Body Text format was one of over 60 tags defined for text elements and tables.

Body Text

Font

Face:	Times
Size:	10 points
Style:	Normal
Color:	Black
Overscore:	Off
Strike-Thru:	Off
Underline:	Off
Double Underline:	Off

Alignment

Horz. Alignment:	Left
Vert. Alignment:	Top
Text Rotation:	None
Hyphenation:	USDICT
Successive Hyphens:	2
Overall Width:	Column-Wide
First Line:	Indent
Relative Indent:	Off
In/Outdent Width:	00,00 picas & points
In/Outdent Height:	1
In From Right to Decimal:	00,00 picas & points

Spacing

Above:	00,00 picas & points
Below:	00,06 picas & points
Inter-Line:	12.00 fractional pts
Inter-Paragraph:	00.00 fractional pts
Add in Above:	When Not at Column Top
In From Left (Left Page):	14,00 picas & points
In From Right (Left Page):	00,00 picas & points
In From Left (Right Page):	14,00 picas & points
In From Right (Right Page):	00,00 picas & points

Breaks

Page Break:	No
Column Break:	No
Line Break:	After
Next Y Position:	Normal
Allow Within:	No
Keep With Next:	No

Tab Settings

Leader Char:	46
Leader Spacing:	2
Auto-Leader:	Off

Special Effects

Special Effect:	None

Attribute Overrides

Line Width:	Text-Wide
Overscore Height:	00.60/10.92 fractional pts
Strike-Thru Height:	00.60/03.42 fractional pts
Underline 1 Height:	00.60/00.60 fractional pts
Underline 2 Height:	00.60/01.86 fractional pts
Superscript Size:	9 points/05.16 fractional pts
Subscript Size:	9 points/01.20 fractional pts
Small Cap Size:	9 points

Paragraph Typography

Automatic Pair Kerning:	Off
Grow Inter-Line To Fit:	On
Letter-Spacing:	0.100 Ems
Tracking:	0.000 Ems Looser
Minimum Space Width:	0.600
Normal Space Width:	1.000
Maximum Space Width:	2.000
Vert. Just. At Top of Para:	00.00 fractional pts
At Bottom of Para:	06.00 fractional pts
Between Lines of Para:	00.00 fractional pts

Ruling Line Above

Width:	None

Ruling Line Below

Width:	None

Ruling Box Around

Width:	None

Screen dumps

We find it easiest to capture and manipulate screens in their native environment, which in this case meant using Macintosh software for screen capture and editing before we moved the graphics to the PC. We used the Capture program to capture parts of the screens (see "Using a screen capture utility" on page 83). Then we edited them in MacPaint, cleaning up stray mouse pointers and painting in pixels and text to simulate features the engineers hadn't quite got working yet (Figure 7). ■ *You can save an entire screen dump, import it into the page layout program and crop it to show what you want (although cropping in Ventura can be tricky). However, if you clip out and save just the portion you need as you're making the screen dump, the graphics files will be smaller and easier to position once you get them onto the PC.*

Table Begins rule

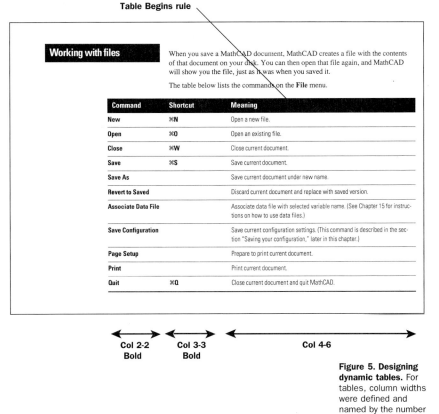

Col 2-2 Bold   **Col 3-3 Bold**   **Col 4-6**

Figure 5. Designing dynamic tables. For tables, column widths were defined and named by the number and position of the page grid columns they were comprised of. The logic of this system helped writers remember the names of the various tags.

Figure 6. Defining style tags for tables. Each column type was defined by a style tag that specified its width and whether it would print in plain or boldface type. The style tags allowed row depth to be determined "on the fly"; the deepest entry determined the depth for the entire row. This made it easy for writers to make the tables fit the data. Although many characteristics had to be specified for each column style, most of them could be copied directly once the first few styles had been defined.

Keeping track of the graphics

We were working with literally hundreds of graphics files, so it was important to take time to create file-naming conventions that we could refer back to later. For most of our graphics files, we created names in which the first two characters indicated the chapter the graphic belonged to, the next two were its figure number, and the last four provided some indication as to content.

It was also important that the frame anchors (the codes that held the place in the Ventura file for the graphic to be brought in) match the figure names. Because there were so many figures, separate subdirectories of illustrations were created for each chapter. ▌ *In Ventura, graphics files are not actually incorporated into the page description code. Instead, a tag is placed in the file that provides an on-screen representation for the graphic element and that calls it when it's time to print. That means that changes to the graphics files are automatically incorporated into the page layout, as long as the file name is kept constant. This is also true for certain file formats, such as TIFFs, in PageMaker on the PC and on the Mac.*

Equations

At the time we were setting up the pages, the MathCAD code didn't allow the PostScript generated by the program to save the equations as encapsulated PostScript (EPS) files for placement into Ventura. So, except where we were

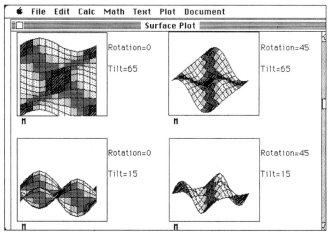

Figure 7. Capturing screen elements. With the program called Capture screen-capture screen dumps from the Mac could be cropped at the time they were made. This saved having to crop them in a bitmapped illustration program such as MacPaint or in Ventura Publisher. MathCAD windows, dialog boxes or individual mathematical elements could be selected and saved as graphics.

Operator	Appearance	How to type	Operator palette	Comments
Derivative	$\dfrac{d}{dt} f(t)$	t [Option]D f(t)	$\frac{dy}{dx}$	All variables in the expression $f(t)$ must be defined. The variable t must have a scalar value. $f(t)$ must be scalar-valued. Returns a scalar.
Addition	x1 + x2	x1 + x2	+	If $x1$, $x2$, or both are scalars, scalar addition. If $x1$ and $x2$ are vectors or matrices of same size, vector or matrix addition.
Subtraction	x1 − x2	x1 − x2	−	If $x1$, $x2$, or both are scalars, scalar addition. If $x1$ and $x2$ are vectors or matrices of same size, vector or matrix subtraction.
Addition with line break	x1 ... + x2	x1\x2	$\frac{x...}{+y}$	Calculates same as addition.

Ascreen-capture utility is a useful tool for taking a "snapshot" of work being done on-screen or printing out a paragraph or two from a longer document when type quality isn't important. But for writing software documentation, a screen capture program is practically a necessity.

HiJaak is a screen capture utility for the PC. Black-and-white Macs have a built-in function for making screen dumps — pressing **Command-Shift-3** saves the entire screen as a MacPaint file called Screen 0, Screen 1 and so on. **FKeys**, a series of utilities, also provides screen capture for color Macs through the **Command-Shift-7** key combination.

There are two drawbacks to using either of these two key-combination screen capture methods on the Mac. First and most important, they don't work when menus are being held in the pulled-down or popped-out position or under any other conditions that require that the mouse button be held down while the "picture" is taken. So if software documentation is your goal, they probably won't be sufficient to provide the graphics you'll need. Second, they snap the entire screen, which means that any time you want something less than that, you have to edit the resulting file in a paint program.

Camera, a desk accessory for the Mac, solves the first problem. Choosing Camera under the apple menu brings up a dialog box that lets you set a time-delay of several seconds before the picture is snapped. This allows you to pull down a menu or click your way through nested dialog boxes before the "shutter" is activated.

Capture solves the second problem. Pressing an assigned key combination (or the **F13 key**, if you have an extended keyboard), gives you a cursor with which you can draw a selection rectangle around the part of the screen you want to capture.

Screen capture utilities seem to be increasing in sophistication. It's worth checking to see what's new and how it will serve for what you want to do.

using screen dumps of equations for illustration, we decided that it would be far more cost-effective to paste in a few printouts rather than to wait until the code was debugged (Figure 8).

Using anchors

We knew our chapters would have to survive revision after revision. The engineers were constantly changing the dialog boxes, menus, icons and so forth as they coded the software. But the writers couldn't just wait until everything was frozen. (Typically it takes six months to write a robust document for a software product.) They needed to lay out the pages with graphics in position so that the alpha and beta testers could check that the documentation was indeed complete and accurate. When graphics changes occurred — for example, when a new dialog box was created for the Local Plot Format — a new screen shot was created and saved with the same name as the old file. When this was copied over the old file in the PC, Ventura would load the chapter as always, only now it would be using the new version of the Local Plot Format figure without any changes to the document itself.

Ventura made text revision easy, too. We used Relative, Automatically At Anchor, accessed by choosing Anchor from the Edit menu, to "anchor"

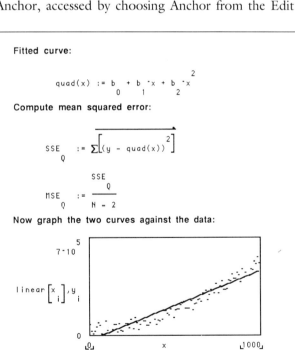

Figure 8. Incorporating printouts. Sometimes electronic pasteup isn't the best solution. Since EPS versions of MathCAD output were not readily available as pages were being composed, space was left for laser printouts such as this to be pasted onto electronically output page layouts.

graphics files to specific places in the text of the document. That meant Ventura would keep them in the same relationship to the text, no matter what changes had to be made to the text (see "Anchoring" below). If the text got longer, for example, the graphic was moved farther down the page; if the graphics file was updated, Ventura placed the newer version in the right location automatically when we opened the chapter. ▌ *You can either enter "anchors" within Ventura or type them in the text with your word processor.*

Anchoring

In Ventura, as well as in other page layout programs, you can ensure that the frame for a graphic element appears in close proximity to the text that refers to it, even when editing changes are made to the text. A frame (Ventura's place-holder for a graphic element) is linked to a place in the text by giving an anchor name to the frame and then putting an anchor marker in the text. The anchor name is assigned in the Frame mode by choosing Anchors & Captions from the Frame menu and typing the anchor name. The anchor spot is marked in Text mode by placing the cursor at the spot in the text where you want the graphic to appear, selecting Ins

Special Item from the Edit menu, choosing Frame Anchor and then typing the anchor name of the frame in the Insert/Edit Anchor dialog box that appears, as shown in the lower box. Finally, choose where you want the frame to appear relative to the text anchor; Ventura provides four choices as shown in the screen dump below:

Fixed, On Same Page As Anchor When the text moves to a new page, the frame that holds the graphic will occupy the same location as on the previous page.

Relative, Below Anchor Line The graphic is anchored directly below the anchor text. But this choice doesn't update the screen automatically as text changes. You

have to select the Re-Anchor Frames Command from the Chapter menu (or by pressing Ctrl-B) to have the picture move to the new location.

Relative, Above Anchor Line The graphic is anchored directly above the anchor text. Once again, you have to select the Re-Anchor Frames command from the Chapter menu (or by pressing Ctrl-B) to move the picture to the new location when text has been changed.

Relative, Automatically At Anchor This choice is used mostly for small pictures within the text, so that they automatically move with the text. The picture is moved automatically as the text is edited.

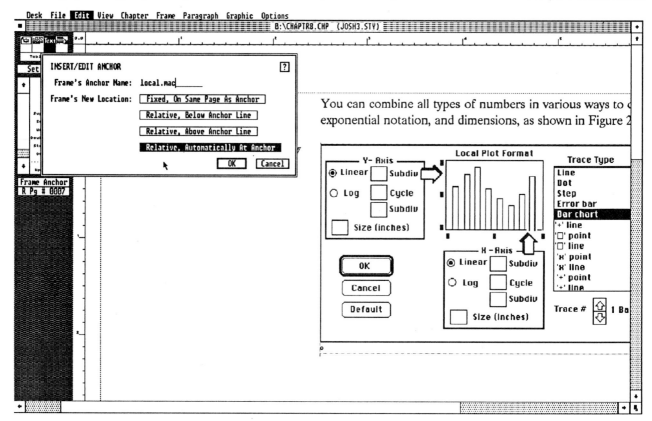

Chapter openings and cover

We set the chapter titles in 24-point Univers 67 type. To turn them sideways on the page, we used Ventura's ability to rotate paragraphs to a vertical orientation (Figure 9). ▮ *Text can be rotated in 90-degree increments. However, to select text once it has been rotated, you have to select where the text would have been had it not been rotated. Often you can use the position of the first letter as the starting point for the selection.*

The cover (shown on page 75) was laid out in Ventura, where type, page size and keyline were specified. But the artwork was stripped in by the printer. The printer stripped in art that we supplied for the section and chapter opener pages, as well as simpler tints for screen-dumped elements (see Figure 7) and running heads.

In retrospect

To sum up, the typographical elegance of Ventura combined with the new lexicon of combining screen portions with procedural text created a compact, dynamic, accessible manual for Macintosh users. The key ingredient, however, was a trusting, communicative relationship between the writer and the designer.

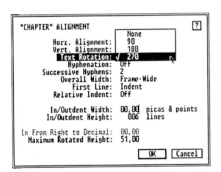

Figure 9. Rotating type. For chapter opener pages the 24-point Univers Condensed type was set and selected. Then Text Rotation was chosen from the Alignment dialog box, accessed through the Paragraph menu, and a 270-degree rotation was applied. Screened artwork for chapter opener pages (and facing pages) and for section openers was provided by Imprimatur Design Systems and stripped in by the printer, who also provided the tint for the running heads.

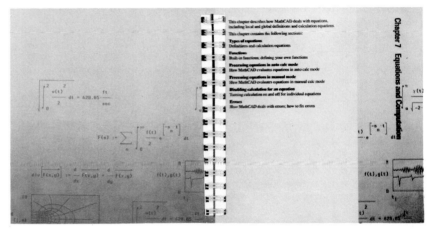

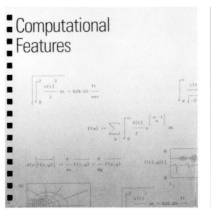

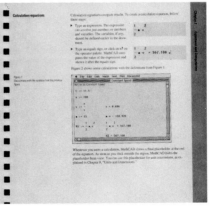

PORTFOLIO

Michael Sullivan

"Today I constantly hear people brag that 'such-and-such software program can do anything' — but I ask, why not use the best tool for the job instead? To master computer tools, you have to be able to make informed decisions on how to best use the tools at your disposal. Knowing only one application will distort your ability to discern what is efficient. This is analogous to a carpenter using only a radial-arm saw to create his furniture — sure, it can be done, but why would anyone want to use a radial-arm saw as a lathe?

To be effective, the new designer will be required to know and master at least a dozen different programs (maybe more). Why are there no decent "panacea" programs out there? Because different problems require different specialized tools. Ventura can do things that PageMaker can't and vice versa. Adobe Illustrator can do things that FreeHand can't, and so on. Illustrators and artists routinely master several media, even though they may have only one style. Designers will have to master multiple software packages because software is the future media of designers."

C-Worthy packaging was designed in Illustrator 1.1 on the Mac. At that point there was no software available for making color separations. To make separations, a master grid was designed and "Saved As" six times. Some elements were deleted from each of the six files, and the remaining shapes were filled in with color.

The **Aspen Plus documentation** had originally been produced by the client on a Wang word processor with MacDraw illustrations. When it was redesigned in Ventura, the logical process of developing the style sheet identified some problem areas that required extensive reworking. Covers were designed on the Macintosh.

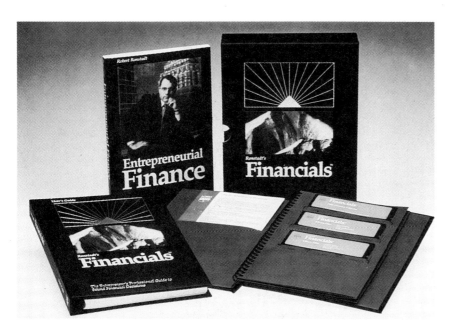

The **Ronstadt's Financials packaging** won second place in Ventura's Technical Documentation competition. Logos and the illustrations inside were developed in Illustrator on the Macintosh. Covers were designed and laid out in Illustrator on the Mac, with photographs by Stu Rosner.

The **Interleaf packaging system** was designed on the Interleaf Technical Publishing System on a Sun workstation. Interleaf is a very powerful system for use in workgroups. Because 20 writers worked on this project, a formal process was developed for designing a new style tag, in order to keep styles consistent. Interleaf's ability to flag sentences that have changed since the last time the file was opened by a particular user helped keep the project organized.

CHAPTER 7

The Art of PageMaker

Designer

Associate Professor of Graphic Design Ken Carls bought a Macintosh computer in 1988 after returning from a sabbatical leave in Glasgow, Scotland. On his return to the campus of the University of Illinois at Urbana-Champaign, he had discovered that his colleagues, who had wielded pens and pica rulers the year before, were now discussing encapsulated PostScript files and megabytes of RAM. Feeling a bit like a dinosaur, he learned to use PageMaker and has been using it (exclusively, at first) ever since.

Project

The "Art and Design in Britain" poster was one part of a three-piece set of materials advertising a University of Illinois study-travel program offered by the Study Abroad Office in conjunction with the School of Art and Design. I decided that the poster must be "Pop" enough in flavor to attract college students, but serious enough to convince their parents who would be expected to fund $10,000 for a year of foreign study. Beyond that were the logistical require-ments: The poster had to fit in an envelope for mailing and it had to carry a pad of mail-back cards. The series of three pieces was done in PageMaker 3.0, with one small part carried out in SuperPaint, on a Macintosh SE and a Mac II. Some images were scanned with an Apple Scanner and saved in PICT format. The poster was proofed on a LaserWriter and finally printed on a Linotronic L-300 at 1270 dpi.

The "Art & Design in Britain" materials were chosen for the Showcase One design competition sponsored by the Association for the Development of Electronic Pub-lishing Technique (ADEPT). Parts of the text in this chapter were excerpted from a speech to ADEPT by Ken Carls which was later published in ADEPTations, *the asso-ciation's journal, and is reprinted with the permission of ADEPT.*

**PROJECT
OVERVIEW**

Design process

I approached the flyer, poster and brochure the same way I work on all my computer design projects. I believe that graphic design is architectonic; that is, it's constructed and communicates in much the same way that architecture is and does. When I start a project, there are no sketches. I work directly on the Mac with no preconceptions. I put something down, and then I'm confronted with two choices: (1) keep it, or (2) change it. The piece spins itself out from there. The marvelous advantage of working this way is that the whole piece remains one evolving sketch until it's done.

The plane was treated differently in each of the three pieces. In the flyer it was photocopied and pasted down on the mechanical. For the brochure it was scanned and used in its original proportions. I had the printer make a mask to leave white behind the images of the plane on the front and back covers to keep the plane "whole" as it overlaid both the light green of the background and the yellow of a round shape. For the poster the scan was stretched a bit to fit the space available for it. No mask was needed, because the plane was placed entirely on the green background.

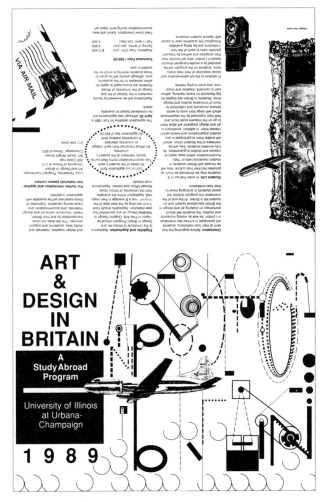

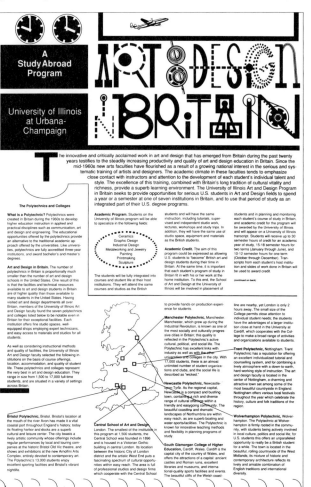

The flyer was the first of the three pieces in this set of materials. I got the copy one week before we had to take the printed flyer to a conference. There was no time to do something exotic; it had to be something purposely cheap. I called a local newspaper publisher and found out that he could print and deliver 3000 copies in four days. So I went to work. I had taught all day; it was 7 p.m. and I sat down at the computer, just planning to crack this open. The next time I looked up it was 10:30, and the next time I looked it was 4 a.m. and the flyer was finished.

With the exception of the map, all the design elements in the brochure were created in PageMaker by overlaying shapes, letters and lines. To make the row of waves at the bottom of the page, a single circle was created, masked with a white rectangle and copied. Copying was done in stages. After the first partial circle was copied and its duplicate was arranged beside it, the pair was copied and arranged, then the row of four, the row of eight and so on.

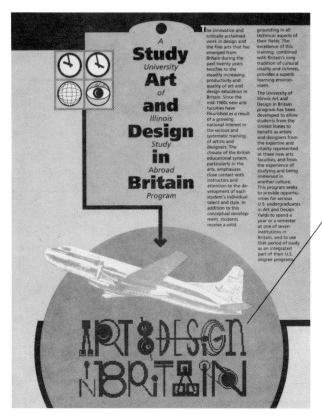

I really liked using exaggerated bitmaps as part of the design. In using the computer, as in any design process, you should allow the technology to enter into the process. If we're going to use the computer, why should we be ashamed to show it. Are we supposed to keep it chained to the bed in the attic so that no one will know that's how we did it?

Working with the client

Instead of designing to fulfill a client's wants or likes rather than his needs, I like to design things that will do what they need to, but perhaps not in the way the client would have expected. In this project I had more than the usual amount of freedom. The client was the Study Abroad Office, in conjunction with the School of Art and Design. Study Abroad provided copy and proofread the first Laser Writer draft. The School of Art and Design saw the poster for the first time when it came back from the printer. As I'd been involved in the Study Abroad program, I was able to add things I knew about a particular school being described in the materials. And if the text didn't fit quite right with the page design I was developing, I'd see what I could take out. It was really quite an irregular way of working.

The graphic elements on the page spreads for the brochure (the third project in the series) were combinations of filled and unfilled shapes, lines, letters and scanned drawings and photos.

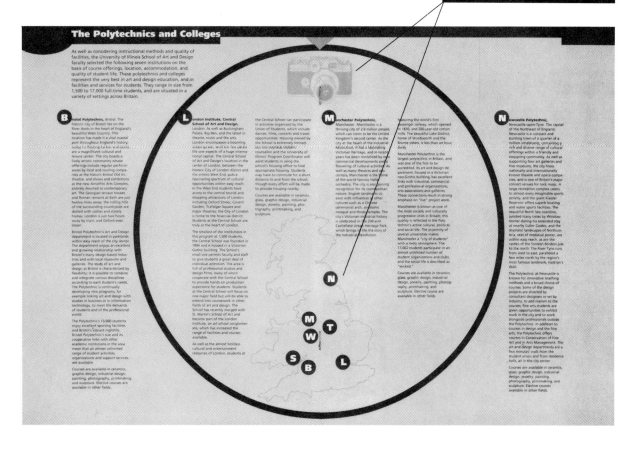

Development of the poster began after the flyer had been completed, and many elements from the flyer were reused "as is" or modified. All elements except the scan were originated in Page-Maker, either when the flyer was composed or when the poster was put together. The only other program I would use at all in developing the poster was SuperPaint — to group the PageMaker elements that made up the "Art & Design in Britain" lettering and to give it a bitmapped look.

Starting out

I keyed in the text, making a separate Microsoft Word file for each separate section of the information. The page was then set up in PageMaker at full size, 17 x 22 inches. Beyond its dimensions, the master page was assigned no other specifications. And there were no Styles defined. For styles to work you have to have some sort of preconceived idea of what you're doing, and I didn't. The poster was built without plans.

I always design in black-and-white first and then add color, and this poster was no exception (Figure 1). (I think this is primarily because I start designing at home, where I have an SE.) I moved text blocks around and experimented with various type treatments. All type was from a single family — various sizes and weights of Frutiger. Type size was used to define text elements. For

Figure 1. Designing the page. The poster was constructed in PageMaker in black-and-white on the SE. Then patches of color were added on the Mac II with Page-Maker's drawing tools.

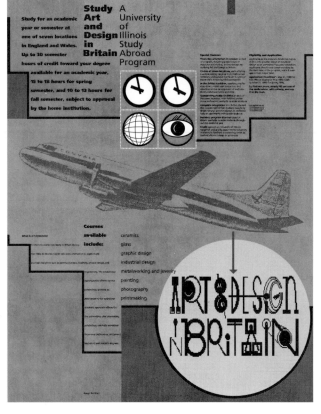

example, 9-point Frutiger was used for both text (Roman) and title (Bold) of "What is a Polytechnic?". The text and title for the list of courses available — which were somewhat interlaced with "What is a Polytechnic?" — were made easy to identify as a separate unit by their size (18 points). Both sections were set on 35-point leading (Figure 2). Thick (12-point) lines, which bled off the page, were used to help organize the various blocks of text.

When I moved into color, I retained the lines but constructed the basic page of two rectangles of "slate dark" (100 percent Pantone 5635, a gray-green color), two rectangles of "slate light" (40 percent gray-green), five overlapping rectangles of "slate" (60 percent gray-green), a red circle and rectangle (Pantone Warm Red) and a large yellow circle (Pantone 128) (Figure 3). The red arrow, used to attract attention to the mail-back cards, was constructed of line pieces (Figure 4).

Figure 2. Identifying text blocks. Text blocks were juxtaposed in a stair-stepped format. Uniform leading was important to the overall design, while variation in type size kept the text blocks distinct.

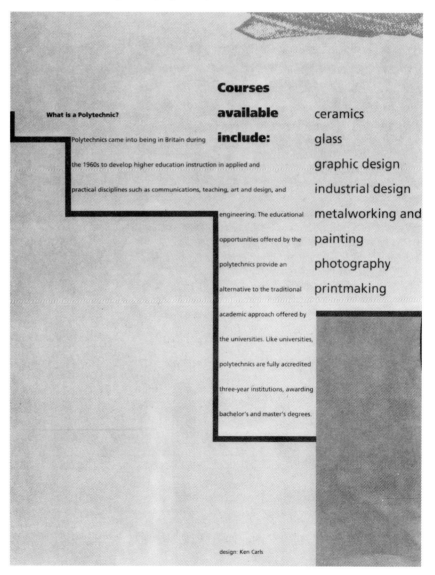

design: Ken Carls

Graphic images

I wanted the poster to talk about several things. First, I wanted it to make some statement about the differences between the USA and Britain. In that connection, the clocks show that when it's 10 a.m. in Champaign, Illinois, it's 4 p.m. in Britain. (I considered an image for an American morning cup or coffee juxtaposed with a British afternoon cup of tea, but couldn't work out how to state that difference clearly visually.) Second, I wanted to talk about the experience of foreign study, seeing the world and opening one's eyes. The globe, the eye and the airplane simply talk about the travel involved (Figure 5). I had to be careful with the airplane (Figure 6). It had to be an upward, positive image; the design of this poster came just on the heels of the Pan Am crash over Scotland with a group of American foreign study students aboard.

"Art & Design in Britain" letter forms

Using PageMaker's graphics tools, I had constructed letters to form the words "Art & Design in Britain" for the flyer (Figure 7). I decided to try an exaggerated "computer" look, so I selected the desired elements, copied them to the clipboard and then pasted them into SuperPaint, which grouped them (Figure 8). ■ *A draw program (or desk accessory) can be very useful if you're using PageMaker's tools to construct graphics. Since PageMaker has no grouping function, it's easy to accidentally knock an element out of line. But you can Shift-*

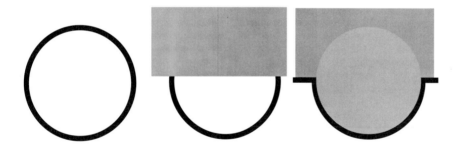

Figure 3. Masking a half-circle. A rectangle of slate light (Lines, None; Shades, Solid) was sandwiched between the black circle (Lines, 12 pt.; Shades, None) and the yellow circle (Lines, None; Shades, Solid).

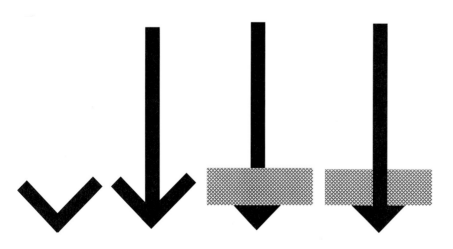

Figure 4. Constructing the arrow. The arrow was assembled from 12-point red lines. A yellow mask created a triangle of red, and Bring To Front was used to pull the vertical line forward.

select all elements of a graphic, cut them to the clipboard, open a draw DA, paste them into the DA's window, group them, and take them back to the PageMaker page, where they can be moved or resized as a unit, and you won't accidentally knock them apart.

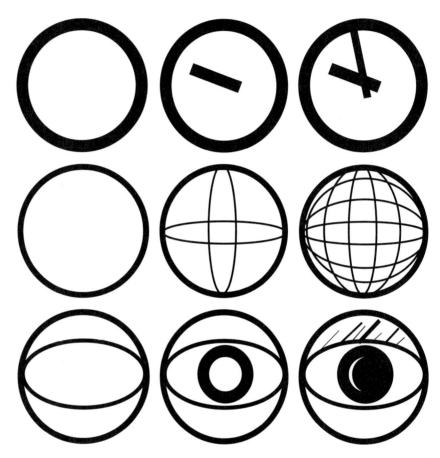

Figure 5. Assembling a square of graphics.
The graphics block was surrounded by a yellow dashed line. Note that the spaces in the dashed line are the paper color rather than the background color behind the lines. Clocks (drawn using the ellipse tool with the Shift key held down) were assembled with 12-point lines and Paper fill, with 12-point hour hands and 8-point minute hands. The globe started with a 6-point circle with Paper fill; 2-point ellipses with no fill were added. The outer circle of the eye had no fill. The slightly offset pupil circle was black with a Solid fill. (For more tips on using graphics tools in page layout programs, see Figure 4 in Chapter 1 and "The computer draws itself" on page 99.)

Figure 6. Placing the airplane. The airplane was scanned from a photo and saved as a one-bit TIFF file. It had the right character — it represented travel and taking off without looking too up-to-date and real.

Figure 7. Assembling letters from shapes. The letters shown here were formed as follows. **R:** A 12-point vertical and an 8-point slanted line were drawn over a circle formed with a thick dashed line with no fill. A circle with a 12-point Reverse line and Solid black fill were offset. **&:** Circles of patterned lines were stacked, a slanted line was added and anther circle of thick dashed lines was laid on top. **G:** Nested offset ellipses were formed of square-dotted lines; straight lines and a patch of yellow were added to complete the letter. **N:** To form this letter, the same pattern was used to draw both an ellipse (masked by a rectangle as shown here) and a straight line. **IN** (in "BRITAIN"): This letter pair was assembled from layered lines and circles of various weights. The cog wheel at the center of the N consists of (back to front) a black 2-point circle with no fill; a ring of empty space; a thick dashed-line circle filled with Solid black; and finally, a smaller black circle with a patterned (three-part) reversed line. This last reversed circle, by iteself, accounts for the center black dot and the three white and two black rings surrounding it. Teeth on the crossbar of the N were made by placing square-dotted black lines beside solid black lines.

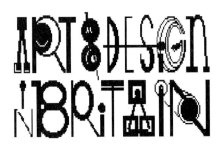

Figure 8. Developing the "computer look." The constructed lettering from the flyer was copied and transferred through the clipboard to the paint (bitmapped) mode of SuperPaint. The exaggerated bitmapped look resulted from stretching the image when it was placed back in PageMaker.

The mail-back cards

The card was designed as a separate page in the PageMaker file. It included most of the "Art & Design in Britain" lettering. This gave the cards a "designed in" look; they didn't look like an appendage as these cards often do. The back of the card included text and rules for a response (Figure 9).

Producing the poster

Once the PageMaker files had been completed, they were output as spot color separations at 1270 dpi. The files had to be reduced to print on the Linotronic L-300, so the printer was given reflective art at a reduced size and the appropriate amount of trap was built in when the negatives were made.

Since the pads of mail-back cards had to be attached by hand after the posters had been folded, the printer was worried about getting the registration between poster and pad exactly right. I felt it would be just fine if the registration wasn't exact — it wouldn't hurt the look of the poster at all. In fact, I was looking forward to the "hand-applied" look, but very nearly all of the posters were perfect.

Success

The Study Abroad Office sent out posters to over 1500 colleges. The response (number of mail-back cards received) was high (about 800 returned cards), and we've had a hard time keeping this poster up on our own walls in

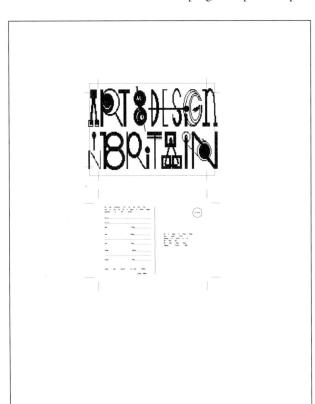

Figure 9. Designing the matching card. The front of the postcard matched the exaggerated bitmap of the poster. The back provided space for a response. The card was set up as a page in the poster file, to be output at the same time and at the same reduction.

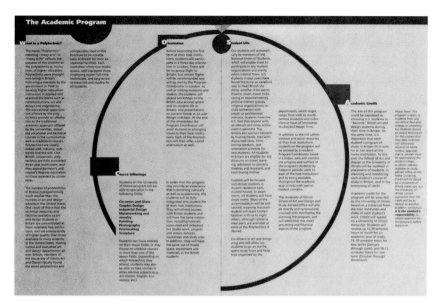

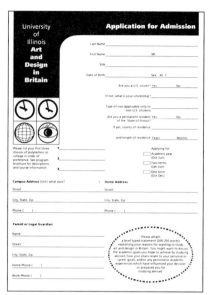

Champaign because the students keep stealing them. You tell me if this is a measure of success.

Brochure and application forms

When students returned the postcards, they were sent a brochure and a set of application forms. The brochure was printed in the same colors as the poster and postcard. Since the text was much more extensive than it had been in the poster, graphics used on the page were large and open, and type size was relatively small and constant. Initial caps reversed out of red circles were a new element developed for this piece; they guided the eye to the beginning of each new text block (Figure 10). ▌ *In PageMaker, to print reversed lettering in spot separations, choose both Spot Color Overlays and Cutouts in the Print dialog box.*

The application forms were black-and-white, businesslike, but still very closely associated with the other materials by the graphic elements used throughout. In the end, the Study Abroad materials formed a cohesive set, but each item also had its own distinctive look.

In retrospect

If I had it to do over again, what I would do differently is everything. Whenever I sit down at the keyboard, I'm there to compose. Standardized form left me when the computer put back into my hands the tools necessary to generate type and images. I no longer need to explain to an outside supplier what I want my type to look like or to a production person where I want something pasted down. (Besides, if I had spec'd type for that poster where it changes 14 times and there are all these indents and runarounds, it would have cost a million dollars to have someone set it.) Design is once again completely in the hands of the designer, which we haven't experienced since the 19th century. So if I were to redesign the poster, who knows what it would be today. But it certainly wouldn't be the same.

Figure 10. Coordinating materials. The Study Abroad brochure was printed in color with initial caps of Frutiger UltraBlack reversed out of red geometric shapes. The application forms incorporated graphic elements from the brochure but were printed in black-and-white.

**The computer
draws itself**

The illustration of the Macintosh at bottom right was created in Page-Maker, not in a drawing program. And it wasn't at all tricky or difficult. The tools that are built into Page-Maker (and some other page layout programs) can do a lot more than create simple charts or lines. And graphics created within the program often print more quickly than imported graphics.

Basic shapes first

Set your Preferences for picas, make sure your rulers are showing and that Snap To Guides is active. Begin with the overall shape. Pull out ruler guides to enclose an area 10 picas wide by 13½ picas high. Then Draw a rounded-corner rectangle within the guides (**a**). While the rectangle is selected, set the corners to the smallest radius possible. (In PageMaker 4.0 this is done by selecting Rounded Corners from the Element menu and selecting the top center button.) Now set the Fill to 20 percent black and the Lines to None.

Next, make another rounded-corner rectangle (**b**), with the same corner radius, about 8 picas wide by 7 picas high, also filled with a 20 percent black. Make sure the line thickness is .5 points and then reverse it (so the line becomes white). Position this outer perimeter of the screen indentation at the top center of the large rectangle.

Next, make another rounded-corner rectangle (**c**) with the same corner radius and width as the previous one but only 1 pica high (or copy **b** and change the height). Choose None from the Lines menu (under the Element menu) and fill with a 40 percent black. Align it with the top of the previous rectangle to form the shaded part of the screen indentation. Using Copy and Paste, put a duplicate of that rectangle at the bottom of rectangle **b**, and change it to 10 percent black to form the highlight at the bottom of the screen indentation (**d**). Work in 200 percent size to make alignment and sizing easier.

The last screen rectangle (**e**) is 7 picas wide by about 5½ picas high. Fill it with solid black and center it over the other rectangles to complete the screen portion of the Mac.

Details lend realism

Now add a few elements to give the Mac some finishing touches. Make a very small rectangle to begin the disk slot. Make it black, and set the line style for Reverse — that makes a small highlight around the rectangle so it will stand out from the body of the Mac. Position the small rectangle to the right and about two-thirds up from the bottom of the Mac to the screen. Extend a black line from the left of the rectangle to finish the slot.

Now for shading the base. Use the rectangle tool with Fill set to 30 percent black and Lines set for None to cover up the bottom 2 picas of the Mac with a rectangle (**f**) the exact width of the Mac. To further enhance the effect, add another rectangle (**g**) about ½ pica high, set to 40 percent black, at the top edge of rectangle **f**. Although it doesn't blend with the other shadow rectangle, it does add to the illusion of depth. Adding an apple for the logo is just a matter of dragging out a rectangle about 6 picas (1 inch) wide with the Text tool, typing Shift-Option-k, and setting the type to 8-point Helvetica. Position the apple as shown. You're done. (The apple prints from LaserWriter printers only. To print it to a Linotronic imagesetter, we set it very large on-screen, made a screen dump and traced it with Streamline.)

To add an active window to your Mac, place a white rectangle (with square corners) over the black screen. Then make a screen dump of what's presently on your screen (see page 83 for information on making screen dumps). Next, Place the screen dump on your PageMaker page, shrink it by holding down the Shift key as you drag a corner point, and position it over the white rectangle on the screen.

To keep all the pieces of the drawing together, "group" them using the Scrapbook or a drawing DA.

— *Adapted from "Make a Mac" by David Doty in* ThePage *newsletter, issue number 13. Reprinted with permission.*

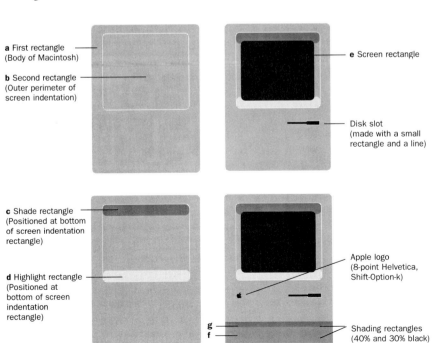

a First rectangle
(Body of Macintosh)

b Second rectangle
(Outer perimeter of
screen indentation)

c Shade rectangle
(Positioned at bottom
of screen indentation
rectangle)

d Highlight rectangle
(Positioned at
bottom of screen
indentation
rectangle)

e Screen rectangle

Disk slot
(made with a small
rectangle and a line)

Apple logo
(8-point Helvetica,
Shift-Option-k)

g
f Shading rectangles
(40% and 30% black)

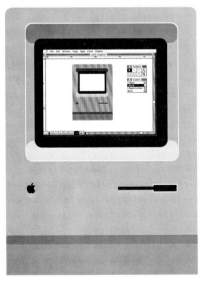

Ken Carls

"I really can't overemphasize that for me, the computer has become a real construction tool. Because it lets me do things that I would never do if I had to do it by hand. I never thought that way when I had a pen in my hand. The design was much more formulaic when I was working by hand, specifying the type for someone else to produce; it's very different when you can sit there and look at it and change it yourself. The machine has given me and my students one wonderful gift and one disability. The gift is that the possibilities have multiplied tremendously. There are no limits. Responsibility for good decision-making increases. Not only do we have more opportunities to make beautiful images, but we also have more opportunities to make terrible mistakes."

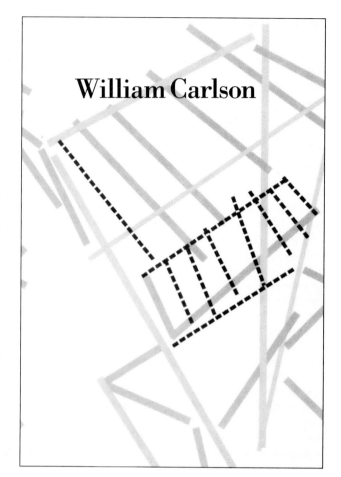

This piece, an **exhibition catalogue** for a glass sculptor, needed to be as pristine and classical as his work. The form of the book is light and transparent, so that the focus is on the work of the artist rather than on the design of the cata-logue. The first piece Carls attempted on the Mac, the cata-logue was designed in PageMaker. The type for the cover was printed on a translucent vellum jacket, with the graphics printed in color on the cover underneath.

The letterhead and envelope were the first pieces of an **identity program** for Architectural Spectrum, an architectural design firm that balances its work between renovation of historic buildings and new construction. Preliminary sketches were done in PageMaker, but it became clear that the design would work better in FreeHand. The mark was designed to refer to the name block used to identify blueprints; the color is reflex blue. The spheres comment on space, volume and geometric solids that architecture is composed of. The logotype is Frutiger, with reference to the classical Roman alphabet (with the use of the V as a U), and then the V is inverted to make the A. The type portion of the design is conspicuously "constructed."

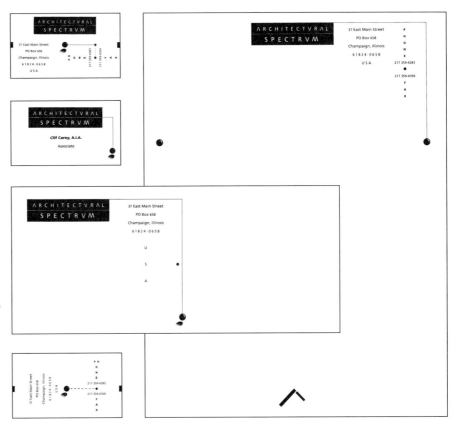

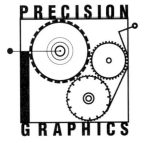

Many preliminary sketches (some of which are shown here on the left) were constructed with Page-Maker's graphics tools for Precision Graphics, a technical illustration and type-setting company. An exploration of designs that incorporated concepts of paper, printing and technical precision and efficiency led to a final Cubist-inspired mark (shown on the right), which was executed in Illustrator. The mark and logotype are used variously in the company's printed pieces. The **type bill** shows one application of the identity.

C H A P T E R   8

An Emphasis
on Style

Designer

Laura Lamar is an art director and typographic designer specializing in publication design. A partner in San Francisco design studio MAX, she also teaches typographic design and Macintosh production skills at the California College of Arts and Crafts. Former art director of *San Francisco Focus* magazine and of Communications Design in Sacramento, she attended UCLA and Scripps College in Los Angeles. Since opening MAX in 1986, she and her partner, illustrator Max Seabaugh, have specialized in electronic design and illustration on the Macintosh for the computer industry as well as for traditional publishing clients.

Project

San Francisco: A Certain Style was designed for publisher Chronicle Books with Ready,Set,Go on a Macintosh IIcx with a Radius two-page full-color monitor. Also important in the development of the project were an Apple Scanner, used to make FPO illustrations for the silhouetted photos, and a Canon NP 9030 Laser Copier, used to make scaled position-only prints for mechanical paste-up. The book was proof-printed on a LaserWriter Plus and output on resin-coated paper on a Compugraphic imagesetter at 1200 dpi.

Design goal

The aim in designing and producing *San Francisco: A Certain Style* was to present the remarkably talented, diverse community of San Francisco architects and interior designers through a book that showcased their designs with full-color photos, to celebrate the individuality of the glorious rooms behind closed doors in the environs of San Francisco. The "coffee table book" was designed to the publisher's size specifications — approximately 10 x 10 inches — a typical size for books of this kind.

Working with author and photographer

Writer Diane Dorrans Saeks, photographer John Vaughan and I prepared and presented six spreads to sell the book to the publisher. After two years of photographing and editing the photos, the writing of the text began in earnest. The project involved close interaction among the three of us, with photo editing, writing and page design going on simultaneously.

Initial capitals for the main sections were "hand-drawn" in Adobe Illustrator 88 by Max Seabaugh, copied from a script face in the Berthold type catalog with the permission of the type house.

Elements of a typical section opener spread included a full-bleed photo, title, text with initial cap, caption and a footer with a page number.

Grand Style

An occasional minor earthquake or rumbling temblor shakes the calm of the City and reminds residents of a more precarious time when an earthquake and fire destroyed its heart. Otherwise, San Francisco seems to have been standing on these hills forever—or at least longer than a mere 140 years or so. ¶ Grand mansions and patrician palazzi edging the bluffs of Pacific Heights and circling Lafayette Park give the distinct impression that they set up residence centuries ago. Solid fortunes made from sugar, gold, railroads, and real-estate speculation provided these grandstand positions, their proud profiles, and the classic Mediterranean-and European-influenced architecture. ¶ In fact, in 1776, the San Francisco Bay that greeted Lieutenant Colonel Juan Bautista de Anza and his band of Spanish settlers was sandy, wind-swept, and wild, with few trees to provide shelter. The rocky hills and headlands beyond the north tower of the Golden Gate Bridge today give some idea of the terrain. Few new settlers arrived on this hardship post in the 60 years following the establishment of the Presidio and the mission. ¶ Around 1835, an Englishman, William A. Richardson, built a house in what is now Portsmouth Square, and the village of Yerba Buena began. A straggly collection of pueblos, huts, tents, and tacked-together shacks huddled around a cove and provided shelter for those first San Franciscans. California was proclaimed part of the United States by treaty in 1846, and soon the land to the north and south of Market Street was surveyed, and rough streets and paths crisscrossed the hills. Fortune seekers arrived. The Gold Rush was on. ¶ City lots in those days may have been sold for as little as $90. But with later speculation, an acre could increase in value from $500 to $20,000 in just a decade. ¶ In the 1850s and 1860s, the fanciest part of town was Rincon Hill. Andrew Hallidie's invention, the cable car, tamed steep Nob Hill in 1873 and gave instant status to the area. As more lines were added, Russian Hill became a desirable address. ¶ In the years between 1870 and 1906, as the City boomed, thousands of houses, most of them Victorian-style, were built. San Francisco extended west from grand Nob Hill, east from South Park, and south beyond the Mission. Grand boulevards like Van Ness Avenue and Dolores Avenue were lined with impressive mansions. Handsome houses in well-tended gardens stood in solitary splendor in Pacific Heights with grand vistas of the Bay.

After extensive refurbishing directed by interior designer Anthony Hail, the main residence of Filoli is now open to the public for viewing. To recreate the interiors as they looked in the twenties, Hail gathered together furniture and paintings bequeathed by Lurline Roth, one of the estate's residents, and special pieces loaned from the Getty Museum, the California Palace of the Legion of Honor, and the M.H. de Young Memorial Museum. *Previous pages:* The ballroom at Filoli with murals painted in 1925 by Ernest Peixotto, a well-known illustrator. The chandelier was said to once hang in the Hall of Mirrors at Versailles. Crystal sconces have amethyst drops. *Opposite:* The refurbished Filoli dining room has Chippendale-style chairs and an eighteenth-century Dutch cabinet. Filoli, a half-hour drive south of San Francisco, may be visited by advance reservation (415-364-2880).

Grand Style **23**

AN ARTIST'S HOUSE, BERKELEY

Across the Bay from San Francisco stands a bucolic Berkeley property discovered by a local artist in 1976. Formerly part of a large estate, the cow barn/granary/milking shed/hayloft was originally designed in 1908 by John Galen Howard, the campus architect for the University of California Berkeley from 1905 to 1930. ¶ With thoughtful renovation by architect Chuck Trevisan, the old barn is now the home of the artist's family. Down the hill, a horse barn eventually became their guest cottage. "I don't think Howard would recognize these buildings even though they're remodelled in the style, spirit, and symmetry of the original," said Trevisan. ¶ A shady colonnade was added and later enclosed to create a family room and bedroom. A new swimming pool and patio were built by the artist, his wife, and their three sons, using old bricks and tiles from the property. A new pergola and trellises covered with wisteria ensure privacy. ¶ Still in the planning stages are a new dining room and a renovation of the kitchen. In the meantime, the family's glorious acre offers them the very best retreat just 20 minutes from the City.

"We repaired and updated all the old buildings on the property without changing their style or scale. They had to look as if they had always been there," said architect Chuck Trevisan, who planned the changes. Sheltered by stands of eucalyptus and a redwood grove, the property includes a new swimming pool and patio and a retro-new house, formerly a barn.

A "Design and Style Resources" section at the back of the book included black-and-white photos, some of which were silhouetted. These silhouetted photos were the only ones for which scans were used as placeholders.

Ready,Set,Go's ability to set up horizontal rows as well as vertical columns provided a five-column by five-row page grid for placement of photos, text and captions. Nonprinting rules (two each, horizontal and vertical) were used on each page to provide visual guides for bleeds, and additional placement guides for photos that did not bleed but needed to extend beyond the last grid column.

SAN FRANCISCO CATALOGUE: DESIGN AND STYLE RESOURCES

Haas-Lilienthal House
2007 Franklin Street,
San Francisco,
(415) 441-3004
Built in 1886, the gray house is a classic storybook Victorian. The fully furnished house was lived in until 1972 when it was donated to the Foundation for San Francisco's Architectural Heritage.

Octagon House
2645 Gough Street,
San Francisco,
(415) 441-7512
Gray with white trim and quoining, the house was built in 1861, and is now a Colonial museum set in a quiet garden. Acquired in 1952 as their headquarters by the California Colonial Dames of America.

Whittier Mansion
2090 Jackson Street,
San Francisco,
(415) 567-1848
The 30-room Richardsonian-Romanesque 1896 mansion was fitted at the turn of the century with gas-electric fixtures and an Otis elevator. Home of the California Historical Society.

Designer Ron Mann's *Shadow* vases are available in three sizes and finishes ranging from verdigris to sandcast bronze. Each has its own special character. Available from the *Ron Mann Designs* studio, 497 Caroline Street, (415) 864-4911 (Through a designer or architect).

DESIGN AND STYLE STORES

These stores are our top choices for an only-in-San Francisco treat. Superbly displayed merchandise, out-of-the-way locations, and unique points of view are here in spades, thanks to a savvy collection of local entrepreneurs. Brilliant, single-minded, visionary, hard-working, and idiosyncratic, these store owners make their businesses special and inspiring. Many of the stores sell handcrafts of Northern California you won't find elsewhere.

Accession
388 Hayes Street,
San Francisco,
(415) 861-3191
Handcrafted and antique accessories. Antique textiles and masks.

Aerial
The Cannery,
2801 Leavenworth Street,
San Francisco,
(415) 474-1566
The out-there owners sell only what they love—an ever-changing collection of architectural prints, art books, accessories,well-designed sporting equipment, and fun stuff. Water bar. Store designed by architect Richard Altuna.

Agraria
1156 Taylor Street,
San Francisco,
(415) 771-5922
Maurice Gibson and Stanford Stevenson make the most elegant potpourri and soaps. A very chic (and wonderfully fragrant) store. Catalogue.

San Francisco designer David Best's sidetable of colorful laminate on wood from Limn, 457 Pacific Street, (415) 397-7474.

Arch
407 Jackson Street,
San Francisco,
(415) 433-2724
Architect Susan Colliver's colorful, graphic store sells supplies for designers, architects, and artists. Fun place.

Bell'Occhio
8 Brady Street,
San Francisco,
(415) 864-4048
Claudia Schwartz and Toby Hanson hand-paint and sell ribbons, charming tableware, antiques, and wonderfully idiosyncratic treasures.

Bloomers
2975 Washington Street,
San Francisco,
(415) 563-3266
In an expansive new shop, bustling Bloomers sells glorious flowers, vases, ribbons, and baskets.

Pine table with tapered legs (48" by 24") crafted by Tony Cowan. Custom order this and other designs from The Cottage Table Company, 550 18th Street, (415) 957-1760.

Virginia Breier
3091 Sacramento Street,
San Francisco,
(415) 929-7173
Also at Ghirardelli Square, 900 North Point Street, San Francisco, (415) 474-5036. A fine gallery for viewing contemporary and traditional American crafts, including furniture and tableware.

Builders Booksource
1817 4th Street,
Berkeley,
(415) 845-6874
With an accent on the practical, this well-stocked store includes books on interior design, gardens, architecture, and materials. Catalogue.

The Cottage Table Company
550 18th Street,
San Francisco,
(415) 957-1760
Craftsman Tony Cowan custom makes fine classic hardwood tables to order. A rare find. Shipping available. Catalogue.

Cottonwood
3461 Sacramento Street,
San Francisco,
(415) 346-6020
Well-edited Southwest style. Accent on beautiful craftsmanship.

Susan Cummins Gallery
32 Miller Avenue,
Mill Valley,
(415) 383-1512
Fine ceramics, crafts, and paintings.

Dandelion
2877 California Street,
San Francisco,
(415) 563-3100
Ostensibly a gift emporium, this superbly stocked store sells books, tableware, accessories, beautiful things.

Decorum
1632 Market Street,
San Francisco,
(415) 864-DECO
Impeccably restored authentic art deco and Moderne in an expansive store opposite the Zuni Cafe.

Filamento
2185 Fillmore Street,
San Francisco,
(415) 931-2224
A neighborhood favorite. Style-concious furniture, tableware, rugs, and gifts.

Floridella
1920 Polk Street,
San Francisco,
(415) 775-4065
Jean Thompson and Barbara Belloli sell the most beautiful flowers in a glorious store full of fragrant blossoms and new ideas.

Flush
245 11th Street,
San Francisco,
(415) 252-0245
Brand new. Interior designer Chuck Winslow and Rosemary Klebahn created a rich world of beautiful objects. Linens, furniture, antiques, Venetian glass.

Black leather "Oxford" club chair designed by Michael Vanderbyl for Bernhardt has small cast aluminum feet. Available through Risa Ogroskin Associates, 149 9th Street, San Francisco, 94103, (415) 552-0655.

I mplementing the design for *San Francisco: A Certain Style* began with master pages set up to be 66 picas by 66 picas. This page size was an inch taller and wider than the actual book pages would be. The extra space allowed a way to indicate where photos would bleed off the page and also provided space for a text block that would keep track of what stage of the project each laser proof represented (Figure 1). To set guidelines for placement of text, photos, captions, headers, initial caps and footers with folios, a custom five-column by five-row grid was established by making entries in the Grid Setup dialog box, accessed by choosing Grid and then Design Grid from the Special menu. Crop marks were included to indicate page corners.

The content of the photos would determine where the pictures would be cropped. This meant we would need maximum flexibility in sizing photos. So guides were added to establish more photo boundary possibilities. Since Ready,Set,Go doesn't provide guidelines, dashed lines were drawn with the line tool where guides were needed (see Figure 1), and Don't Print was checked in the Line Specifications dialog box. That way, the guides would show on screen but not on proofed or printed pages. Outside lines indicated the extent of bleeds, and inside lines provided another guide for placement of photos, between the last full column and the edge of the page (see page 105).
▮ *Design Studio, with its pasteboard metaphor, provides ready-made nonprinting guidelines.*

Typefaces

Aside from the full-color photos, type would make up the only other elements on the pages. The type had to be visually interesting and elegant, but it couldn't be too formal and, most important, it couldn't be allowed to compete with the pictures. Two contrasting type families — Palatino and Futura Condensed — were chosen.

Palatino type at 12.09 points on 15 points of leading was chosen for the text on section opener pages, which was styled with a ragged right margin. Twelve-point paragraph symbols (Shift-Option-8) from the Zapf Dingbats font were used rather than indents (Figure 2). They made it clear where new paragraphs started and added graphic interest, but kept the "shape" of the text as clean and simple as possible. On section opener pages the text spanned four of the five grid columns. The combination of large size, serif face, open leading and ragged right margin contributed to the readability of the broad text block. Section titles were set in 36-point Palatino Italic.

On residence spreads Palatino text was set two columns wide. Whereas on the opening page of each section the type filled the entire available text space on the first page, on the second page and on residence spreads, text ended without reaching the bottom of the page. Headings for residence sections were set in 12-point Futura ExtraBold all caps letter-spaced at .25 em (Figure 3).

Figure 1. Designing master pages. Right and left master pages were set up to be large enough to allow placement of photos that would bleed. A custom 5 x 5 grid was then established within the print area. Extra guidelines needed for photo placement were drawn with graphics tools since, unlike DesignStudio and PageMaker, Ready,Set,Go does not provide non-printing guidelines other than the grid elements.

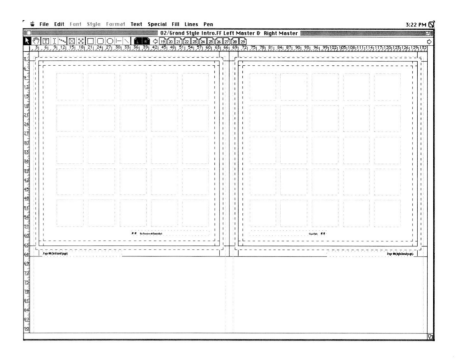

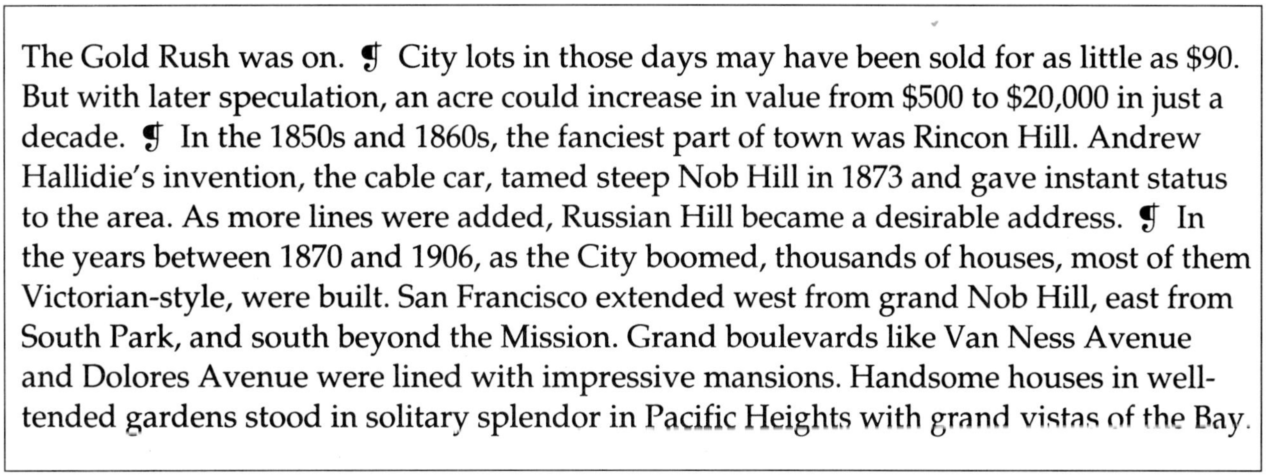

The Gold Rush was on. ❡ City lots in those days may have been sold for as little as $90. But with later speculation, an acre could increase in value from $500 to $20,000 in just a decade. ❡ In the 1850s and 1860s, the fanciest part of town was Rincon Hill. Andrew Hallidie's invention, the cable car, tamed steep Nob Hill in 1873 and gave instant status to the area. As more lines were added, Russian Hill became a desirable address. ❡ In the years between 1870 and 1906, as the City boomed, thousands of houses, most of them Victorian-style, were built. San Francisco extended west from grand Nob Hill, east from South Park, and south beyond the Mission. Grand boulevards like Van Ness Avenue and Dolores Avenue were lined with impressive mansions. Handsome houses in well-tended gardens stood in solitary splendor in Pacific Heights with grand vistas of the Bay.

Figure 2. Delineating paragraphs. With Zapf Dingbats symbols rather than indents marking paragraph breaks, text could be designed as a single solid block on each page where it was used.

AN ARTIST'S HOUSE, BERKELEY

Figure 3. Designing headers. Titles for the residence spreads were set in Futura ExtraBold, all caps. The characters were letter spaced and the title was placed at the top of the page, aligned with the outside margin. Occasionally this alignment rule was broken to accomodate the crop of a photo (see page 105).

In John Dickinson's Victorian firehouse, the sky-lit ceiling and walls are as the designer found them, a mottled topaz. In the hallway, a dresser of *faux ivoire* handpainted by Dickinson. An imposing pair of heads between shuttered windows was acquired from a sale at the Old Spaghetti Factory (a former North Beach landmark) and refinished. *Overleaf:* Dickinson creates his own room patterns with a highly disciplined no-color scheme that emphasizes the outlines of the plaster tables and curvy Victorian chairs in changing light from the south-facing windows. The pair of paintings is by Ralph Du Casse (see his house on page 172).

Figure 4. Styling captions. Bold condensed type added "weight" to the captions in balancing the page design.

A friend of mine said my studio reminded him of a dentist's office in Los Angeles in the fifties," said interior designer Gary Hutton. His Mission District apartment/ studio is located in a one-story building built for light industry in 1946. Still, with its exposed concrete walls, concrete floor, steel-framed wrap-around windows, exposed-beam ceilings, and clean lines, it was the perfect setting for Hutton. He had been looking for a building where he could set up office and use the rooms as a lab for new designs. ⁊ Patterns

Figure 5. Using initial caps. The text in each residence section began with a Futura CondensedBold initial. In the Text Block Specifications dialog box (accessed through Specifications in the Edit menu), Runaround was selected and the Text Repel distance was set to 2 points, so that the text wrapped around the initial.

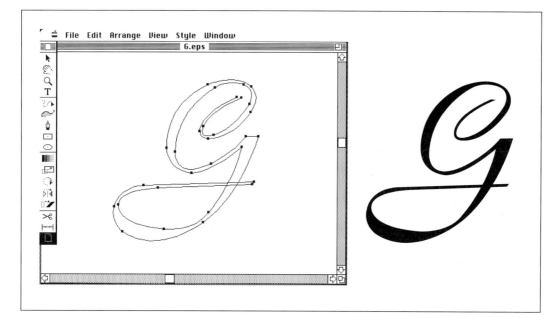

Figure 6. Drawing script initials. A script face from the Berthold type catalog was used as the basis for the calligraphic letters that served as initial caps for section opener pages. The initials needed were phototypeset, enlarged photographically and scanned. Scans were used as templates for tracing in Illustrator by Max Seabaugh. The fee charged by Berthold for typesetting and photographically enlarging the characters included payment for permission to copy the letter forms.

Futura CondensedBold at 9 points on 12 points of leading was used for captions, which were always written as single paragraphs (Figure 4). Again, ragged right styling was used.

Initial caps

Two kinds of initial caps were used in the book. To begin stories on spreads about the residences, 50-point Futura CondensedBold was inset in the first three lines of text (Figure 5).

We wanted a script face for the decorative caps on the section opener pages, but at that time there were very few digitized script faces, and none of them seemed right for this project. We found an interesting face in the Berthold type catalog. It had been designed for type on invitations and so forth, and the largest size available was 12 points. We asked Berthold if we could buy permission to redraw the characters in PostScript. The characters we needed were set at 12 points and enlarged photographically. The fee for permission to digitize the type was included in typesetting charges. We scanned the enlarged type and traced it in Adobe Illustrator. The result was a "hand-drawn" digitized face based on, but not strictly the same as, the face we had started with. The initial caps were placed in picture blocks and sized to span eight lines of text and to extend slightly above the text block (Figure 6).

Running feet

The Futura ExtraBold 8-point verso and recto folios were the most prominent element of running feet (footers), which were set from the center inward at the bottom of each page. Left-hand (verso) footers included the book title in 7-point Palatino Italic (Figure 7); right-hand footers included the section title in the same face (see page 105). Since photos were cropped according to content rather than to fit within margins, many bled off the bottom of the page. Footers were eliminated on these pages, even if it meant leaving both pages of a spread unnumbered.

Managing the photos

Working together, the writer, the photographer and I had arrived at a set of photos that could be used for the book. After the initial selection, I was given free rein in deciding what photos would go where and which ones to delete. I planned the spreads for each residence section to provide the best pacing, in terms of content and overall coloring. Ready,Set,Go (and now DesignStudio) has a wonderful feature that allows you to see a set of thumbnails on the screen and even move pages around within a file by dragging the thumbnails into place (Figure 8).

I worked with the writer to determine the order of residences in each section of the book. I made suggestions about which residences shouldn't fall together sequentially, based on the content and layout of individual residence spreads. Each section opener and residence section was saved as a separate file.

46   *San Francisco: A Certain Style*

Figure 7. Styling and placing the footer. The weight of the Futura ExtraBold folio balanced the length of the lighter Palatino Italic in the footers, which were placed so they extended from the horizontal center of the page toward the gutter.

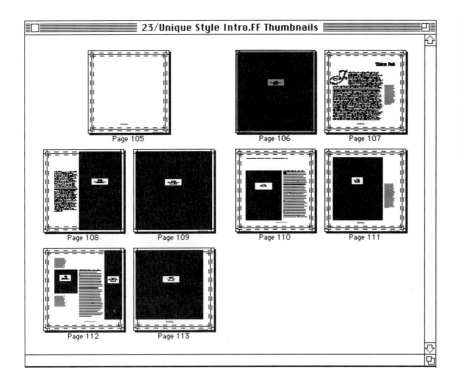

Figure 8. Rearranging thumbnails. Ready,Set, Go's thumbnails view (also found in DesignStudio) allows deletion and re-arrangement of pages. This is especially useful in a book like this, in which spreads don't have to be in a particular order but pacing is important.

Scanning photos and placing them in the electronic pages would have made the files too large and unwieldy. Instead we used black windows to hold places for the pictures. I used a technique that I use in any project involving photos — placing a slug (a type block) within the window with identification and sizing information for the photo that will go there (Figure 9). ■ *Ready,Set,Go/Design Studio has a Picture Block Specifications dialog box, accessed by choosing Specifications (from the Edit menu in Ready,Set,Go, or from the Object menu in DesignStudio), that tells the dimensions of a selected graphic element. This provides an easy way to double-check the windows for photos against the actual measured sizes of pictures.*

For silhouetted photos of chairs in the "Resources" section, it made sense to use silhouettes in the electronic layout so that I could see how photos and text blocks would interact. Since the photos existed as 35mm color slides but I needed only the shapes and not the color information or the detail, I used a "trace-and-scan" process to get the electronic files I needed: First I used a light table and tissue to trace the outline of each of the chairs. Then I enlarged these tracings on my photocopier, and finally I scanned the enlargements to get the electronic place holders to incorporate into the page layouts (Figure 10).

Figure 9. Using photo slugs. Labels identifying the photos that would go into windows on the pages helped both designer and printer in matching photos to their page spreads.

Production

Output was done at 1200 dpi on a Compugraphic 9600. I sent the service bureau a "San Francisco Styles System Disk" that included System files and fonts, along with the disks that held the files for the pages (Figure 11). ■ *Sending System files and fonts with a page layout job ensures that outputting the job will not run into compatibility or font-numbering problems between the*

Figure 10. Keeping it simple. Pencil sketches drawn on tissue by tracing 35mm slides on a light table were enlarged with a photocopier and the copies were scanned and saved as PICTs for placement in page layouts. Keeping the sketches simple and the files small saved computer time and storage space. Scans were used only for silhouetted photos, which appeared in the "References" section; all other photos were represented by rectangular windows.

system that generated the page layout file and the system that operates the imagesetter. ■ *If you're already quite sure of font-numbering compatibility between your system and your service bureau's, instead of supplying the fonts themselves, you can choose Fonts Used from Annexes under DesignStudio's Document menu to provide the service bureau with a printed list of fonts specified in the file.*

We wanted to provide the printer with mechanical boards for each spread, so we output the pages on resin-coated paper and pasted them up. We made acetate overlays for all pages, with scaled and cropped photocopies of the photos pasted in place. With FPO photos, slugs in the windows and labels on the photos, the printer had no trouble identifying which photo went where.

In retrospect

Ready,Set,Go's (and now DesignStudio's) on-screen thumbnails feature is a godsend on a picture-book project like this one, for which pacing of the graphic elements in the spreads is of paramount importance. Being able to immediately see the result of moving pages around electronically saves lots of time and paper. Now that DesignStudio provides the best of Ready,Set,Go's features as well as some great ones that originated with PageMaker (such as nonprinting guidelines and a single pasteboard common to all pages), it provides a wonderful environment for designing grid-based pages with a great deal of flexibility.

SFC&FAM S.v.6.02		
Name	Size	Kind
Clipboard File	1K	System document
Finder	105K	System document
FuturCon	27K	document
FuturConBol	29K	document
FuturExtBol	30K	document
General	14K	Control Panel doc.
Key Layout	5K	document
Keyboard	5K	Control Panel doc.
Laser Prep	28K	LaserWriter docu.
LaserWriter	64K	Chooser document
System	332K	System document

Figure 11. Sending a System disk to the service bureau. A System that included any nonstandard fonts used in the book was sent to the service bureau along with the files for the pages. Using this System to output the files ensured that there would be no conflict of System versions or font identification, which can occur when a file is created on one Macintosh system and output on another. Also included in the System folder were printer drivers and other System software.

PORTFOLIO

Laura Lamar

"Once upon a time, we blithely sent our copy to a typesetter, who toiled to achieve a perfection that we took for granted. Today we must assume responsibility for the perfection of our electronic files, and find we must pay attention to the details ourselves. Quality is as much the responsibility of the designer as it ever was; we can't blame the hardware if we've chosen the wrong software. And we can't blame the software if we haven't learned to use it properly. We have to insist on quality to help raise, and then maintain, the level of work being produced on the computer."

With a vertical emphasis established with text columns, **A Report from the San Francisco Craft and Folk Art Museum** was designed and produced in PageMaker.

The **San Francisco Style brochure** was originally designed and produced conventionally. It was later reproduced (as shown here) with ColorStudio, LetraStudio and DesignStudio as a demonstration for the 1989 Aspen Design Conference. Production time was cut to one fifth.

The **CCAC Founders Day Celebration invitation** was designed and produced in DesignStudio for the California College of Arts & Crafts. The "5," "0, "S" and "CCAC" were created with LetraStudio. The two pages (outside and inside) were spot-color separated from DesignStudio to paper base art and two layers of film positive overlay.

C H A P T E R   9

The Proof of the Catalog…

Designer

John Odam received a "straightforward British art school education" at the Leicester College of Art and Design. He designed book covers in London for three years before moving to the United States in 1968. He worked for several publishers and designed textbooks for CRM, publishers of *Psychology Today*, before becoming a freelance designer. He began working with a Macintosh in 1986 and has rapidly come to the forefront of designers working with electronic media. John is the art director of *Verbum* magazine and design director of *Step-by-Step Electronic Design* newsletter.

Project

The Journeys travel brochure/catalog was a very straightforward, humble kind of layout and production project. It didn't call for any kind of new wave ultrapostmodern approach. Journeys sells adventure tours, so the design for the brochure could be fairly simple, allowing the photographs of the beautiful places to come through. While completing the project, we derived some emblems from the Journeys logo, developed a technique for making relief maps in FreeHand and used scans of 35mm slides to position color photos in our layout.

We used primarily a Macintosh II with a Radius two-page color monitor, a Macintosh IIcx, a DataFrame 80 MB hard disk drive, a 45 MB Mass MicroSystems Syquest removable media hard disk drive, a Barneyscan slide scanner, PageMaker 3.02CE, Microsoft Word and the Aldus FreeHand PostScript illustration program.

**PROJECT
OVERVIEW**

Working with the client

The previous Journeys brochure had been published electronically a couple of years before. At that point the pages had been laid out in PageMaker 2.0. To do the new edition, we went back to the original PageMaker disks, exported the text as a Microsoft Word file and used it to work out the initial layout for the current catalog. We submitted laser proofs of the initial layouts to the client and also supplied floppy disks with exported text files in Microsoft Word format that included "style tags" that would automatically apply type specs to the text when it was again placed in PageMaker. For this first round of laser proofs, we put in rectangles as place holders for the photos (because they hadn't been supplied yet) and for the maps (because they were in the process of being drawn). Because there is no provision for proportionally enlarging rectangles and ellipses drawn in Page-Maker, we drew place-holder rectangles for photos and illustrations in FreeHand (a PostScript drawing program) and placed them in the PageMaker file. Unlike graphic

elements created in PageMaker, these imported elements can be proportionally enlarged or reduced by holding down the Shift key and dragging on a corner handle. We were redesigning the Journeys logo, which had served the company well for 10 years but now needed updating, at the same time we were developing the catalog layouts.

The people at Journeys put the newly tagged text files into their Macs and used Word 4.0 to make the necessary changes — the dates of the trips, the names of the guides, new routes they would take and whatever new features or trips they had added since the last edition. Then they sent the text files back to us, along with their entire 35mm slide collection.

We placed the revised copy in our PageMaker layout. We also chose photographs to use in the layout and made on-screen "for-position-only prints" (FPOs) with a Barneyscan device. Then the client flew out from the Journeys offices in Ann Arbor, Michigan to our studio in Del Mar to "proof" the layouts on-screen. We also provided him with laser proofs to

check the text. We made the last set of revisions together while he was in our studio. Mostly we were dotting i's and crossing t's. But there was still some shuffling going on — one tour was being discontinued, and areas of the world were being shifted from one position in the book to another.

A logo to indicate family treks was assembled from a FreeHand drawing of three figures, and rectangle and circle shapes which were drawn in PageMaker.

For section headings we used large Korinna type with a filled rectangle behind it and a stylized banner below it. Banners were drawn in the Aldus FreeHand program and rectangles in PageMaker.

Colorful relief maps created in FreeHand and saved in encapsulated PostScript (EPS) format, were placed on the pages to indicate terrain and Journeys routes. Flat atlas-style maps of the continents showed the Journeys areas of operation. Both types of maps were used in silhouette form to make the pages more lively than a bounded rectangular format would have.

Throughout the book, the Journeys Style logo was used with black type on a colored background to head a description section that told about the kinds of services provided to travelers in a particular location. The logo itself is a busy little emblem; almost like the illustration on a wine bottle, but the trail, mountains and hiker convey the kind of travel Journeys provides, and the bird, grasses and pagoda represent the environments in which the travel is offered. The logo had too much detail to reduce well, so simplified versions were prepared for section headers.

It's hard to overstate the importance of the role played by photos in the Journeys catalog/brochure. The page design often placed the photos of Journeys destinations in central positions, where they would attract "browsers" to read the surrounding text. The photos have no border. Sometimes I use a rule around photos, but for this brochure it seemed a little fussy.

Photos were separated and stripped in conventionally by the printer. But color scans saved as PICTs were used for on-screen comping and proofing.

The ragged right columns of text conveyed a relaxed, informal feeling about Journeys travel. But vertical rules and the highly structured, consistent presentation of information conveyed an impression of careful organization. A black keyline and the pastel, nearly neutral border area also contribute to a sense of stability in Journeys and the adventures being offered.

Bright colors were used in the logos (see page 123) and the type for schedules, levels of difficulty and captions to convey a lively, exciting, upbeat feeling that would add extra appeal to the idea of traveling with Journeys.

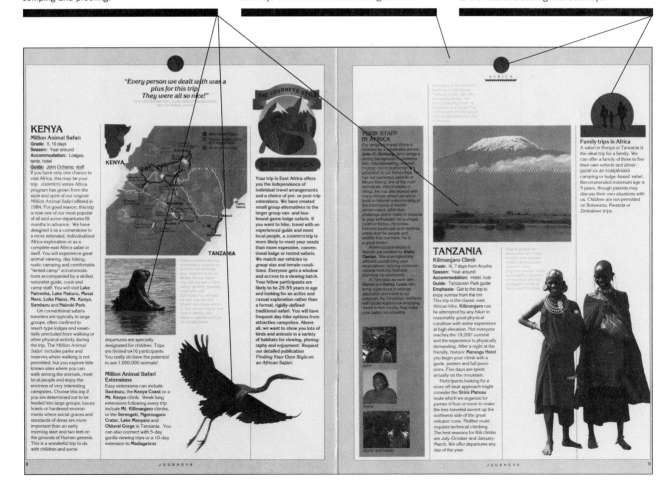

One of the difficulties you're likely to encounter with a brochure like the Journeys catalog is that the client always needs to put more and more and *more* information and pictures into a given number of pages, and the result can tend to look very cluttered. The previous Journeys catalog had suffered from that. Every square inch of the 8½ x 11-inch format was filled up with photos or text or something. The current catalog had been assigned more pages. Of course, they were running more trips, but even so we were able to put more white space into the design.

Establishing the layout

A typical page in the Journeys catalog consists of photos, text, a map (imported from FreeHand), a little symbol to show what part of the world is being described, and possibly also the Journeys Style logo (developed in several programs, finished in FreeHand and imported). We built some white space into the page by using a sinkage at the top of the page, and we used a four-column grid (Figure 1). The symmetry of the page was completed by adding a running head at the top and a running foot at the bottom, with folios at the lower outside corner of each page. The text was designed to be ragged right, and the bottoms bounced, because we thought it would give an informal flavor to the copy and because we were using narrow columns. But we added vertical rules between columns to stabilize the look of the page and to give it a sense of order. A keyline defined the "active" part of the page. Only two fonts were used in whole catalog — the Korinna family and plain old Helvetica.

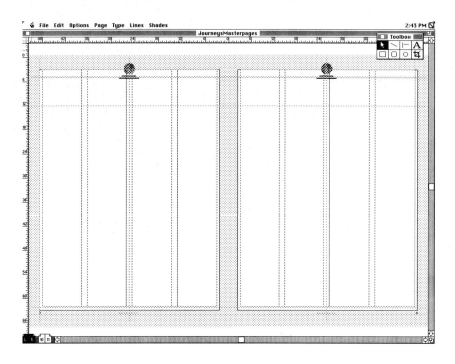

Figure 1. Setting up the pages. Master pages for each PageMaker file included the white "live" area of the page, the benday border area, column guides and rules to define the four-column grid, the header including a small logo, and the footer (the word "Journeys" and the folio). Horizontal guidelines indicated the baseline for text that violated the top margin, the margin itself and the baseline for the footer.

Breaking the rules

The symmetry of the page is one of the underlying rules of page design. In this case it was perhaps honored more in the breaking than in the observance. Due to the particular requirements of a page or the odd shape of a map, the symmetry was broken out of. But it was underlying, there all the time, so it helped give the brochure a rhythm.

Top margin We had decided that the first line of text would start a couple of inches down the page to give a wide top margin, but we also knew that the top margin wasn't inviolate. It could be used for photos that needed to rise up above that sinkage, for bits of maps, for quotations from satisfied customers and for a place to put an occasional caption, but nothing else other than the running heads (Figure 2).

Four columns We also decided that any two of those four columns could be run across as a wider measure if necessary. On the opening page of each continent's section, for instance, the introductory text runs across two columns (Figure 3). We also tended to use the central two of the four columns on each page for photos and maps. Putting the photos in the middle established a rhythm through the book, anchored the page and made the photos the center of attention. After all, it's the photos, the graphic elements, that draw potential travelers into the idea of going to the different countries — "Africa looks exciting," or "These rare animals in the Galapagos . . ." — and then once interested, they'll start to read the details of what the trips are, where they go and when. The grid gave us the flexibility to vary our column widths and make the photos one, two, three or four columns wide. In some places, the text ran a little heavy and we had to use all four columns for copy.

Figure 2. Creating space. The 2-inch top margin was designed to build some white space into the otherwise very full pages, as shown on the opening page (a). Maps (b), photos (c), captions and logos (d) were allowed to extend into the margin space.

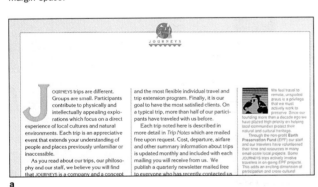

a

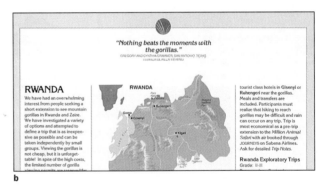

b

c

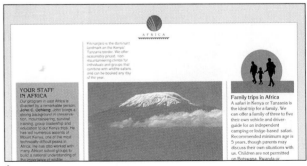

d

Vertical rules

Without the vertical rules, the pages might have looked a little chaotic. ▌ *If you try to use justified text and fixed bottoms with text in narrow columns, you're likely to get some awfully bad breaks and widows. But when you have unjustified text with bouncing bottoms, you usually need to have vertical rules between the columns.*

In deciding whether to put in the rules, I did what I usually do if I'm not really sure whether some element is necessary. I put it in, then I take it out, and then I decide which way looks better. Everything on the page has to have a *raison d'etre*, a reason to be there. ▌ *Electronic page design has made it easy to use the "decision by subtraction" method. If you can't make up your mind about whether an element belongs on the page, take it out, look at it again, and if it doesn't make a bit of difference whether it's there or not, leave it out. If it does make a difference, decide whether it's positive or negative and act accordingly.*

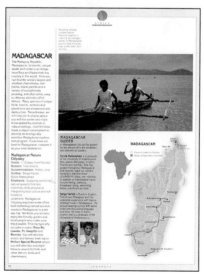

Figure 3. Using a flexible four-column format. The four-column format allowed text to run one or two columns wide. The central columns were often used for photos and maps, but this arrangement varied with the need to accommodate the information required on particular pages and spreads.

Type choices

The two fonts — Korinna and Helvetica — are different enough so they contrast, and we used them for different purposes. As a rule, if I use a serif face for one thing, I use a sans serif for the other.

The Journeys company has been using Korrina in all their literature since 1979. Korinna is a serif font, which makes for a little more humanistic appearance. And although it's a bit ungainly, it's very distinctive and it's become very closely identified with Journeys (Figure 4). They like it, and I've resisted the temptation to change it arbitrarily to something else. I think that with a few possible exceptions, it's not so much the font you choose that's important, but where you put it, how big you make it and how it works in concert with everything else. In a lot of circumstances, any number of different fonts would do.

We used Korinna for display type and basic text. Korinna sets up a little loose, so all the text columns were set at 80 percent word spacing and –4 kerning. First of all, tightening the spacing made the text more compact — we could get more words into a column. Also, it improved the color of the type — the "grayness" that the body of text contributed to the overall page design. I tweaked around with the spacing until I got it to work. ▌ *Most type looks better with spacing reduced a little bit. You want to be cautious about space reduction if text is justified, however, because when it's justified, space is both added and subtracted depending on whether a line is tight or loose. And if you tighten up the spacing on justified text, you're going to get some very tight lines.*

Once all the columns of text had been flowed in, I hit Command-A to select all. I went to the Type menu and chose Spacing and typed in the word spacing and the kerning I had decided on. I knew the text would lose the spacing and kerning information when I exported it to Word in order to send it to the Journeys company on disk for editing. I was using "creative pessimism," anticipating that I'd have to go back in and spec the text again. But when I checked it after it had been reimported, I was pleasantly surprised.

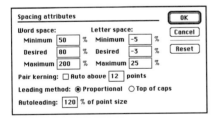

Figure 4. Incorporating the "Journeys" typeface. Adobe's Korinna typeface was used for headings, subheads and text. Text was set at 9.5 points on 11.5-point leading. Text color was adjusted by tightening the Desired Word Space to 80 percent and setting kerning (Letter Space) at –3 in the Spacing Attributes dialog box.

The possibilities for personal discovery and adventure are limitless on a JOURNEYS trip in Latin America. The land is hauntingly beautiful and incredibly diverse. Ruins of great empires beckon modern exploration and mysteries of ancient Indian civilizations live on through traditional cultures. Your local guides not only share their knowledge of ecology, archaeology and indigenous culture, but take you

▌ *One of the little quirks of PageMaker 3.0 was that you could apply spacing to an entire selected text block, but you couldn't apply it as a Style. In other words, you could spec your text and Style it in terms of its point size, leading, font, weight and so on. But you couldn't put into the Style any information about word spacing or kerning. However, a spaced and kerned text block would always retain those particular spacing attributes. The text acted as a kind of spacing place-holder. So when copy was exported, updated and flowed back in again, if you selected that original text block and you chose Replace Selected Text in the Place dialog box, the new text would assume the spacing of the text it was replacing. In PageMaker 4.0, you can control spacing as just described or by including it in the Style for a paragraph.*

We used Helvetica for captions and map lettering because of its clarity and simplicity (Figure 5). The public sees Helvetica as "plain print" — it's just there, it's informational. We also used it for footnotes, lists of items, number of days in a trip, grade level of difficulty and for the folios. When we needed to make the Helvetica type stand out a little, we used color — red for headings, blue for captions.

Putting in the photos

We took all slides we had selected for the brochure and scanned them with the Barneyscan. We used the Barneyscan software to reduce them down to 150K color PICTs, and then we placed them on the PageMaker pages. They looked tremendous on the screen.

We also found it relatively easy to simulate the effect of a silhouetted halftone. We used the brush tool in the Barneyscan software to outline any objects we wanted to pull out from the photos and silhouette, and then with the paint pot we went in and cleaned out all the background, turning it to white. This made color silhouetted halftones that could be put in and used to set up type runarounds (see Figure 3). PageMaker's Text Wrap function was used to repel text around silhouetted photos. (For more information about using the Text Wrap function, see "Wrapping type" on page 57.)

As on-screen FPO prints they sped up the layout process tremendously. We were able to see each spread on the screen with all its color elements — the color photos, bendays, colored type, maps and so on. The client could make the kinds of decisions that might have taken one or two weeks of back-and-forth in the mail right there on the spot. And he came away with a sense of what the thing was going to look like in terms of its overall feeling and color in a way that he never could have done if he hadn't come and seen it. ▌ *A large color monitor is a very good tool for showing clients what their pages will look like. You have to caution them, of course, that the colors they see on the screen, although close, are not absolutely accurate. Blues and greens will print darker and less vivid than they appear on many monitors, while reds, oranges and browns tend to be fairly close.*

YOUR GUIDES IN LADAKH
Our Ladakhi leadership team exemplifies and defines the high standard of local leadership we try to incorporate in all of our trips. We have worked with the same staff in Ladakh since we began trips here in 1983. Each year comments of our trekkers reach higher levels of praise for their skills. You will be well cared for. You will eat well. You will believe you are in very capable hands. Tsering Wangchook and Tsering Norboo guide our treks and orchestrate the difficult logistics of our trips. Tsering Phunchok manages all the trekking transportation needs. Sonam Phunchok is always improving both his personal knowledge of local history and religious traditions and his ability to interpret these subjects for you. If you have an interest in Buddhist traditions of Tibet and Ladakh, you will want to be on his trip. If there were a grand prize for the best meals under the most difficult preparation conditions, it would surely go to Tsering Dorjee and his kitchen staff.

Figure 5. Including a sans serif face. Helvetica type was used for the "Guides" sections as well as for maps, captions and information presented in lists.

Trapping

In general, I don't take any special precautions for trapping. I've found that in working with process color I've never had to worry about that. Even with Pantone colors, I send the work out as it is and see what I get. If the printer says "There's no preparation here for choke and spread," then I'll say, "Well, how much do you need?" And then I can go back in and tweak it.

But providing for trapping ahead of time is rather like sitting down at the dinner table and putting salt and pepper all over your food before you've even tasted it. You should taste it to see if it *needs* anything. You run a test.

Everything that I've run has *been* a test. We did a whole college psychology text full of FreeHand diagrams without any choke and spread. But we did that in process color up to color, and we made the palette so that every color except those at the really pale end of the spectrum had a little bit of each of the four process colors. Kiss fit.

If I can see what sort of mess we get, then I can see what kind of adjustments to make. Otherwise I might overdo it and end up with something worse than if I'd left it alone. It's like tuning a fiddle, you have to hear the sound to know whether it's sharp or flat.

Working together, with the pages on-screen, the client and I could make decisions about position, size and overall color effect (see "On-screen color proofing" on page 124). It was a real luxury to be able to see all of that before we got all the way through to press proofs. He could look at the screen and say, "Oh, we're mentioning this country here. Why don't we move this picture a little closer to where it's being mentioned?" At this point nothing had been committed: Nothing had been committed to separation. Nothing had been committed to real type. It was all just laser proof for the type and color on the screen. (Now it's possible to get a better on-screen view of type in place with the other elements of a page. See "What you see is getting better" on page 71.)

Developing the logos

The Journeys company had decided that the simple logo that had served them for 10 years needed to be updated to reflect their expanded offerings. So while we were designing the brochure, we also redesigned the logo in FreeHand (Figure 6). We also pulled elements from the circular logo to represent different continents in the running heads. A "Journeys Style" logo was designed to indicate special features of their programs in a particular part of the world — for example, "The Journeys Style in Tanzania" (see page 117).

Making the maps

Maps of continents were traced in FreeHand from scans of atlas-style maps provided by the client (Figure 7). The relief maps showing hiking trails and roads were made in FreeHand by illustrator Jill Malena, using a combination of layered PostScript outlines, scanned pencil drawings of mountain elevations and layered solid and dashed lines (Figure 8). To give a more dynamic

Figure 6. Developing logos. The original Journeys logo (above) was redesigned in FreeHand using both flat and graduated fills. Header logos were derived by pulling out the pagoda (for Asia), the grasses (for Africa) and the parrot (simplified) (for the Americas). For the Journeys Style marker, we added a banner.

look to the page layout, maps were created as country silhouettes rather than placing the countries within rectangular frames.

Color separation

For this brochure, the printer was giving us a quote that included all the stripping and all the color separations of the photos. It's hard to beat the separation prices you get under those conditions, so we decided we'd send the printer the slides to separate and we'd provide 1270 dpi repro of the PageMaker files. ∎ *Although a brochure may include four-color photos and screened colors, if type and keylines are the only parts you're outputting electronically, medium resolution serves very well.*

Bendays and tint boxes that had been entered in the PageMaker file were converted to keyline boxes and called out on the overlay. But we left the scanned photo PICT files on the repro to serve as FPO prints.

FreeHand does good color separations, so we provided the logos and maps as loose separated film, but once again we left the FPO images on the PageMaker page. For anything that was to be used more than one time, we provided it once and the printer duplicated it and stripped it in. We were able to put several of the maps and logos on one page to save on stripping costs. We made no particular preparations for trapping color, except that where type appeared on a tinted background, it was overprinted rather than knocked out (see "Trapping" on page 123).

Printing

The Journeys company arranged printing through a print broker, who located O. G. Printing Productions, Ltd. in Hong Kong. An initial run of 55,000

Figure 7. Tracing atlas-style maps. Continent maps were traced in FreeHand from maps provided by the client. The corner point tool was used to outline the continents and wtihin them the areas where Journeys operates. Outlines were formed of straight line segments rather than curves and were filled with flat color. Areas of operation were filled with a lighter shade. Maps were saved in EPS format and placed on PageMaker pages.

█ On-screen color proofing

Color scans really pay off when you can sit down with your client in front of the screen and show him or her exactly what each page is going to look like with all the color photos in position. It's hard to overstate the excitement and enthusiasm on the part of the client. It really helps cut down decision-making time and takes out a large degree of uncertainty. It's more like an on-screen press proof than an on-screen comp. The client can see all kinds of possibilities because it's so realistic-looking, even though the thing is still in electronic form.

The color scanning process can produce very good results, but at this point no color scan is likely to give you as good a four-color process halftone as you can get by conventional separation. Also, the resulting files are huge and take a long time to output. The film ends up costing almost as much as conventional separations, and then you can pick holes in the color balance and so forth. In the cold light of day, one ought to be very careful about promising clients that one can deliver four-color separations from the desktop.

I'm not sure whether it's worth getting a slide scanner just for on-screen color proofing, but it might well be. Service bureaus are charging around $25 a scan. My sense is that they want to price it so they can (a) make some money and (b) be competitive with the alternative route, which is to make a black-and-white dog print and glue that down. But then if it needs to be resized, you're back where you started.

copies of the four-color, 40-page catalog/brochure was made on Japanese glossy art paper supplied by the printer at a printing cost of 55 cents per piece.

In retrospect

When you use electronic page design methods, it's important to think ahead about how much work is involved between the finished on-screen layout and the files that will be sent to the output service. The layout has to be pulled apart into pieces, step by step — and that takes time. For the Journeys brochure, first of all, we had to strip out all our tints and convert them to keylines. We left our photos in FPO, because as PICTs they wouldn't slow down the output time significantly.

Another important lesson we learned was to be careful not to put too many complicated FreeHand files (maps and logos) on a single page, and to print them right from FreeHand. For example, in a related project, I once set up a page that had 12 Journeys business cards, each one with a logo, of course, which is fairly intricate. The job crashed, so we had to cut down to six per page. This was with the old Linotronic raster image processor (RIP); the RIP3 probably wouldn't have any trouble with the original 12-card page. But you can get greedy, putting a whole lot on one page, trying to save money on separations, and end up with nothing.

Figure 8. Drawing relief maps. Country outlines were drawn in FreeHand and filled with flat "safari" colors. Each country map was cloned twice and stroked with thick strokes in two blue shades to indicate surrounding water. (On landlocked sides the blue lines were cut and removed.) Mountains were indicated by scanned pencil sketches of texture, incorporated into the FreeHand drawing. A "snow" fill in shades of light gray and white was drawn in FreeHand and layered between the base and the pencil-sketched texture. FreeHand's ability to fit type to a path was used to mark rivers and other physical features. Travel routes were indicated by solid and dashed lines marked with symbols from Adobe's Carta font.

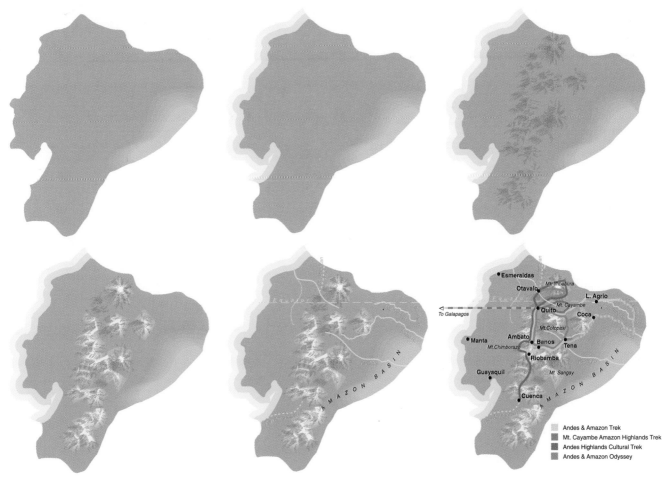

PORTFOLIO

John Odam

"As a general rule, I'm not the kind of designer who's too grid-bound. There are certain things that I'll stick with absolutely. I'll have one or two things in the page design that are absolutely rigid, no exceptions. But I tend to be a little on the loose side with page layout. That's probably why I don't get on so well with programs like ReadySetGo! and QuarkXPress — once you've laid in your railway tracks, you're on time but you're not likely to deviate from the course. I tend to go off the page with things. If I've got a nice graphic, I'll throw it all over the place. It's kind of like jazz. You've got a beat and a chord progression, and that's given, but you can sometimes take a little solo and go off on a tangent. If you know what the rules are, you can break them."

All type and rules for ***Grand Canyon Visual*** were set and placed traditionally. But the Macintosh and Page-Maker were used to arrive at a layout that satisfied the designer and provided a rough for the typesetter to follow. The electronic design process made it possible to meet the layout challenge of combining title page, copyright page, table of contents (with photos) and graphics credits in a single page.

The PageMaker 3.0 layout for ***Del Mar Looking Back*** was based on a three-column grid, with the inside column on each page being used for floating art and brief captions, while the two outside columns allowed uninterrupted flow of the text. Folios and running heads were place about a third of the way down the page in the margin. TIFFs were imported as placeholders for the art. The author had supplied no subheads, so initial caps were used to break the text into manageable chunks for the reader. All type was set in the Cheltenham family of faces.

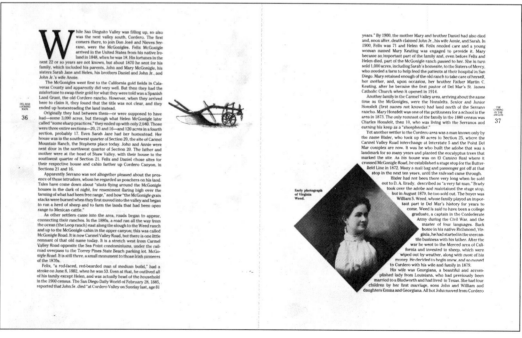

For this spread in **Verbum** magazine (issue 3.4), the article title and description of the Imagine event were set, rotated and colored in FreeHand. The typography and page geometry were executed in Aldus PageMaker Color Extension and converted to Visionary format with the V.I.P. interface. The spread was then produced using the Visionary/Scitex system.

A five-column PageMaker layout was used to design pages for Wayne Weiten's **Psychology, Themes and Variations,** published by Brooks/Cole. The book was electronically dummied but conventionally typeset, as the publisher wasn't ready to commit to "desktopping" it. The page design can accommodate illustrations of five different widths, four of which are shown here. The main headings break both text columns, clearly announcing a change in subject matter.

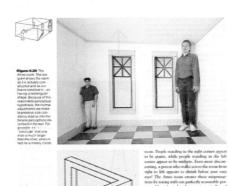

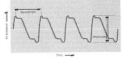

CHAPTER 10

The Mac Connection to Scitex

Design team

Gene Hammond Designs +, Inc., located in High Point, North Carolina, began in 1974 as a royalty-based product design firm serving the gift, housewares and home furnishings markets. With income contingent upon how well a product sold, the firm became seriously interested in knowing how to maximize that result. This led the company to offer marketing support services to ensure that products are shown to their best advantage from conception to production and on to sales. Many times this means developing the manufacturer's identity along with their product. So other services have been added, such as packaging design, point-of-purchase displays, sales literature, order forms and trade show exhibits, to increase the probability for success.

The company now offers complete marketing and new product development services to its clients. The integrity of a product's design is maintained through all phases so the marketplace perceives the dedication of the company to the product and its image. Computer technology has increased the efficiency of integrating design and marketing support.

Project

This sales brochure was one of ten graphics projects for a product line manufactured by Allspace, a housewares manufacturer based in Commerce, California. Packaging and another brochure were already in process when this project was started, so it was necessary to adhere to already established graphic motifs. Because so many jobs were going to use the same photography, timing became a critical factor.

At the time, Visionary (QuarkXPress-like software that links the Macintosh to high-end color prepress functions such as color correction and separation on Scitex Color Response equipment) was the only software capable of handling all the projects within the given time frame and budget. The program's ability to reuse blocks of copy, four-color tint areas, layouts and separations was instrumental in dropping the time and costs in these and subsequent projects.

The brochure was produced using a Mac II with 8 MB of RAM, running Visionary and FreeHand software; a Cutting Edge internal 85 MB hard disk drive; a 44 MB Syquest removable hard drive; a Mitsubishi 13-inch 8-bit color monitor; a Howtek Scanmaster with transparency option; a 9600 baud Telebit modem; Mitsubishi, Howtek Pixelmaster and QMS color printers; a LaserWriter IINT; a Scitex prepress color system; and a pen plotter.

The text was input in Visionary, the Allspace logo was developed in FreeHand, and the photographs were scanned in with the Howtek Scanner with a transparency option.

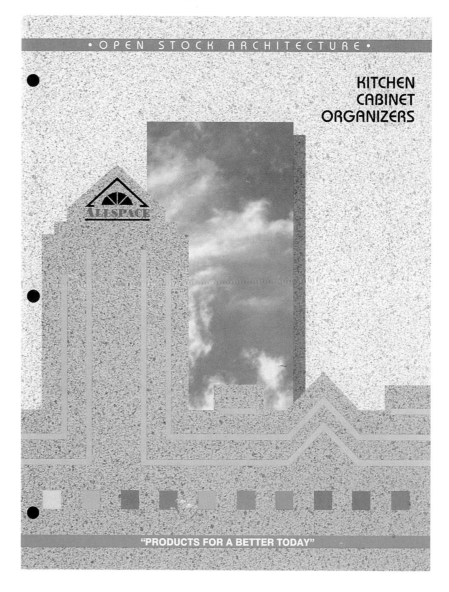

**PROJECT
OVERVIEW**

Design goals

The aim of this brochure was to help motivate potential retailers to carry the Allspace product line. We wanted to show the features of the product and convince the retailer that it would practically sell itself.

Design elements from the first brochure would be used in this one and carried over to the others that would follow. The product is a system of white storage elements. Our goal for the printed materials was to display a utilitarian product in a way that made it bright and attractive. To show the organizers in use and to make the graphics lively, we photographed the white shelves and bins, filled with brightly colored items, on a dark, neutral background in a rectangular format. We also silhouetted photos of the packaging and the Project Center merchandising system.

Using Visionary

With Visionary, prepress tasks such as layout, design, typesetting and four-color separations could be managed within the office under the control of the design team on our computer. The product photographs could be scanned and separated digitally on the Macintosh for use in creating packaging, literature and advertising. These same digital files could be used over and over at different sizes without paying for additional color separations and with no loss of quality. This represents an impressive savings to the client by reducing turnaround time and being able to generate color comps before committing a layout to four-color film. As the designer's and client's color changes were noted on the color proofs, the color corrections were made to the original digital file, so that any recall of this image would also be color correct.

Visionary has many of the same features and functions as the QuarkXPress page layout program. Both applications allow direct entry of text, providing spell-checking and search-and-replace editing functions. And both use a system of parent and child boxes as the method of placing text and graphic elements on the page (see "QuarkXPress" in Chapter 2). If a text or picture box is created inside another box, it becomes a child of that parent box, and the elements within move when the patent box is repositioned.

The map on the back cover of the brochure was drawn by hand.

The sky and the granite texture on the cover were scanned elements. The design of the cover implementing these graphic elements was a takeoff on the "open architecture" concept of the product line.

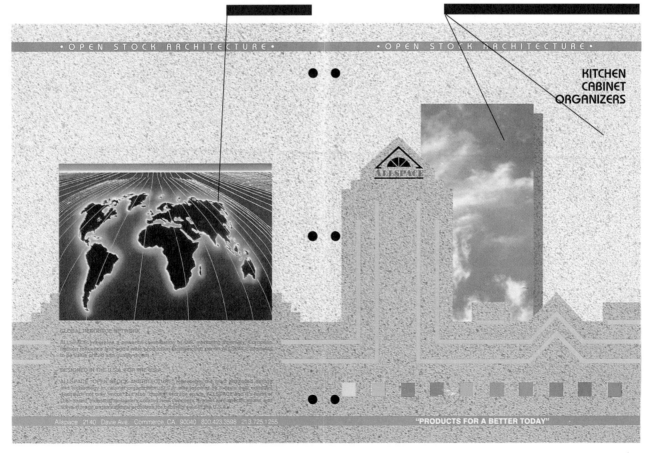

Working with the client

We have a long history of doing work for Allspace, which has led to a level of trust that was essential in getting this job done on time. The director of sales and marketing for Allspace often passed us the task of approving comps and proofs. When Allspace *did* need to see the pages, we printed them out on the LaserWriter so that we could fax proofs to the client. This sort of approval was used as an interim step while we were in the process of producing the job. At critical stages in the project, color comps from the Mitsubishi, QMS and Howtek printers were sent to the client via overnight mail.

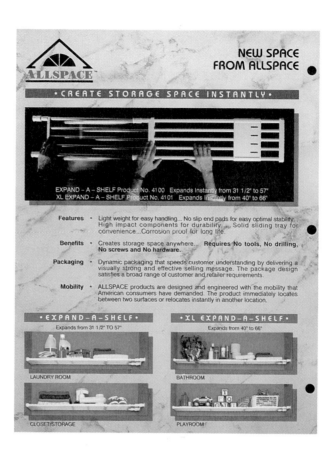

The insert sheet displayed new products added to the Allspace line. As in the brochure itself, colorful items and dark, neutral background rectangles helped to display the functional, white product.

Since many of the elements, such as the product photos and some of the copy, already existed in digital format, building this brochure was just a matter of bringing these elements into position in this document.

Color bars were used to highlight type for page headings, subheads and the text for the guarantee.

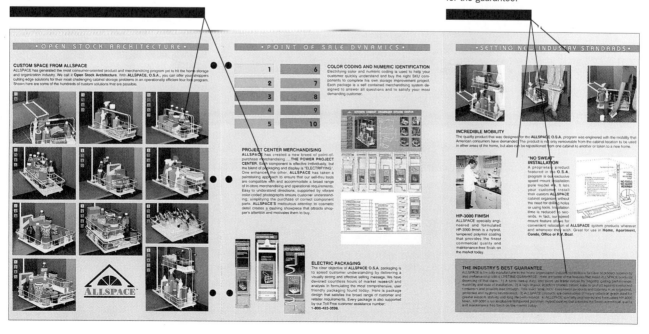

From a tissue pencil comp with dimensions, the brochure was set up as two 11 x 25-inch horizontal pages and two 8½ x 11-inch vertical pages. As this piece was the first we had attempted in Visionary, it took between 10 and 14 hours to set up the basic framework of the brochure. After that, we started to piece it all together, calling out colors, bringing in the photographs and so on.

Type

All text and display type, except the Allspace logo, was typed directly into Visionary. The typefaces used in the brochure — Bauhaus for the headlines and Helvetica for the body copy — helped convey the "architectural" form-follows-function nature of the product (Figure 1). They carried through with the presentation of the product as the simple solution, often harder to create, but true to the materials.

Images

The images for the brochure consisted of four-color photos that we shot ourselves, line art and the Allspace logo created in FreeHand, and geometric shapes created in Visionary (Figure 2). The photos that would be used in the final layout had originally been scanned with the Howtek Scanmaster with enhanced Howtek scan software. We had also originally used Visionary's built-in scanning package for fast, low-resolution scans to be set in the page layouts as position shots as we developed the first brochure. For this brochure, we were able to utilize low-resolution scans from the Scitex, since they had been developed during production of the first printed piece. ▮ *Low-resolution scans allow the designer to implement the design with color in place, sizing and positioning the images along with the text blocks. The scans also provide the ability to print fairly accurate-looking comps from a color thermal printer. ▮ If a document must go into production before linked scans from the Scitex are*

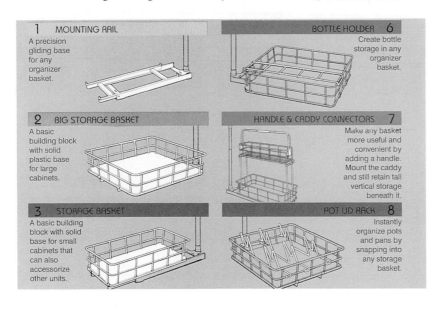

Figure 1. Choosing type. The Helvetica face is very straight-forward and func-tional looking, like the Allspace product. Bauhaus type also has a simple, elegant look. Its monoweight strokes and open curves look similar to the wire elements that make up the kitchen organizers.

available, the Scitex production house can use these position scans as a guide for placement and sizing to later position their high-resolution scans.

▌ Linked scans from a Scitex production house are actually two files created by the Scitex from one set of transparencies. One is a low-res scan (72 dpi) that is passed back to the designer to size, crop and use for layout purposes. The other is a high-res scan that they keep to output to the film plotter. The scans are encoded with a link that actually replaces the low-res scan in the document with the high-res scan at the same position, scale and rotation before the file goes to the film plotter. Because they are high-resolution and digital, these separations can be used over and over again with any magnification value from 50 percent to 200 percent with no loss of quality.

Visionary's parent-and-child box arrangement was useful for moving elements from the file for the first brochure to this file. By clicking on a parent box, we could move it, with all its "children," into position on the new page.

▌ Once a box is placed inside another to become its child, it can't be moved out of its parent except by cutting and pasting.

The installation drawing was line art saved as a FreeHand EPS (encapsulated PostScript) format file. Placed in a picture box, it became a parent for both the white background (a color bar) and the text for the installation instructions (Figure 3).

Visionary's polygon picture window allows picture boxes to be created in any shape composed of straight lines. This allowed us to do our own masking on some simple shapes. The three elements in the "electric packaging" on

Figure 2. Unifying the graphics. The architectural look of the Allspace logo was reflected in the "cityscape" created for the front cover. Granite and sky textures were from scanned 35mm transparencies. Visionary's polygon window was used to mask the shape of the skyline, and its graphics tools provided the light gray lines.

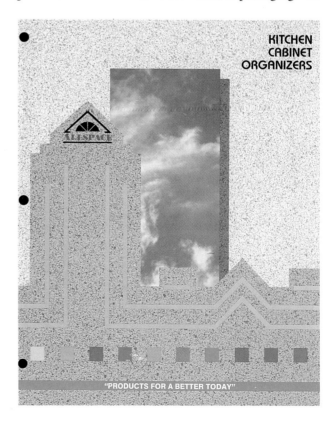

page 2 of the brochure were one scanned photograph that was imported through a polygon picture box. The box was shrunk around the images, dropping out the background to silhouette the three packages (Figure 4). The building on the brochure cover was formed by creating a polygon window to mask the scanned granite texture (see page 130).

Text elements were made transparent so that the scanned background or the color bar would show through. All color bars were specified as Pantone colors, which were then separated into process colors (cyan, magenta, yellow and black) for printing. We made a point of making sure the client understood that the comp colors were not "Pantone-correct." They were "pleasing colors," chosen so that we could feel pretty secure they were right, but final judgment was withheld until a Matchprint was made.

In retrospect

Electronic publishing technology served us very well on this project. This piece was originally intended to be a sheet-fed job on a six-color press. Due to time constraints, production was completed on a six-color web press. This press change did cause some anxious moments, but with the Scitex connection we were able to replot the film to compensate for the characteristics of

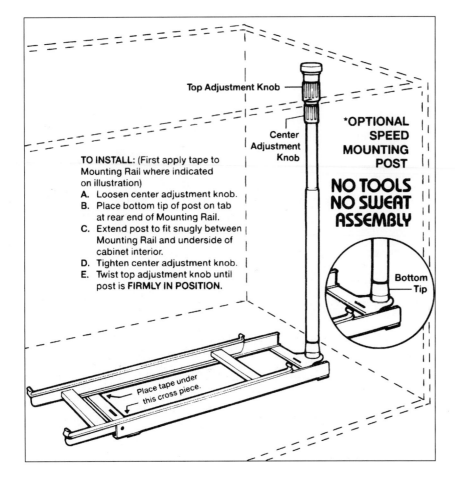

Figure 3. Assembling an illustration. The picture box that held the line art for the installation drawing also served as a parent box for the background rectangle of white and for the text box that held installation instructions.

the web press. The map on the back cover was drawn by hand and we ran into problems reproducing it in a curved format (see page 130). Today we would draw the map on the computer.

We would also handle the type below the map a little differently. Short of running a press proof, we couldn't tell exactly how dark the granite was going to be. We had intended to run the type in black, but in looking at the color comps it was very hard to tell whether it was going to be legible or not. That was when we made the decision to run it in a color. We wanted a color with very high density to be sure that we would get good coverage, so we made the type almost a process blue. It turned out that black would have been the better choice in this case, but we were afraid that the black type would have been lost in the dark granite. Knowing that going to film is certainly the most expensive part of the process, but also knowing it's the only way to judge a concern such as this, we could have cropped down to this part of the page, duplicated it, set the type in both blue and black, gone to film and to plate and run a press proof. So for about $200 we would have known exactly what both options were going to look like.

**Figure 4.
Silhouetting with
the polygon window.**
The three packages
were silhouetted
from one scanned
transparency. The
photo was placed on
the page and a
polygon window was
tightened around the
three elements.

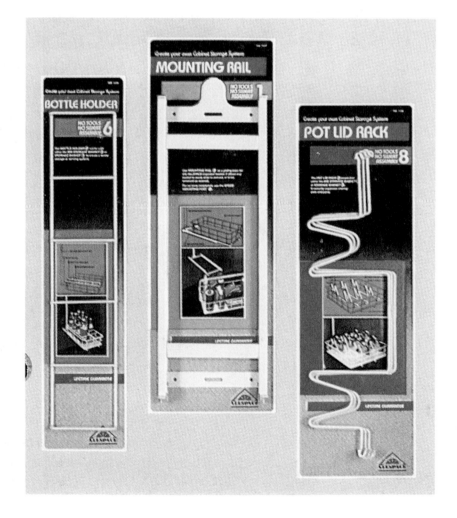

Gene Hammond

"The capabilities of the Scitex are enormous. Since we now have prepress options such as the ability to call out color on the Macintosh, scan in and manipulate photos, and perform many other time-consuming tasks, it's nice to see technology capitalizing on all our hard work. The Scitex takes every bit of information from our files and outputs that information to film. Rather than creating a black-and-white mechanical from an imagesetter that a printer must recreate in terms of color breaks and so on (the traditional stripping method), the Scitex plots our instructions directly to film."

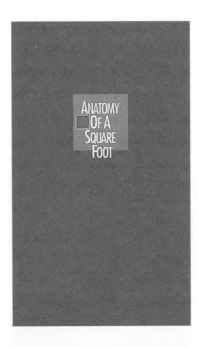

Peter Hollingsworth, who works closely with Gene Hammond Design, used FreeHand to design the **Anatomy of a Square Foot** brochure for Hayden Design Associates, Inc. The printer did not only the stripping of continuous-tone photos and the printing, but also the Linotronic output. Hollingsworth took advantage of these circumstances to let the printer take responsibility for the trapping. He delivered the FreeHand file on disk and the printer added trap where it was needed by overprinting the strokes that defined the geometric shapes and the type. The brochure was printed in seven spot colors and the four process colors.

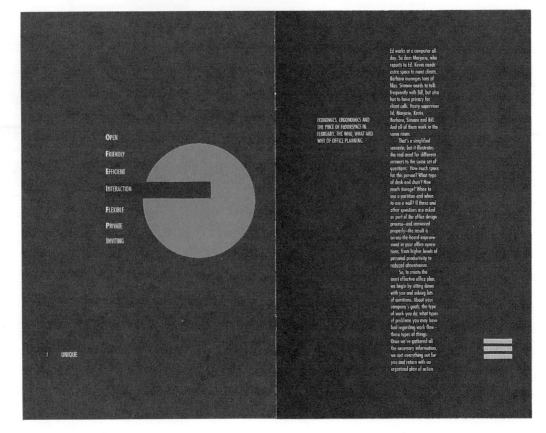

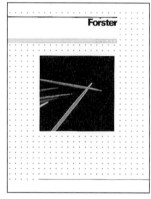

The **Forster brochures** were laid out in Page-Maker in two spot colors and separated through the program. Continuous-tone photos were stripped in traditionally.

The **Placewares post-card** was designed and laid out in Aldus FreeHand. Lettering for the logo had been re-created in Font-ographer from hand-drawn lettering. Problems with banding on the graduated fill were partially resolved by turning the piece 90 degrees in the Free-Hand file so that the negative film was output at a different angle by the Lino-tronic imagesetter.

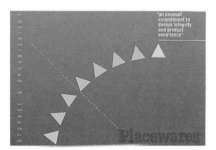

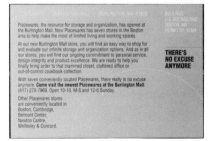

The **Allspace pack-aging** was designed using the same Visionary system used for the brochure described in the body of this chapter. Many of the type, graphic and background texture elements from the brochure were reused in the packaging.

CHAPTER 11

Package Design With Forethought

Art Director and Designer

Art director Clement Mok studied at the Art Center in Los Angeles. After working in New York for the entertainment division at CBS, he was lured back to the West Coast to join Apple Computer as it was developing the Macintosh. He spent over five years designing in-house at Apple and then established his own studio — Clement Mok Designs — in San Francisco. The studio provides a full range of design services for clients both inside and outside the microcomputer industry.

Designer Charles Routhier received a B.A. in Art Studio from Rhode Island College in Providence, where he worked as a designer for five years. He moved to San Francisco in April 1988 to become a senior designer for Clement Mok Designs.

Project

We started working with Farallon Computing, marketers of PhoneNet, MacRecorder and several other products for microcomputers, when the firm had reached a critical point in its corporate development. It was undergoing phenomenal growth. In terms of design, this meant that the company needed to project itself as a larger corporation. Farallon needed to do everything from sharpening up its logo and revamping its software interface to establishing a new look for its packaging and publications.

At the time we got involved, Farallon was using the logo, publications and packaging that had been developed in-house when the company was a much smaller operation. The limitation of the in-house approach became apparent as the company's volume and product line got bigger. For instance, any time a customer wanted two or three different items together, Farallon produced another box and added a cover. As a result, many different box sizes were used to pack products individually and in various combinations. One of the company's biggest sellers, PhoneNET, was being packed in a small, clear plastic box reminiscent of fishing lure packaging.

Farallon had also started a vigorous advertising campaign, placing ads in the back of *MacWeek* every week. And the marketers liked the corporate tone that Robert LaPointe Advertising had established in developing the ads. Our job was to help the company grow, developing a logo, packaging and a publications style that established the new Farallon corporate ID and that made sense in terms of cost.

We used MacDraw for early presentations to show the client the structure of the packaging we were proposing. We used Adobe Illustrator 88, which we were very familiar with, for both illustration and page layout for the packaging. We also used Aldus FreeHand for some special effects we couldn't get with Illustrator. And we used PageMaker for a lot of the publications design, with SuperPaint for editing screen dumps (illustrations made by capturing on-screen displays) and LaserPaint for separating color screen dumps. Farallon delivered copy for manuals and package inserts on disk in Microsoft Word to be placed in the PageMaker files. Our hardware included the Macintosh IIx, a LaserWriter IINTX and an Apple scanner. Finished art was produced as pasted-up mechanicals that included Linotronic L-300 output at 2540 dpi.

**PROJECT
OVERVIEW**

Design goals

Our objective was to design Farallon's packaging, establishing the corporate look and feel as well as the package structure. The problem was partly a corporate identity issue.

A growing company can't afford to tie up a lot of space and money in packaged product inventory. But on the other hand, it can't afford to risk being unable to fill an unusually big order on time because of the need to wait for packaging to be printed. On-demand turnover of product can be a life-or-death issue. So our goal was to design packaging that could meet the somewhat unpredictable demand Farallon would face as the market for its products developed.

Working with the client

Part of our job was to make it all work — the approach that had been established in-house at Farallon by Lisa Cort, marketing communications manager, the tone the ad agency had set and the new materials we would be developing. The people at Farallon wanted to stay very much involved in the development of all the materials that represented their company. We worked closely with them to set a tone and style for each new kind of print material we developed, so they could apply them later.

We kept costs in mind from the beginning. Early in the design process we checked with fabricators of packaging materials to make sure a design we planned to use would work with the printing process we'd chosen and that it wouldn't cost too much to produce.

Part of the job of designing Farallon's packaging was to redesign the logo and establish standards for its use, as shown in this excerpt from the *Corporate Styleguide*.

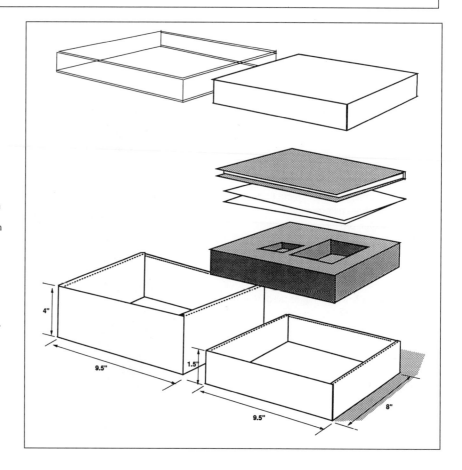

The first plans presented to Farallon for a packaging system were drawn in MacDraw. Drawings showed a clear plastic sleeve (top left). At first a single, shallow lid was planned (top right), but we later decided to make the lids as deep as the bottoms. Diagrams showed how manual, warranty and foam to hold a product would fit in the box, and that the boxes would share the same "face" dimensions and could therefore use the same cover illustration.

Twelve paintings were used in the cover illustration. Nine of them were painted to represent the nine products Farallon was marketing. For example, the speaker painting in column 2, row 3 represents MacRecorder. The useof the traditional medium (oils) and the presence of people in the pictures created the look and feel Farallon wanted to represent its communication products. Three empty land-scapes were included in the grid to allow for ex-pansion of the product line.

The bulleted arc motif used in the product boxes was also carried through in the template designed for disk labels.

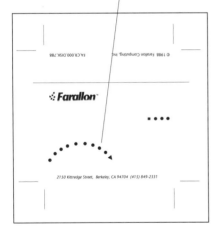

Each of the Farallon products has its own ID color, which is printed on the side of the box sleeve and overprinted with a dot screen that remains constant throughout the product line.

Bulleted arcs cross the package fronts to help tie the products together in shelf displays. "Entry" and "exit" points are consistent from package to package.

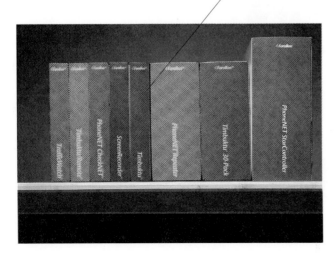
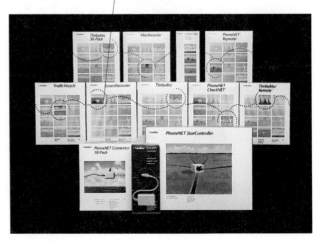

Our first suggestion in designing a new logo was to drop the word "Computing" from Farallon's original corporate mark. We proposed a new logotype with the letter "o" being a partial circle formed of round and square bullets drawn with Illustrator's shape tools. But eventually plain type was chosen to complement a graphic element that Farallon wanted to retain from the original mark (Figure 1). We chose Stone Sans extrabold italic for the logotype. ▌ *We often convert the logotypes we design to Illustrator artwork. This can be done by printing the type, scanning the print and using the scan as a template for tracing (with curve tools, with the autotrace feature or with Adobe Streamline) or by using SmartArt or Adobe Type Manager to provide the on-screen template. Conversion to a PostScript graphic element provides a convenient way to modify type. It also allows flexibility in output — the output device doesn't have to be equipped with the font used in the logo in order to print it.*

Typefaces

We had chosen the Stone Sans family of typefaces for the logo and other high-visibility pieces that projected the Farallon corporate image. The Stone faces had been designed to look good on the Macintosh screen, and we knew that about half of the Farallon products would be viewed on-screen. Susan Kare,

Figure 1. Developing the logo. Farallon's original logo (top) needed updating to better represent the growing company. We proposed a design that included a bulleted "o" (center), but the bullets didn't work with elements of the logo that Farallon wanted to retain, so we arrived at a compromise (bottom).

formerly with Apple and NeXT, also used Stone Sans in revamping the Farallon interface (Figure 2), and we wanted to make sure there would be a nice crossover from the on-screen interface to the documentation and packaging.

We also included Franklin Gothic in our design specification because it was more readily available than Stone. Most of Farallon's documentation would be produced on the computer, but we didn't want other vendors who might be contracted to produce documentation to be locked into Stone Sans if they didn't have access to it.

The packaging concept

We decided to develop a packaging design strategy that would greatly reduce the number of different boxes Farallon would have to stock. The basic idea was to use only three kinds of boxes, each of which could hold several of Farallon's different products. The fewer kinds of boxes and the more versatile each box could be, the more flexibility Farallon would have in packaging their products to meet demand.

The individual products packed inside the boxes would be identified by printed clear plastic sleeves that fit over the boxes and by insert cards (inserted between the back of the box and the clear sleeve) that presented detailed information about the hardware and software inside. Since the sleeves and cards didn't require die cutting and could be produced more quickly than the boxes, they would be easier to produce on demand. Box bottoms, lids and

Figure 2. Matching the interface. Susan Kare used Stone Sans type as well as the traditional Chicago font in redesigning Farallon's interface. Choice of typeface was important in making sure that product, documentation and packaging showed a consistent, coherent style.

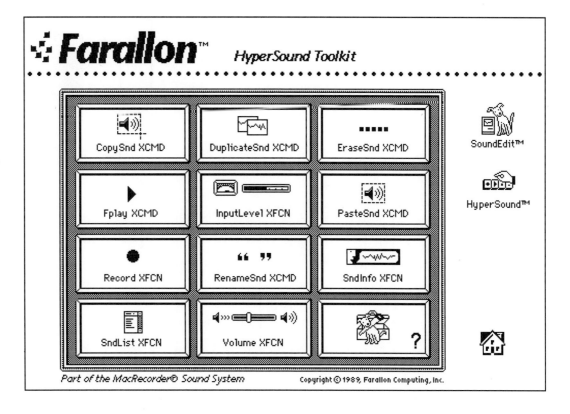

sleeves would be delivered flat for folding and assembly. The printed clear plastic would also be glued to form sleeves as they were as needed.

The first package

The first package we developed for Farallon was also the smallest and simplest — a new presentation for the PhoneNET product. Part of the problem with the fish tackle box they'd been using was that people couldn't see the connector at the end of the PhoneNET cord, and they needed to see it to choose the kind that matched their particular hardware. We took the simplest approach — letting the product show through a clear plastic sleeve — so Farallon wouldn't have to print and stock a lot of different boxes (Figure 3). We examined many different kinds of plastics for degree of transparency, weight, availability and printability of the surfaces.

When we priced the printing and cutting of the package elements, we found that in the U.S. it would cost about $1.75 to manufacture the package. There was no way it made sense to box a $40 to $50 connector and cable in a package that expensive. So we looked to Taiwan, where the package could be made for about a quarter of the cost, including shipping.

We made the two side panels of the package identical to each other, consisting of type on a coarse halftone dot screen (generated as a FreeHand

Figure 3. Designing the first package. The first Farallon package we designed was for PhoneNET. A clear plastic sleeve would let both the connector and the product information card show through so that customers could be sure of what they were buying.

In the end, the box design was not exactly as shown here. We chose a plastic material that was strong enough that the bottom of the box could be formed of two flaps instead of being continuous with both front and back faces of the package. So we changed to a wraparound (rather than a "wrap-under") design, which saved on materials and assembly.

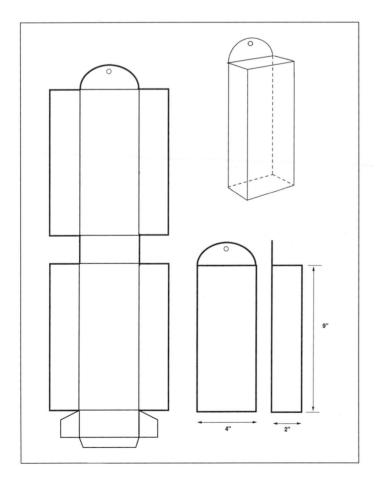

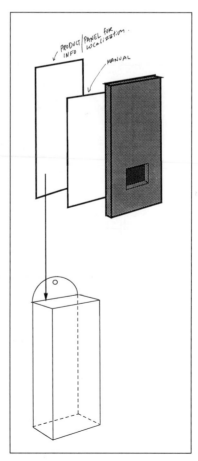

file) over a solid panel of a Pantone yellow. (As packaging, manuals and advertising and marketing materials were developed, each product was assigned its own particular color.)

The type elements for front and sides of the packages were set in Illustrator because at that time PageMaker 3.0 didn't provide for precise control of kerning, and we were having kerning problems with Stone Sans. ▋ *In addition to kerning of type, illustration software provides for more precise measurement and placement control, both through dialog boxes and through the ability to enlarge the view of the artwork more — 1600 percent in Illustrator in contrast to 400 percent in PageMaker.*

We also restructured the PhoneNET manual. In the process, we designed a format for pages and a graphic style for the drawings that would appear in all the Farallon manuals (Figure 4).

The second package design

With the first and simplest design problem solved, we went on to the larger packages. The two larger squarish boxes are basically identical — one a scaled-down version of the other.

The box cover We tried several illustration ideas for the box covers (Figure 5). The thinking that led to our final choice went like this:

- We wanted the covers of the boxes to have a distinctive, consistent, memorable "Farallon" look.

Figure 4. Establishing document format and graphic style. Besides establishing a format for documentation (with styles for text, headings, chapter titles, lists, tables, running heads, folios and so on), the PhoneNET manual set the style (line weights, standardized components and so forth) for Farallon's illustrations and tables.

The manual (3¾ x 7 inches, spiral-bound) had to be small to fit in the packaging. Trimmed, the pages have less than ¼-inch margins. With the small page size and relatively high density of unnumbered illustrations, page bottoms had to bounce to keep graphics in the correct relationship to associated text. The white space that resulted contributed to the open feeling in this compact document, as did the generous leading. Running heads and folios are reversed out of a black band that bleeds off the top of each page.

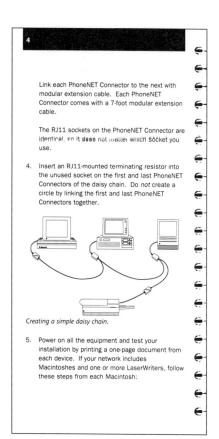

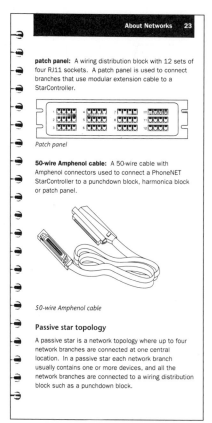

- Since Farallon's products support communication, networking and work groups, we wanted to include people in the pictures that made up the cover illustration.
- By including representations of all the products (or groups of products) Farallon sells in one cover illustration, we could use the same basic box for all the products, varying only the design of the plastic sleeve.
- By including more pictures than there were products, we could allow for expansion of the product line with the maximum efficiency in package production and the minimum disruption of the look of the line.
- We wanted the finished fronts of the boxes, the combined impact of box cover and sleeve, to represent a well-integrated line of unique products, rather than a collection of unrelated gadgets in a generic package.

We settled on a three-by-four-element grid of paintings. Looking at the portfolio submitted by Mark Penberthy convinced us that we had the right illustrator to develop the images (Figure 6). Working with him and with Farallon, we developed a set of ideas for people-oriented paintings to be rendered in oils, to emphasize the human interaction the high-tech products were designed to support. A picture was developed to represent each product. We took 35mm slides of the paintings for documentation. Then the oil paintings were sent out for traditional color separations.

A keyline file was made in Illustrator with a rectangle showing the position of each painting. Placing the logo in the upper left corner as an EPS file completed the front panel.

Three "empty landscapes" were included in the grid of pictures to hold places for products yet to be developed. All three were made from a single painting, cropped and filtered differently to create the variations. There are now a couple more paintings in the works for products under development. When these products are ready, new covers will be printed.

The sky tones used for the side panels of the box were portions of one of the landscapes, enlarged and separated traditionally. When all the parts were done, we pasted up mechanicals and sent them off for camera work to produce the single piece of film the printer required for the die vinyls.

Figure 5. Designing cover illustrations. Experimenting with ideas for the box cover illustration, we tried a comic strip approach, an assemblage of figures composed of fingerprints and a series of Steinberg-like images that included people. The computer played a limited part in this process — we used it primarily to generate type and rules.

Figure 6. Choosing an artist. Mark Penberthy's portfolio included paintings that were amazingly close in style and concept to what we were looking for.

Figure 7. Designing the sleeve. A "target" layer, a halftone screen layer and a type-and-keyline layer made up the artwork to be silkscreened on the clear plastic sleeve for each product in Farallon's line. Shown above are parts of three different sleeves.

Figure 8. Placing the dots. A nonprinting rectangle represented the painting we wanted to target and a large nonprinting circle provided an arc for arranging small circles and triangle. Using the rotation tool with the Option key held down and with Copy selected in the Rotate dialog box, we tried spacing the dots at various degrees of arc until we settled on 12 degrees. (The technique for placing a series of objects around a circle is described in Chapter 3.)

A nonprinting horizontal line intersected a nonprinting outline of the box cover to define "exit" and "entry" points (at left and right edges of the cover, respectively) for additional arcs of circles.

Plastic sleeves The mechanicals for the plastic sleeves were put together in three computer-generated layers — a "target" layer in Illustrator, a FreeHand halftone screen layer, and an Illustrator type-and-keyline layer (Figure 7). We made black-and-white scans of the 35mm slides of the paintings at low resolution (150 dpi) and arranged them to use as a kind of template for the design of the sleeves. For each product, black filled circles and a triangular arrowhead in color were arranged in a partial circle in Illustrator to target the appropriate painting. We aligned the circles and arrowheads on the curve using Illustrator's rotation tool (Figure 8). Additional arcs of circles and triangles led from a consistent "entry" point on the left of the sleeve front to the "target" and from there to a consistent "exit" point on the right. It was tricky to make the arcs look good in relation to the target and the borders of the package front and still keep the entry and exit points consistent so that packages placed side-by-side on a shelf would present a unified appearance (Figure 9).

To help focus attention on the targeted painting, a FreeHand file was set up to produce a coarse halftone round-dot screen that would be printed in white on the front of the clear plastic sleeve (Figure 10). The target dots from the Illustrator file would be overprinted in black. The boxes from the Illustrator keyline file were measured and redrawn in FreeHand. The screen covered the entire square of 12 pictures except a masking rectangle that made a clear window for the painting representing the product to be packed inside the box. We faced two design constraints in choosing the line screen to generate the halftone dots: The smallest dots had to be big enough to hold

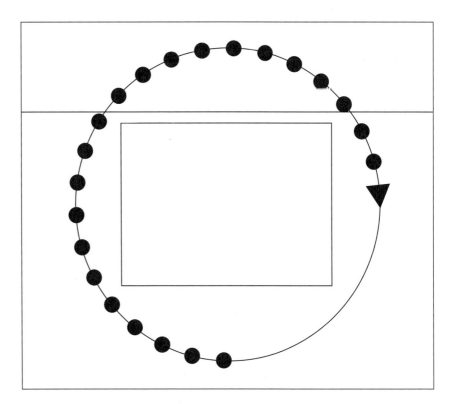

up under the silk-screening process that would be used to print the sleeve. And the largest dots had to be small enough so they wouldn't compete visually with the filled circles that made up the design in the Illustrator file.

We started out using a uniform screen, no gradation, just a matted-out effect. But the single clear window in a uniform screen looked like a mistake in printing instead of an intentional design element, so we went to a gradient fill. We played around with the dot screen, using positive and negative screens, faster and slower transitions, and diagonal blends from corner windows. At one time we even considered going into the PostScript code to change the dot pattern, but we decided it looked fine the way it was. For the two pictures in the middle, we used a radial fill centered on the clear window. For elements in the top and bottom rows and left and right columns, unidirectional fills worked best, with the screen going from sparse to dense as it got farther from the targeted painting. We decided against diagonal fills.

Side panels A FreeHand uniform halftone dot screen was used to overprint a panel of the product's assigned color on each side of the sleeve. To arrive at the design for the side panels, we had the type output on film by the Lino, made underlays from colored paper, and ran the FreeHand screen on acetate on the LaserWriter; we layered them all, looked at it and said, "Yeah, that looks about right" (Figure 11).

Figure 9. Connecting the dots. Arcs of dots run from the left edge to the target to the right edge of the box on the matching Farallon cover sleeves. The sky tones on the top and bottom of each package were derived from one of the original cover paintings, photographed and color-separated by conventional means.

Radial fill

Figure 10. Developing the screens. Screens for muting the cover images were produced with Radial and Graduated black-to-white fills at 0, 90, 180 and 270 degrees, as selected through the Fill menu. The dots were generated by setting FreeHand's Halftone Screen (from Special under the element menu) to Round Dot at 10 lines per inch and the default screen angle.

0 degrees

90 degrees

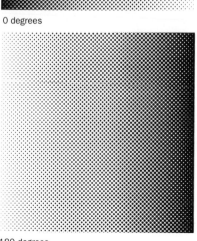

180 degrees

270 degrees

Figure 11.
Designing the side panels. The side panels for the plastic sleeves were arrived at by experimenting with dot screens and type laser-printed on clear acetate sheets and overlaid on colored paper.

Printer's instructions We used Illustrator to show all printer instructions on small, to-scale drawings (Figure 12). ▌ *A scaled-down version of a page layout is an easy way to generate accurate printer's instructions. First a copy of the file is saved under a name different from the original illustration. Then all elements of the page are selected (Select All) and grouped, the scale tool is chosen and Option-clicked on the group to scale the page layout down so that it will fit on an 8½ x 11-inch sheet and still allow room for the instructions and a leader line from each instruction to its page element. The leader lines and notes are added and the page is laser printed. The same technique can be used for page layouts constructed in other PostScript programs, saved in EPS format and opened in Illustrator to have notes added.*

The insert The information card to go inside the back of the sleeve was a pretty straightforward PageMaker layout (Figure 13). The name of the product was set in 18-point Stone Sans type next to the logo at the top of the box. Text was set in 10-point Franklin Gothic on 12-point leading in a single 32-pica column. Black-and-white screen dumps provided by Farallon and cleaned up as needed with SuperPaint were placed on the PageMaker page. Color screen dumps were included in the Page layout as placeholders, and the screen dump files themselves were cleaned up and separated with LaserPaint for stripping into final film.

Figure 12.
Instructing the printer. A reduced version of the artwork was created in Illustrator and marked with complete printing instructions. Although this example was constructed as a new file, such printer's instruction sheets can be assembled from EPS files of the original artwork.

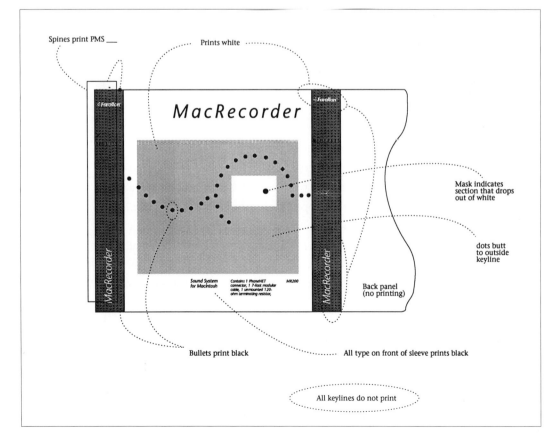

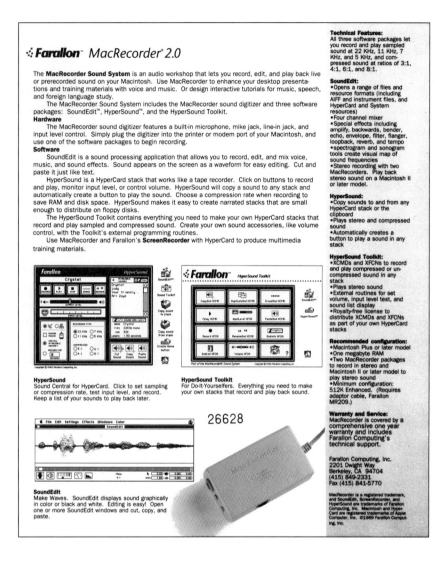

∴ Farallon˙ MacRecorder® 2.0

The **MacRecorder Sound System** is an audio workshop that lets you record, edit, and play back live or prerecorded sound on your Macintosh. Use MacRecorder to enhance your desktop presentations and training materials with voice and music. Or design interactive tutorials for music, speech, and foreign language study.

The MacRecorder Sound System includes the MacRecorder sound digitizer and three software packages: SoundEdit™, HyperSound™, and the HyperSound Toolkit.

Hardware

The MacRecorder sound digitizer features a built-in microphone, mike jack, line-in jack, and input level control. Simply plug the digitizer into the printer or modem port of your Macintosh, and use one of the software packages to begin recording.

Software

SoundEdit is a sound processing application that allows you to record, edit, and mix voice, music, and sound effects. Sound appears on the screen as a waveform for easy editing. Cut and paste it just like text.

HyperSound is a HyperCard stack that works like a tape recorder. Click on buttons to record and play, monitor input level, or control volume. HyperSound will copy a sound to any stack and automatically create a button to play the sound. Choose a compression rate when recording to save RAM and disk space. HyperSound makes it easy to create narrated stacks that are small enough to distribute on floppy disks.

The HyperSound Toolkit contains everything you need to make your own HyperCard stacks that record and play sampled and compressed sound. Create your own sound accessories, like volume control, with the Toolkit's external programming routines.

Use MacRecorder and Farallon's **ScreenRecorder** with HyperCard to produce multimedia training materials.

HyperSound
Sound Central for HyperCard. Click to set sampling or compression rate, test input level, and record. Keep a list of your sounds to play back later.

HyperSound Toolkit
For Do-It-Yourselfers. Everything you need to make your own stacks that record and play back sound.

26628

SoundEdit
Make Waves. SoundEdit displays sound graphically in color or black and white. Editing is easy! Open one or more SoundEdit windows and cut, copy, and paste.

Technical Features:
All three software packages let you record and play sampled sound at 22 KHz, 11 KHz, 7 KHz, and 5 KHz, and compressed sound at ratios of 3:1, 4:1, 6:1, and 8:1.

SoundEdit:
• Opens a range of files and resource formats (including AIFF and instrument files, and HyperCard and System resources)
• Four channel mixer
• Special effects including amplify, backwards, bender, echo, envelope, filter, flanger, loopback, reverb, and tempo
• spectrogram and sonogram tools create visual map of sound frequencies
• Stereo recording with two MacRecorders. Play back stereo sound on a Macintosh II or later model.

HyperSound:
• Copy sounds to and from any HyperCard stack or the clipboard
• Plays stereo and compressed sound
• Automatically creates a button to play a sound in any stack

HyperSound Toolkit:
• XCMDs and XFCNs to record and play compressed or uncompressed sound in any stack
• Plays stereo sound
• External routines for set volume, input level test, and sound list display
• Royalty-free license to distribute XCMDs and XFCNs as part of your own HyperCard stacks

Recommended configuration:
• Macintosh Plus or later model
• One megabyte RAM
• Two MacRecorder packages to record in stereo and Macintosh II or later model to play stereo sound
• Minimum configuration: 512K Enhanced. (Requires adaptor cable, Farallon MR209.)

Warranty and Service:
MacRecorder is covered by a comprehensive one year warranty and includes Farallon Computing's technical support.

Farallon Computing, Inc.
2201 Dwight Way
Berkeley, CA 94704
(415) 849-2331
Fax (415) 841-5770

MacRecorder is a registered trademark, and SoundEdit, ScreenRecorder, and HyperSound are trademarks of Farallon Computing, Inc. Macintosh and HyperCard are registered trademarks of Apple Computer, Inc. ©1989 Farallon Computing, Inc.

Figure 13. Preparing insert cards. A card was designed for each product, to be inserted between the sleeve and the bottom of the box. It described the hardware and software in the package. Text from the card was imported from Word into PageMaker and styled in Stone Sans type. Screen dumps modified in SuperPaint were used as finished art for black-and-white screens and as place holders for color screens that were color-separated in LaserPaint and stripped in as film.

A keyline defined the screened panel of technical information. (Space was left between the technical panel and the bottom illustration for a photo of the MacRecorder, to be stripped in by conventional means later, and for a sticker with the serial number of the product.)

Figure 14. Designing layouts for manuals. Farallon's in-house publications group used established graphic and documentation styles to prepare the MacRecorder user's manual.

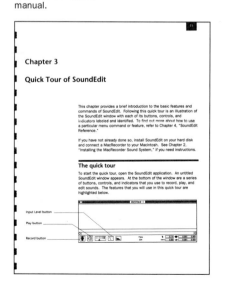

A rectangle was drawn to serve as a keyline for the screened background of the specifications panel at the right of each card. For cards that included color screen dumps and so required color printing, these panels were a screened-back version of the color that appeared on the side of the sleeve. Registration cards included in the package were also color coded, for a quick tally on card return. To save on the cost of printing, if the informational graphics didn't require color, the specifications panel and registration cards were called out as 10 percent black so the cards could be run in one color.

Coordinated manuals

In designing the layout for the MacRecorder manual in PageMaker, we again set the tone and the style for future product manuals. We used Stone Sans for headings and subheads and Franklin Gothic for text (Figure 14). The page design included running heads, folios and horizontal rules at the beginning of each new section and subsection.

Maintaining the style

We developed letterhead and other stationery in Farallon's new look. We also provided a short, simple style guide to help Farallon's employees keep the look consistent (Figure 15) — not a great big, thick graphic standards manual, just a simple guide designed in PageMaker.

In retrospect

If we were starting the Farallon project today, we probably would have used FreeHand for much of the work we did in Illustrator, since we had to use FreeHand to generate the halftone dot pattern, and since FreeHand can align objects like our filled circles and arrowheads along curves. But at the time, we were much more familiar with Illustrator. One of the few things we knew about FreeHand then was that it could generate those dot patterns. Today, even with the improvements in the current version of PageMaker, we still might lay out the packaging in PostScript illustration software because of the precision it provides in placing graphic elements by numerically defining coordinates.

Figure 15. Keeping style consistent. The six-page *Corporate Styleguide* covers the use and placement of the logo, color, typography, heads, body copy and stationery.

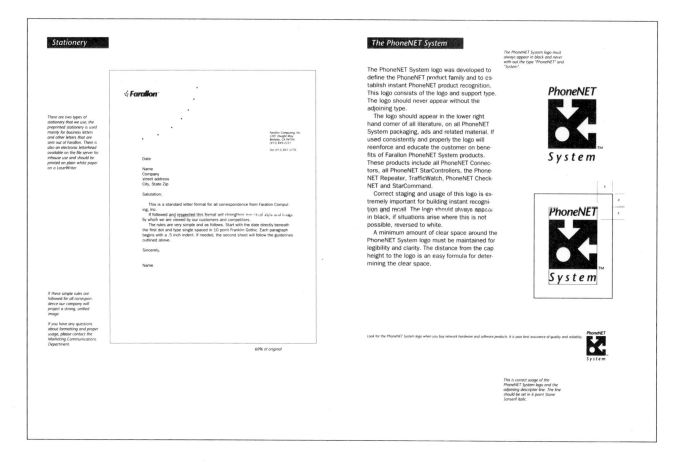

PORTFOLIO

Clement Mok

"My philosophy and approach are the same in designing with computers as with other media. The point is to make the information understandable and compelling. The Macintosh is a tool and it's also an extension to the way I visualize and present ideas. I don't really view it any differently than I view a pencil."

The design for the series of **OmniPage ads,** which included this one of Rick Smolan, had to make a boring task (scanning text) interesting. The idea was to show interesting people doing interesting things with OCR. The ad was laid out in PageMaker with 8-bit AppleScan images of Rick made from contact photos and used as place-holders.

Design development for the **OmniPage packaging** was done in PageMaker and Illustrator 88. The goal was to explain and illustrate in a fun and unexpected way the features of a not-so-understand-able technology.

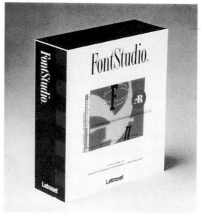

The **packaging** for Letraset's FontStudio was designed using screen capture shots from FontStudio as well as images fom Adobe Illustrator, and was assembled in Ready,Set,Go.

To illustrate electronic design tools to the design community without being trite or overtly cute, the goal was to create something simple and symbolic of the subject addressed. The idea was to use the vernacular of the medium — the visual vocabulary inherent in the software program — and to treat these elements like we would type, color and rules. This **folder** to hold press releases and other promotional materials was designed and produced with Studio 8 and Ready,Set,Go.

Clement Mok **designs**

477 Bryant Street
San Francisco
California 94107
415 777-5315

FAX 415 777-0930
ConnectID Mok5515
AppleLink D2414
Certified Developer

Clement Mok

For his firm's **business cards,** Mok used the California state bear symbol to represent local and regional influences, the apple as an object of play and a symbol of Apple Computer, and the glasses/sunglasses as a cliché California image and as a representation of "nerd glasses," to get across the idea that technosavvy is hip. This small "page" was laid out in Illustrator 88.

C H A P T E R   1 2

Evolution of a Newsletter

Design team

Designing the *Step-By-Step Electronic Design* newsletter was a team effort from the beginning. Editor and art director worked together to arrive at the initial design, and each issue presented its own design and layout challenge to managing editor and production manager. Michael Gosney is publisher and editor of *Verbum*, a journal of personal computer aesthetics. He is also director of The Gosney Company, a computer-focused ad agency and publication producer in San Diego. John Odam, a freelance graphic designer, serves as art director for *Verbum* and for *Step-By-Step Electronic Design* newsletter. Linnea Dayton is managing editor of both publications and is co-author with Gosney of *Making Art on the Macintosh* (Scott, Foresman, 1989) and *The Verbum Book of Electronic Page Design* (M&T Books, 1990). Martha Siebert is the production manager for The Gosney Company and *Verbum*. Janet Ashford is a freelance designer and writer who frequently contributes articles and design services to *Verbum* and The Gosney Company and is a coauthor with Dayton and Gosney of *The Verbum Book of PostScript Illustration* (M&T Books, 1990).

Project

The project was to create a newsletter aimed at graphic designers who had adopted or were in the process of adopting microcomputer design and illustration tools. Dynamic Graphics, publishers of traditional and electronic clip art, as well as *Step By Step Graphics* magazine, decided to initiate a monthly newsletter to provide articles that showed, step-by-step, how various electronic design projects were carried out. They called on the editorial, design and production services of The Gosney Company, which produces *Verbum* magazine. Working with Nancy Aldrich-Ruenzel, editorial director of Step-By-Step Publishing, the firm developed a prototype and began producing issues on a monthly basis. Originally designed to be flexible, the newsletter has gone through minor and major transformations, with new elements being added, a change from two-color to four-color, and transfer of production from The Gosney Company/*Verbum* offices in San Diego to the Step-By-Step offices in East Peoria, Illinois.

The newsletter was originally designed on a Macintosh II in PageMaker, and the first 18 issues were laid out and produced on Mac–PageMaker systems. Then the design was "translated" to Quark XPress. It was proofed on LaserWriter IINT and IINTX printers and was delivered on floppy disks for output on L-300 imagesetters. Other hardware and software typically used in producing the newsletter included an Apple Scanner, various modems (for transmitting files from writers to editor and from editor to production manager), Microsoft Word (for preparation of text), Camera and Capture (for making screen dumps), SuperPaint (for editing the screens) and FreeHand (for logos and editorial illustrations).

Design process

Art director John Odam wanted to create a newsletter design with a sturdy structure but enough flexibility to accommodate the changing size and shape of each issue's illustrations and text. The design needed to be straightforward and intelligible so that other designers could take over the page layout task as needed. And it was necessary to link the style visually to that already used by the parent magazine, *Step by Step Graphics*, though the newsletter was to have it's own character. The first step was to design and print a four-page prototype issue to show the publishers at Dynamic Graphics how the newsletter would look. The design developed by Odam for this preview issue was refined somewhat for later issues, but remained basically the same.

Working with the client

The first 19 issues of *Step-By-Step Electronic Design* saw a transition from two-color to four-color and from one production and layout team to another. Concept, design and content were developed by Michael Gosney and The Gosney Company/*Verbum* magazine team for the publisher, the Step-By-Step Publishing division of Dynamic Graphics. After 14 issues, Step-By-Step took over production of film, and after 18 issues, the entire layout and production process was moved.

During its first year of publication *Step-By-Step Electronic Design* was printed in two colors on letter-size paper with a three-hole punch, like this preview issue. The basic design structure of the newsletter included a three-column format, with two wide columns for text and figures and a narrower outer column for captions, graphic elements and figures overflowing from the main columns. This structure remained unchanged in later versions of the design.

COLOR PALETTE

A palette of six custom colors was created from percentages of CYMK using the Custom Color box from Illustrator's Style menu. ☛ *Using custom colors rather than Pantone colors or CYMK tints allows you to adjust screen colors to look right while working on the poster design, and then easily make universal color adjustments when it's time to output to film.*

I created a custom black made up of 40C, 40M, 40Y and 100K because I wanted a deep black with percentages of all four process colors. ☛ *In Illustrator, elements that are colored using the regular black from the paint dialog box will surprint any colors they're on top of, rather than reversing out as other colors do. Surprinted black can look a slightly different color when it's on top of red, for example, than when it's on yellow.* ☛ *Another advantage of using a custom black is to minimize potential trapping problems in areas where colors abut to black, since the black contains percentages of all the process colors.*

A Zapf Dingbats symbol of a pointing hand was used to introduce a "hint," a highlighted section of text that explained a specific technique. Hints were written to fall at the end of a paragraph and care was taken to make sure that the hint symbol didn't appear as the last character in a line.

THE RIGHT PICTURE is a powerful shortcut to making an editorial point. Big-budget periodicals often commission artwork from a photographer or an illustrator. If at all possible, try to do the same. This gives you the best possible control over quality and such important characteristics as relevance to the editorial content, medium (photograph, computer graphics, line art), and shape and size. Unfortunately, publishers of other than big-budget periodicals often lack the time and money to commission original illustrations. We make do, adapting stock photos or generic clip art and making the most of the poor-quality snapshots we're presented with.

Here are a few ideas for using art more effectively, whether electronic or conventional.

Generally speaking, take a conservative approach to art. Making extreme departures from a normal view may be disturbing — and therefore distracting — to your readers. Use most photographs "square" — that is, with regular right-angled edges. And limit the use of techniques such as floating a photo above a rectangular dropped shadow of itself. Avoid vignetting (making the edges fade out gradually) unless you're illustrating a period piece.

Look for fresh images. Using clichés to illustrate an article is risky. For example, a picture of animals falling out of the sky ("raining cats and dogs") in an article about weather systems can sidetrack the reader instead of providing a direct route to your editorial point. Or, if

you use an already overused image, you run the risk that the article will seem too ordinary or "stale" to be worth reading. On the other

hand, old engravings or paintings — Renaissance art, for example — can seem very fresh in a modern context.

Use repetition to intensify the visual effect of an image. For dramatic effect, use the same image two or three times, changing the cropping, reproduction size, overprinted color, or other element with each repetition. Zoom in on parts of a drawing or photograph, and use the enlarged details to illustrate related parts of the story.

Use pictures or other graphic devices structurally. A small image repeated in the same location on all the pages of a long article helps to guide the reader through the pages and serves as a graphic reminder of the subject matter. Bullets, "flowers" — typographic ornaments like the leaves found in the Zapf Dingbats font — or rules can be used to indicate breaks in text or to distinguish a sidebar from the main article.

Crop in tight to transform pictures. Close cropping emphasizes the relevant portion of an image. Use cropping to focus the reader's eye, and then allow a part of the image — an arm or foot, for example — to pop out dramatically into the adjoining space. Crop all the head shots in a group the same way, and make the faces about the same size — use the width of the eyes as a guide — to unify what might otherwise appear to be a bunch of miscellaneous photos. Make general-purpose clip art seem fresh and apt by cropping in to focus on a minor detail. Change the shape of an image by cropping: one dimension more than the other: Use a square or horizontal portion of a vertical image for example, if it helps make the picture work better.

Manipulate the scale of an image for impact. Presenting a detail very large — a small section of a tapestry, for example — is a useful technique if you don't overdo it. The opposite technique is also powerful: show a landscape in wide slivers, or show a person, doing something that can be understood despite the small size, in a 2-inch square. Fiddling with scale, like exaggerating verbally, should be done sparingly, or the technique will lose its impact, and it's possible your publication will seem less credible to the reader.

Distortion can be dangerous, especially with graphs. Resist the impulse to make the numbers look better by graphic sleight of hand. The reader who realizes she's been deceived about the bottom line by false vertical emphasis on a bar or line chart will not be receptive to your publication's point of view, no matter how persuasive the copy.

The Graphic Eye

Picture Perfect
by Kathleen Tinkel

Beginning desktop publishers often lament that their work looks "unprofessional." In this column designer/writer Kathleen Tinkel helps you develop your own sense of good design by discussing basic design elements and how to apply them in the electronic studio.

Cropping is a powerful technique for tailoring images to your message or for removing distracting irrelevancies. Add drama by letting portions of the image pop out of the frame.

Each of the regular columns was identified with an icon that bled off the top outside corner of the page.

After the first year of publication, the newsletter went from two-color throughout to eight pages of four-color and eight of two-color.

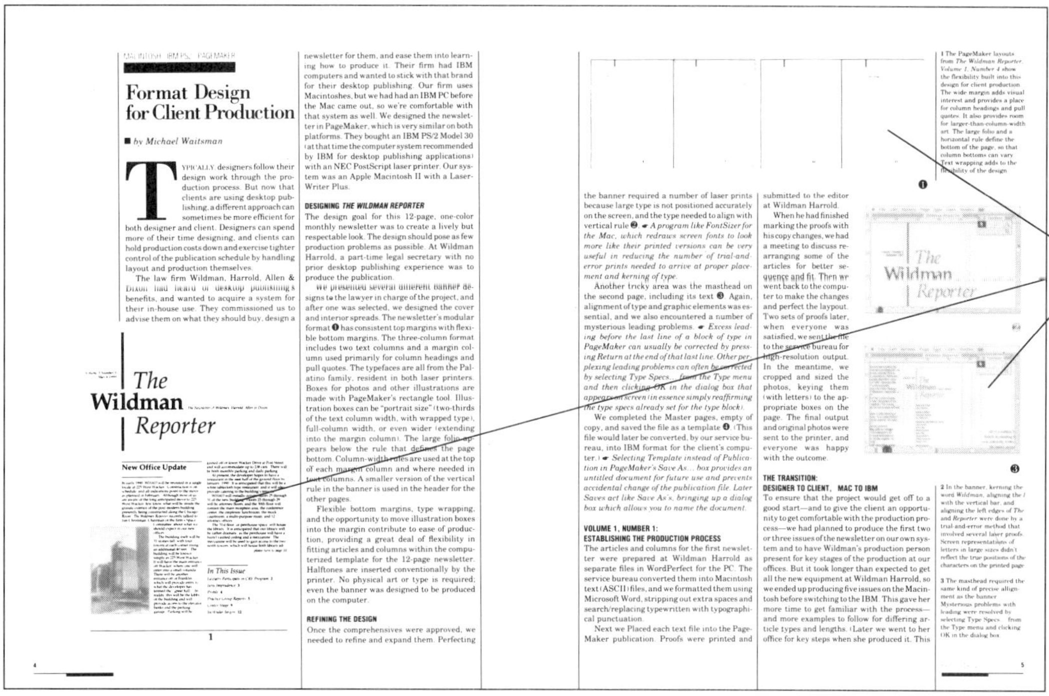

Format Design for Client Production
by Michael Waitsman

TYPICALLY, designers follow their design work through the production process. But now that clients are using desktop publishing, a different approach can sometimes be more efficient for both designer and client. Designers can spend more of their time designing, and clients can hold production costs down and exercise tighter control of the publication schedule by handling layout and production themselves.

The law firm Wildman, Harrold, Allen & Dixon had heard of desktop publishing's benefits, and wanted to acquire a system for their in-house use. They commissioned us to advise them on what they should buy, design a

newsletter for them, and ease them into learning how to produce it. Their firm had IBM computers and wanted to stick with that brand for their desktop publishing. Our firm uses Macintoshes, but we had had an IBM PC before the Mac came out, so we're comfortable with that system as well. We designed the newsletter in PageMaker, which is very similar on both platforms. They bought an IBM PS/2 Model 30 rat that time the computer system recommended by IBM for desktop publishing applications) with an NEC PostScript laser printer. Our system was an Apple Macintosh II with a LaserWriter Plus.

DESIGNING THE WILDMAN REPORTER

The design goal for this 12-page, one-color monthly newsletter was to create a lively but respectable look. The design should pose as few production problems as possible. At Wildman Harrold, a part-time legal secretary with no prior desktop publishing experience was to produce the publication.

We presented several different banner designs to the lawyer in charge of the project, and after one was selected, we designed the cover and interior spreads. The newsletter's modular format ❶ has consistent top margins with flexible bottom margins. The three-column format includes two text columns and a margin column used primarily for column headings and pull quotes. The typefaces are all from the Palatino family, resident in both laser printers. Boxes for photos and other illustrations are made with PageMaker's rectangle tool. Illustration boxes can be "portrait size"—two-thirds of the text column width, with wrapped type; full-column width, or even wider (extending into the margin column). The large folio appears below the rule that defines the page bottom. Column-width rules are used at the top of each margin column and where needed in text columns. A smaller version of the vertical rule in the banner is used in the header for the other pages.

Flexible bottom margins, type wrapping, and the opportunity to move illustration boxes into the margin contribute to ease of production, providing a great deal of flexibility in fitting articles and columns within the computerized template for the 12-page newsletter. Halftones are inserted conventionally by the printer. No physical art or type is required, even the banner was designed to be produced on the computer.

REFINING THE FORMAT

Once the comprehensives were approved, we needed to refine and expand them. Perfecting

the banner required a number of laser prints because large type is not positioned accurately on the screen, and the type needed to align with vertical rule ❷. ◼ A program like FontSizer for the Mac, which redraws screen fonts to look more like their printed versions can be very useful in reducing the number of trial-and-error prints needed to arrive at proper placement and kerning of type.

Another tricky area was the masthead on the second page, including its text ❸. Again, alignment of type and graphic elements was essential, and we also encountered a number of mysterious leading problems. ◼ Excess leading before the last line of a block of type in PageMaker can usually be corrected by pressing Return at the end of that last line. Other perplexing leading problems can often be Placed by selecting Type Specs... from the Type menu and then clicking OK in the dialog box that appears on screen (in essence simply reaffirming the type specs already set for the type block).

We completed the Master pages, empty of copy, and saved the file as a template ❹. (This file would later be converted, by our service bureau, into IBM format for the client's computer.) ◼ Selecting Template instead of Publication in PageMaker's Save As... box provides an untitled document for future use and prevents accidental change of the publication file. Later Saves act like Save As's, bringing up a dialog box which allows you to name the document.

**VOLUME 1, NUMBER 1:
ESTABLISHING THE PRODUCTION PROCESS**

The articles and columns for the first newsletter were prepared at Wildman Harrold as separate files in WordPerfect for the PC. The service bureau converted them into Macintosh text (ASCII) files, and we formatted them using Microsoft Word, stripping out extra spaces and search/replacing typewritten with typographical punctuation.

Next we Placed each text file into the PageMaker publication. Proofs were printed and

submitted to the editor at Wildman Harrold.

When he had finished marking the proofs with his copy changes, we had a meeting to discuss rearranging some of the articles for better sequence and fit. Then we went back to the computer to make the changes and perfect the layout. Two sets of proofs later, when everyone was satisfied, we sent the file to the service bureau for high-resolution output. In the meantime, we cropped and sized the photos, keying them (with letters) to the appropriate boxes on the page. The final output and original photos were sent to the printer, and everyone was happy with the outcome.

**THE TRANSITION:
DESIGNER TO CLIENT, MAC TO IBM**

To ensure that the project would get off to a good start—and to give the client an opportunity to get comfortable with the production process—we had planned to produce the first two or three issues of the newsletter on our own system and to have Wildman's production person sit in on all the equipment at Wildman Harrold, so we ended up producing five issues on the Macintosh before switching to the IBM. This gave her more time to get familiar with the process and more examples to follow for differing article types and lengths. � Later we went to her office for key steps when she produced it. This

❶ The PageMaker layouts from The Wildman Reporter Volume 1, Number 1 show the flexibility built into this design for client production. The wide margin adds visual interest and provides a place for column headings and pull quotes. It also provides room for larger-than-column-width art. The large folio and a horizontal rule define the bottom of the page, so that column bottoms can vary. Text wrapping adds to the flexibility of the design.

The
Wildman
Reporter

New Office Update

In This Issue

1

❷ In the banner, kerning the word Wildman, aligning the l with the vertical bar, and aligning the left edges of The and Reporter were done by a trial-and-error method that involved several laser proofs. Screen representation of letters in large sizes didn't reflect the true positions of the characters on the printed page.

❸ The masthead required the same kind of precise alignment as the banner. Mysterious problems with leading were resolved by selecting Type Specs... from the Type menu and clicking OK in the dialog box.

Each page spread of the newsletter involved a careful fitting together of text and graphic elements. The strong but flexible design made it possible to accommodate graphics of any size or proportion.

The
Wildman
Reporter

4

5

nitial design requirements called for a 16-page, two-color newsletter with 8¼ x 10½-inch pages and a three-hole punch along the inner margin. John Odam chose a three-column format, with the outside margin used for captions, the authors' biographical blurbs, small figures, and larger figures flowing over from the two main columns. The two inner columns were reserved for article text. Interline spacing (of titles, bylines, text and subheads) would be consistent, but column bottoms would be allowed to "bounce."

Setting up master pages

John used PageMaker's master pages to set up the features that would appear on every page (Figure 1). He specified a three-column format, which produced three equally wide columns, and then dragged the margin and gutter lines into position for his customized column widths.

Choosing type

Working with editors Gosney and Dayton, Odam developed a style sheet for the newsletter (Figure 2). New Century Schoolbook, an easily read serif face, was used in justified columns of 9 points on 11-point leading for the body copy, while 9/11 Helvetica Condensed Light Bold was used for the all-caps subheads, with a line space above. ∎ *A bold, all-caps subhead on the same leading as the text makes the subhead stand out but ensures that text will align from column to column all the way down the page. Because there are no descenders, leading doesn't need to be increased to accommodate the heavier type.*

A one-line kicker above each feature article would list the software being featured and was set in 9-point Helvetica Condensed Light. It was under-

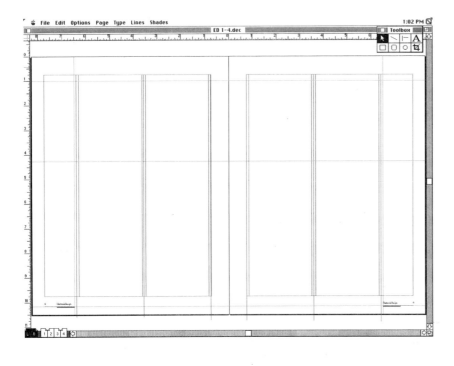

Figure 1. Designing master pages. This master page spread shows the basic three-column design (featuring a 1¼-inch outside column and two inner columns of 2⅝ inches each, with 1-pica gutters) and the down rules, folios, running feet, margins and guidelines that stay the same on each page. The two guidelines at the top indicate alternate starting places for text and graphics.

scored with a 12-point solid rule. Main article titles were set in 36/33 Bodoni type, at first in all caps and later in upper and lower case. Secondary article titles were set in 25/24 Bodoni. ■ *Display type (as in headlines) is often set on leading smaller than the type size and is also kerned (the letter spacing is tightened between individual pairs of letters); with large type less space is needed between letters and between lines for visually pleasing results. But reducing the leading may mean that an occasional two-line headline will have to be rewritten to avoid collisions between ascenders from the lower line and descenders from the upper.*

The byline was in italicized body text, but 1 point larger. It was preceded by a square bullet (typed as a lowercase n) from Zapf Dingbats. A large initial cap (96-point Bodoni) began each article and the text was wrapped around it. The first few words of the text were set in small caps, to provide a transition from the initial cap to the rest of the body copy. Captions were set in 7/8.5 New Century Schoolbook and were made flush left to further differentiate them from the body copy. Author biographical blurbs were the same as captions, but in italic.

A special feature called a "hint" was created for use within the body copy (see page 156). A hint is an especially useful bit of specific advice on how to achieve an effect being discussed in the text. To call attention to the hints, they were set in italicized body text and preceded by a Zapf Dingbats symbol of a pointing hand (Shift-8 on the keyboard). The hints, along with the captioned figures, provided a way for readers skimming an article to pick up useful tips and to gain a quick understanding of the flow of a project.

Figure 2. Establishing styles. The art director and editorial staff worked together to create style specifications for various elements of type. A typical article includes a kicker, two-line title, author byline, initial cap, subheads, captions and the author's biographical sketch.

Many articles would also include sidebars. These were set off in hairline rectangles and styled with an 18/17 Bodoni headline, a 12-point rule, and text in 8/9.5 New Century Schoolbook (Figure 3).

Custom-made bullets

Within the body copy, figure references were indicated by an 11-point serif numbered bullet from the Zapf Dingbats font. This was done to match the figure reference style already in use in *Step-By-Step Graphics* magazine. Bullets 2 points larger than the text seemed to look better with the New Century Schoolbook type than did bullets of the same point size. The figures themselves were labelled with a larger, 14-point numbered bullet.

The bullets provided by the Zapf Dingbats font go from 1 to 10 in both serif and sans serif, black and reversed styles (see "Finding the numbers" on page 164). But because some articles might include 11 or more figures, John Odam used Fontographer to design a set of additional bullet numbers. To do this, he first typed the Zapf Dingbat bullets in FreeHand and enlarged each one to completely fill a letter-size sheet. These sheets were scanned and the scans were opened in Fontographer to serve as templates. It was difficult to get all of the two-digit number combinations, especially the 12, to fit within the bullet circle. Odam had to form "ligatures" of some of the pairs by reducing the size of the serifs (Figure 4). He created bullets for the numbers 11 through 19, struggled to fit a 20 inside the bullet, and then decided that articles would just have to be limited to 19 figures! He named the font Dingbat Numbers. ▮ *Software that has become available since the Dingbat Numbers were developed could simplify the development process. For example, Adobe Type Manager, which can provide smooth screen images of type in large sizes, could be used in place of the scanning process; or Metamorphosis could be used to automatically convert characters to PostScript graphics outlines; and Art Importer could be used to assign custom symbols generated as PostScript outlines to keys on the keyboard.*

Using the Styles and Color palettes

To streamline the production process and ensure consistency, John used PageMaker's Define Styles function to give a name to each type element (Kicker, Subhead 1, Caption and so on) and defined the type specifications for each. Fine points, such as the 11-point space before each subhead and a flush-left first paragraph for the body text, were added at this time. John also assigned a color to each element; either black (for the body copy, titles and captions) or blue (for the kicker, initial cap, subheads, and "hint" hands). (For tips on using the Styles menu, see "Using styles in PageMaker" in Chapter 2.) ▮ *A shortcut for opening the PageMaker Styles or Colors menu (rather than making a selection from the Options menu) is to type Command-Y (Command-E in versions before 4.0) or Command-K, respectively.*

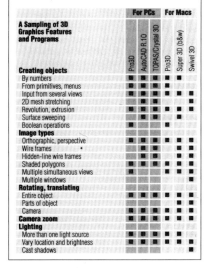

A Look at 3D Graphics Software

AMONG 3D GRAPHICS programs for pc's are several with features especially suitable for graphic designers. Seven of these programs — merely a sampling of this rapidly developing genre — are listed in the chart below. Solids can be created by specifying dimensions numerically, by choosing from building blocks supplied by the program, or by drawing a shape and revolving or extruding it (as described for the Angel Studios logo). Some programs also allow the user to form objects by pushing and pulling points of a 2D mesh, stretching this grid to form a 3D model. Surface sweeping involves changing a 2D form as it's simultaneously moved through space to create a 3D solid; for example, a circle could be enlarged and swept to generate a solid cornucopia shape. In combining forms, Boolean operations make possible the subtraction of one solid from another (as the prism was subtracted from the pyramid in the Angel Studios logo) and the embossing of a raised pattern onto a solid's surface.

The artist can see and modify a solid in orthographic (plan and elevation) or perspective views. Solids are made up of polygonal surfaces. Wire-frame views show the edges of those surfaces; hidden-surface wire frames hide edges that would be screened from view by closer surfaces. Objects or camera (the viewpoint) may be rotated or moved through space; some programs allow movement of parts of an object, and some even allow the user to limit or coordinate motion of various parts. Lighting can be varied.

A Sampling of 3D Graphics Features and Programs	For PCs			For Macs		
	Pro3D	AutoCAD R.10	TOPAS/Crystal 3D	Pro3D	Super 3D (b&w)	Swivel 3D
Creating objects						
By numbers	■	■	■	■	■	
From primitives, menus	■	■	■	■	■	
Input from several views	■	■	■			■
2D mesh stretching			■			■
Revolution, extrusion	■		■	■		■
Surface sweeping			■			■
Boolean operations	■	■		■		
Image types						
Orthographic, perspective	■	■	■	■	■	■
Wire frames	■	•	■	■		■
Hidden-line wire frames	■	■	■	■		■
Shaded polygons	■	■	■	■	■	■
Multiple simultaneous views	■				■	■
Multiple windows				■		■
Rotating, translating						
Entire object	■	■	■	■	■	■
Parts of object					■	■
Camera	■	■	■			■
Camera zoom	■	■	■	■	■	■
Lighting						
More than one light source	■	■	■	■	■	
Vary location and brightness	■	■	■	■	■	
Cast shadows					■	

Figure 3. Styling sidebars. Sidebars were set off in boxes and could be one, two or three columns wide. The body and headline type was the same as for articles but set smaller. Sidebars often contained figures or tables, which were created in FreeHand and placed in the PageMaker layout. Helvetica Condensed Light type was used for figure text.

Figure 4. Designing Dingbat Numbers. To make the two-digit numbers fit within the bullet size, Odam had to trim serifs and squeeze the numbers together.

John chose a blue (3155 from the Pantone Matching System) as the second color for the newsletter because he knew he would often want to use percentage screens to set off figures or as backgrounds for whole page spreads. Blue would work well when screened back to 20 percent. John used PageMaker's Define Colors function to simulate this blue on the screen.

Features and columns

During the newsletter's first year of publication, each issue of *Step-By-Step Electronic Design* included two feature articles and three regular columns: "In the Trenches" by Steve Hannaford, a regular contributor (with a technical bent) to *Verbum* and other publications; "The Graphic Eye" by Kathleen Tinkel, an electronic designer and writer with particular interest in type and in the business aspects of graphic design; and "Questions and Answers" by the editorial staff. Other regular elements included a "Calendar" of computer design events, a "Resources" section of brief book and product reviews, and a "Get Info" section that provided source information for all products mentioned in the issue. The main feature article always began on page 1. To differentiate between a feature article and a column, Odam created a slightly different placement of elements for the title page of each (Figure 5).

Creating column icons

Each regular column featured a two-color icon placed in the outside column above the title, where it bleeds off the top and side of the page (Figure 6). Small one-color symbols were also created to highlight the "Get Info," "Calendar" and "Resources" sections. Odam produced all the icons in Free-Hand using scans of his rough initial sketches as template guides. The icons were saved as EPS files and placed in the PageMaker layout. Each column icon was designed to be used either on a left-hand or a right-hand page, allowing for changes in the sequence of articles and columns in each issue.

Figure 5. Identifying articles and columns. Kickers, titles and bylines for feature articles begin at the top left of the page, in the body text column. Titles and bylines for contributor's columns appear in the narrow outside margin.

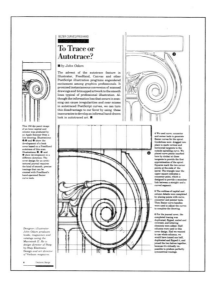

Two-color separations

The three original two-color icons included graduated fills that varied from 100 percent black to 100 percent magenta. Though eventually printed with blue ink, magenta was chosen for the electronic art because it generates the 75-degree screen angle that's considered ideal for printing a second color with black. For the first nine issues of the newsletter, these icons were separated and printed to film through FreeHand and the negatives were stripped into the film for the page layout mechanically. By the October 1989 issue the production team was using Aldus's new PageMaker 3.02 Color Extension, so the FreeHand graphics could be placed as EPS files and separated along with the rest of the page through Adobe Separator.

Creating a nameplate

Other elements that appeared in each issue of the newsletter included the nameplate on the cover, a table of contents, a masthead and brief production notes. Dynamic Graphics asked The Gosney Company to produce a nameplate similar to that used for *Step-By-Step Graphics*. The team developed a nameplate that featured a solid black rectangle, the Step-By-Step logotype in reverse, and the words "Electronic Design" rendered in white and graduated grays. John Odam was supplied with photostats of the Step-By-Step logotype and of "Electronic Design," rendered at Dynamic Graphics. Because the typeface used for the logotype was not at that time available as an Adobe font, John used Streamline to autotrace a scan of the stat. The Streamline document was opened in Illustrator 88, saved as an Illustrator 1.1–compatible file, and then opened in FreeHand, where he refined the autotraced drawing (Figure 7). The nameplate appeared on both cover pages.

Building in flexibility

The Step-By-Step team knew that the issues would vary greatly in graphic content, depending upon the types of illustrations or page design projects being described. It was also important that each graphic appear in sequence and on the same page or page spread as the text that referred to it. To ensure flexibility, Odam designed the newsletter to "give" in various directions when spacing of text and figures became tight. For example, the bottom of each column of text usually aligned at the same place, but didn't have to reach the absolute page bottom. The narrow outside margin could be used for the placement of small graphics and also to accommodate larger graphics that wouldn't fit comfortably in the width of one or two text columns. The variable sinkage at the top allowed for articles that ran shorter than usual on text (this rarely happened!) and the bullets that label figures could be placed either above or below them and could violate the top and bottom page margins. Sidebars could be the width of one text column, or two text columns, or of one text column plus the outside column, or could spread across the whole page. Screen dumps (transparent bitmaps in black-and-white) could be

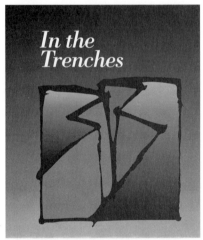

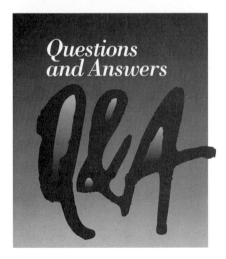

Figure 6. Using column logos. Two-color icons were created in FreeHand as signature graphics for each regular column.

Figure 7. Creating a nameplate. The nameplate for *Step-By-Step Electronic Design* was designed to follow the style already used by *Step-By-Step Graphics* magazine. The logotype and script type were auto-traced in Streamline. Odam opened both auto-tracings in FreeHand for further refinement. To keep the centers of the B and P's open so that the background color would show through, he drew these letters as continuous closed paths. To create the shadow behind the script lettering, Odam cloned the white script, added a stroke to make the clone thicker, and then filled it with a graduated fill and placed it behind the original.

The nameplate, table of contents, subtitle and volume information, masthead and production notes appeared in the same positions on the front and back covers of each issue.

grouped together and placed over a 20 percent blue screen. With these flexibilities balanced by the newsletter's strong underlying structure, fitting the text and graphics for each issue became a challenging but not frustrating exercise of fitting puzzle pieces tightly together (Figure 8).

Evolving styles

As the newsletter evolved during its first year of production, various style elements changed and some new elements were created. One addition was a tinted background of 20 percent blue on pages at the center of the newsletter that included a special article or a series of shorter articles with related contents. Some of these features required the creation of special "bugs," or graphic symbols, to highlight the theme being presented: for example, power-user tips, time-saving techniques and so on (Figure 9).

Working with contributors

Because regular columnists Hannaford and Tinkel live and work on the east coast, communication with them was by telephone, mail and modem. Both sent in their column text by modem via MCI Mail. Kathleen used Desktop Express, which allowed her to send formatted Microsoft Word files, rather than just ASCII files, as well as illustrations. Other writers sent their articles either by modem, on floppy disk or as hard copy. (For suggestions on preparing copy for page layout, see "Getting the text in shape" on page 9). In all cases, managing editor Linnea Dayton prepared the final Word file for placement in PageMaker. Working with John on his monthly article, which later became a fourth column called "Design Workshop," was more immediate, since he lived and worked locally. Because his articles featured mostly graphics and only a small amount of text, he would write and design within the newsletter's page format and provide a PageMaker layout as well as a Word file for editing.

Producing the newsletter

John Odam laid out the first two issues of the newsletter, training Martha Siebert, The Gosney Company's production designer, to take over the job of fitting articles and graphics into his design. By the March 1989 issue, Martha was doing the layout on her own, with Odam providing a final design check and suggestions. She started with the PageMaker templates and simply performed a Save As to rename each for the current issue, removed the previous text, and then added the new. It worked best to break the newsletter into units of one to four pages, depending on the length of each article.

For each article and column, Martha received clean, edited text in Microsoft Word, along with a page imposition (where in the newsletter the article or column would fall) and the graphics. Some graphics were in the form of EPS files, and some were bitmapped or PICT files, either from a paint-style application or screen dumps designed to show an application's interface or a particular function in use. Occasionally there were TIFFs produced by image-editing software. The screen dumps were either supplied by the author or were created in-house by using an application file and a desk accessory, either Camera or Capture.

Finding the numbers

Although most of the bulleted numbers in the Zapf Dingbats font can be found through Key Caps, the desk accessory that displays a picture of the keyboard and the locations of lowercase, uppercase, Option and Option-Shift characters, some require sequences of key combinations that aren't displayed.

❶ Option-d	① Option-u
❷ Option-w	② Option-=
❸ Option-Shift-p	③ Option-Shift-'
❹ Option-p	④ Option-Shift-o
❺ Option-b	⑤ Option-5
❻ Option-9	⑥ Option-Shift-=
❼ Option-0	⑦ Option-,
❽ Option-z	⑧ Option-.
❾ Option-'	⑨ Option-y
❿ Option-o	⑩ Option-m

❶ Option-space	① Option-Shift-/
❷ Option-' Shift-a	② Option-1
❸ Option-n Shift-a	③ Option-l
❹ Option-n Shift-o	④ Option-v
❺ Option-Shift-q	⑤ Option-f
❻ Option-q	⑥ Option-x
❼ Option-hyphen	⑦ Option-j
❽ Option-Shift-hyphen	⑧ Option-\
❾ Option-[	⑨ Option-Shift-\
❿ Option-Shift-[	⑩ Option-;

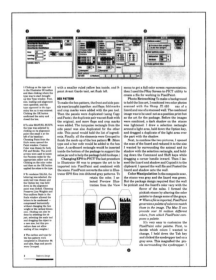 

Figure 8. Designing for flexibility. A strong but flexible design made it possible to fit graphics and text together in a coherent and visually pleasing way.

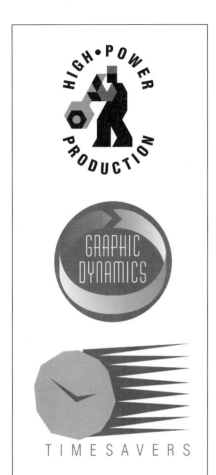

Figure 9. Highlighting themes with graphic symbols. Small one-color symbols were created in FreeHand to highlight subject themes covered in the newsletter. These were composed of screen tints and printed in blue over the 20 percent screen used as a page background.

Some of the articles required illustrations produced by traditional graphic arts processes — for example, four-color separations of slides. For other articles, especially articles about projects produced on IBM PC or PC-compatible systems, using traditional camera processes to photograph the final printed piece or even a printed screen dump was more efficient than trying to deal with file transfers from one platform to another. In these cases, the traditional processes were used.

Siebert relied on her own judgment and design sense to make the text and graphics for each article fit into the allotted space. As the layout for each article fell into place, Siebert and Dayton worked together in front of the computer screen to resize graphics and further edit text to gain space or to resolve loose or tight lines and widows (short lines of text that are visually bothersome). ▌ *To loosen a tight line or fix a widow, you can try adding a discretionary hyphen (Command - hyphen) to break the last word in the line, use PageMaker's kerning function (Command-Option-Delete) to add small increments of space between words in the line until the last word kicks down into the next line, or, if both of those strategies fail, rewrite the text to solve the problem. To tighten up the text, try breaking the last word in the line above the loose line, use Command-Delete to tighten kerning, or, once again, rewrite. Rewriting to shorten often has the salutary effect of making the copy even tighter and more concise.*

Switching to four-color

The newsletter proved so successful during its first year that Dynamic Graphics decided to produce the 1990 issues with eight pages in four-color and eight in two-color. The switch to color required John Odam to redo the column icons and other symbols. He made sure that the colors he chose would also look good when printed in black-and-white, as each symbol might sometimes fall on a color page and sometimes not (Figure 10). The one-color symbols used at the back of the newsletter were also changed to four-color.

Since the newsletter was undergoing major changes at this point, Odam also made further refinements to its overall design. To allow a more flexible layout of the cover page, the nameplate was shifted from the top center to the top right. The script type on the nameplate was made a bit thinner and the gray-tone shadow was changed with each issue to match one of the colors in the art featured on the cover. The same color was also used on the bar that headed each "In This Issue" block, which was also redesigned slightly. John decided to build in more flexibility for the cover page by allowing the shape and placement of "In This Issue" to vary from month to month (Figure 11).

The body text was changed to Adobe's Century Expanded type because John felt the Expanded version of Century was more refined and provided a nicer "color" or copy texture to the page. And despite its name, Century Expanded is slightly more condensed than New Century Schoolbook, so more text fits on each page. ▌ *Century Expanded doesn't include a bold style, but when bold is needed New Century Schoolbook bold can be specified.*

To provide more contrast between the captions and the body text, the captions were changed from 7/8.5 New Century Schoolbook to a sans-serif font, 8/8.5 Helvetica Condensed Light. Article titles were changed from Bodoni to Century Expanded and the initial cap was changed from Bodoni to 84-point Helvetica Condensed Light Bold.

Four-color separations

During the newsletter's first year the editing, design, layout and film production were all handled by The Gosney Company/Verbum team. Siebert worked directly with Central Graphics in San Diego, a well-staffed service bureau and a founding member of the Professional PostScript Alliance (PPA), an association of service bureaus that support the PostScript language. PPA has worked closely with Adobe Systems, Inc. to produce and distribute their Macintosh screen fonts using the NFNT resources, designed to prevent font-numbering conflicts that occurred under the original font-numbering scheme. Siebert produced laser proofs of separations before sending finished PageMaker documents to Central for output on a Linotronic L-300. The laser proofs showed, for example, whether reverse type and windows for photos had knocked out of all four separations. ∎ *In order to make sure that type knocks out of all four-color separations, it's necessary to check Knockouts in the Aldus Print Options dialog box (accessed by choosing Options in the Print dialog box) before printing the PostScript file to disk for separations.* ∎ *When a rectangle in a PageMaker layout is filled with Black, the window shows up only on the Black layer when separations are run. However, designating the window as Registration (from the Colors menu) makes it print on all separations.*

The final film was sent to East Peoria where Step-By-Step art director Mike Hammer and associate art director Michael Ulrich worked with the printer. A set of bluelines and Color Keys was always sent to the San Diego group for approval and any last-minute corrections.

Transfer of layout and production to Peoria

Shortly before the newsletter switched from two colors to four, a transition was made to transfer the output process to East Peoria, although the first two four-color issues were output in San Diego. A second production artist in San Diego, freelance designer and writer Janet Ashford, took on the job of laying out several of the later issues, freeing Siebert to pursue other work at Verbum. In East Peoria, Michael Ulrich supervised production of film, which was done by Input/Output, a service bureau in Normal, Illinois.

After 18 issues had been produced, layout of the newsletter was also moved to the Step-By-Step group in East Peoria, where managing editor Catharine Fishel provided editorial support for Linnea Dayton and assumed responsibility for last-minute editing for fit and widow control. Both Michael Ulrich and the staff at Input/Output were more experienced and comfortable working with Quark XPress than with PageMaker, so the decision was made to switch

Figure 10. Looking good in both color and black-and-white. When *Step-By-Step Electronic Design* switched to eight pages of full color, the column icons that had been created in FreeHand were changed from two-color illustrations to four-color process graphics. But since the icons would sometimes fall on black-and-white pages, they had to look good in monochrome also. The "Design Workshop" icon shown above was developed later, when John Odam's monthly graphic design article became a column.

The icons for the "Calendar," "Get Info" and "Resources" columns (shown from top to bottom) were also redone in color, and their black-and-white versions were revised.

Figure 12. Making the cover more flexible. When the newsletter went from two-color to four-color, other changes were implemented as well. To provide more opportunity for variety in the cover design, the nameplate was moved to the upper right corner and the "In This Issue" was allowed to vary in position and size, as shown in the comps above, which were submitted to Dynamic Graphics for approval.

Figure 13. Changing colors. The switch to four-color also provided an opportunity to change the color scheme. Buff and gray colors were created to highlight features that had previously been printed in blue. The front and back pages of the February 1990 issue (at right) show the implementation of design changes.

programs. Ulrich constructed a template in XPress based on the master elements, styles, letter spacing and word spacing that had been used in the PageMaker issues.

In retrospect

After the first four months of publication, the newsletter had won an award in the Newsletter Awards Competition sponsored by the Newsletter Clearinghouse. After a year, it had a growing readership of 7500 subscribers. All participants in the project had grown comfortable with working "long distance" and with comparing the cost and effort involved in using electronic versus traditional methods of production — and reverting to the latter when it made sense. When the transfer of layout and production was completed after the first year and a half of publication of the newsletter, Dynamic Graphics expressed pride and confidence in a strong product.

PORTFOLIO

The *Gosney Company/*Verbum *team*

"We use Macintosh systems in developing publications, including Verbum magazine and the Verbum Book Series, of course. We also produce advertising programs, collateral materials and more recently, interactive multimedia projects. One of the most important concepts in our work is 'synergy.' In one sense, this means to use the full complement of electronic tools available, combining the use of several programs in the development of a finished design or illustration. We try to use the computer's unique capabilities to achieve something fresh. In many cases, a project will consist of several dynamic elements — a logo, design elements, a background pattern, a scanned photo — that have been planned from the outset for possible use in several forms, such as grayscale, color, 2D or 3D, print or animation. Synergy also means teamwork, and we encourage collaboration from concept through completion of projects, which is often greatly facilitated by the computer tools."

Pictured above: production manager Martha Siebert, managing editor Linnea Dayton, creative director Michael Gosney, art director John Odam, (not pictured: art director Jack Davis).

This full-page **ad for a planetarium industry magazine,** produced with PageMaker 4.0, included a small digital halftone and an illustration with a gray ramp that was developed using Swivel 3D Professional and Adobe Photoshop. The finished ad was output on resin-coated paper with 85-line screen halftones for the photo and illustration. Art directed by Jack Davis.

The **Reidy O'Neil's brochure** is a four-color piece designed with Page-Maker 4.0. The FreeHand logo was placed in the PageMaker file. To produce a comp, color photocopies were scanned, and the scans were touched up in Adobe PhotoShop. Background colors were added in Page-Maker. The file was output on a Tektronix 4693D color thermal printer with a Tektronix Phaser PS (a PostScript RIP) at 80 percent to show the bleed on the comp. Final film, including process screens for the background colors, was output on a Linotronic L-300 imagesetter. The four-color subjects were separated traditionally and stripped by the printer. Art directed and designed by Jack Davis; logo designed by John Odam.

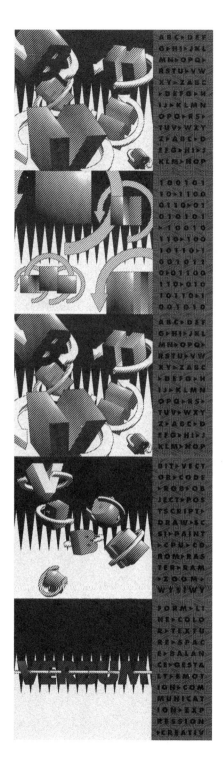

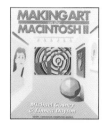

Making Art on the Macintosh II is a 336-page book produced with Page-Maker 3.0 and output on resin-coated paper. Grayscale images were output as negatives and stripped in place by the printer. The cover was designed and output to film using FreeHand, incorporating elements produced using PixelPaint, MacDraw II, Pro 3D and Adobe Illustrator. Large outside margins provided room for spot illustrations and "TIP" boxes created in Adobe Illustrator and placed as EPS files. The margins also allowed for extended illustrations, such as screen dumps, and captions. Art directed by John Odam.

Interactive presentations such as this **HyperCard stack developed for Toshiba** for CD-ROM demo kiosks in Tokyo record stores require page design of a slightly different sort than for printed materials. HyperCard, rather than PageMaker, Quark-XPress or some other page layout program, provided the environment in which the components — new Adobe fonts, PostScript patterns and other Macintosh graphic elements — were assembled for the screen designs. Art directed by Jack Davis.

The **Verbum moving announcement**, a 5 x 14-inch three-fold self-mailer included three-dimensional lettering and arrows created in Swivel 3D Professional. The letters were converted to TIFF files, imported into PageMaker and given a coarse line screen through the Image Control dialog box. The ethnic pattern to the right is from Adobe's Collector's Edition and was edited with Illustrator. The type above the pattern was set in PageMaker. Designed by Jack Davis.

Gallery

The following pages showcase exemplary electronic page design samples from leading designers whose works represent not only excellent design, but effective and innovative use of the electronic tools.

Reactor

Louis Fishauf is creative director of Reactor Art & Design Ltd., a graphic design and illustration firm in Toronto, Canada. He was formerly editorial art direc-tor for Saturday Night, T.O., Executive, The City, Chatelaine and Golf Commentator *magazines.*

Fun With Computers! was designed in Illustrator 88. The pattern in the blue lefthand portion of the poster was created as a custom pattern tile with a transparent background. The pattern could then be tried out over a background of any color. The pattern fill in the yellow ovals behind the "FUN" lettering was from Adobe's Collector's Edition 2, colored yellow. The image of the two scientists was scanned from a 1940s magazine ad with a ScanMan handheld scanner and blown up to show the halftone dot screen. The scan was saved in EPS format so that it could be incorporated into the Illustrator file for the poster.

The equipment list at **Surfer** includes about 30 Macintosh SE's and more than 10 other Macs of various sorts. PageMaker is used for layout, Adobe Illustrator for drawing and some lettering, FreeHand for most titles, Swivel 3D for 3D effects and Microsoft Word for text. Except for some Emigré faces, the magazine staff uses exclusively Adobe fonts — about 200 faces on a 40 MB hard disk used as a font server. A modem is used for remote access — from Hawaii, for instance, during the contest season.

Surfer *magazine*

Jeff Girard is art director of Surfer *magazine and a principal of Victoria Street Graphic Design. A 1980 graduate of Cal Poly, San Luis Obispo, in Graphic Communications, Girard has been designing on the Macintosh since 1984. When he and others started building Surfer magazine on the Mac in 1987, the approach was to avoid computer "tricks" and make a magazine that looked conventionally produced. He says few people seemed to notice the change when the magazine went to desktop publishing. Now the art staff feel freer to experiment with layouts.*

The display typography for **The Boys** is the result of a technical glitch. Jeff Girard was using an outdated version of FreeHand to build the titles in the layout. The Emigré fonts used in the layout are type 3, which wouldn't export correctly. After several tries, he gave up, printed the titles directly out of Free-Hand, distressed them on a photocopier and scanned and placed TIFFs. The effect worked well with the informal layout for the article, which dealt with hot young surfers who were referred to by their nicknames.

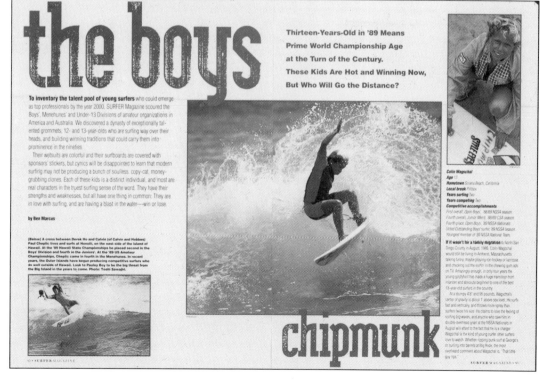

In the opening spread of this **Top 30** article that analyzes the new rankings of the top surfers in the world, the images were assembled on the Scitex Response system, and a mask was created to ghost the separation values in the number 30 back to 25 percent of their normal weight. An offset shadow created the overlay effect.

Jeff Girard got his start at *Surfer* in 1980 doing hand-lettered titles and illustration. Unique typographic design such as the lettering in **The Surf Machine**, done by Girard and Mark Sansom to open an article about state-of-the-art training techniques, was constructed in Adobe Illustrator.

Frankfurt Gips Balkind

Internationally recognized as an innovator in the industry, Frankfurt Gips Balkind is a communications agency formed in 1972 and offering a full range of communications services, with offices in New York and Los Angeles and a public relations affiliate in Washington, D.C. A Network of more than 50 Macintosh computers links the staff of 70 in the administrative, design and electronic paste-up divisions. Stephen O. Frankfurt is a member of the Advertising Hall of Fame. Philip Gips has been named one of the 25 Designers of the Decade by Idea *magazine. Aubrey Balkind has a national reputation in marketing consultation and design management.*

These pages by Frankfurt Gips Balkind were part of the marketing campaign for the syndication of **The Cosby Show** for Viacom Enterprises. QuarkXPress, Type Align, FreeHand and other packages were used to prepare ad slicks, slides, schedules and on-air promotions so that local stations could just drop in their station call letters and logo. The computer allowed a smooth linear progression from comps to final mechanicals.

Why? is an annual report for Time Warner. The challenge here was to create a totally new kind of annual report to reflect the totally new company created by the merger of Time Inc. and Warner Communications. Creative directors Aubrey Balkind and Kent Hunter, along with designer Riki Sethiadi, used FreeHand to design "factoids" — circles, squares and triangles with type that's curved, sideways and vertical. The goal was to create a visual vocabulary in which words and images became interchangeable.

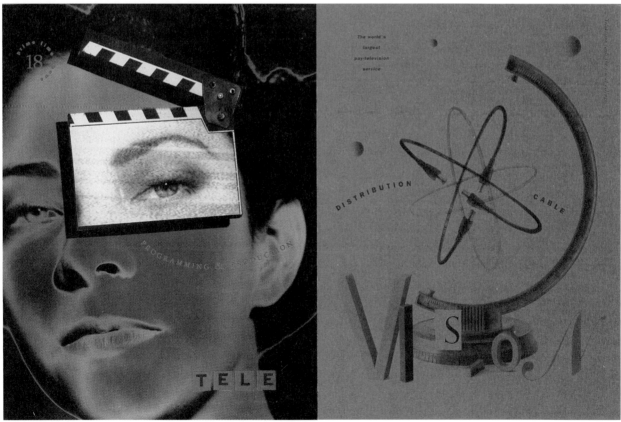

Frankfurt Gips Balkind

MCI World is a newsletter created for MCI communications. It was cited in a desktop publishing awards program for employing the spontaneity available with electronic design techniques without overdoing it. Designer Kin Yuen of Frankfurt Gips Balkind used Illustrator 88, FreeHand, PixelPaint and Image Studio to design the page.

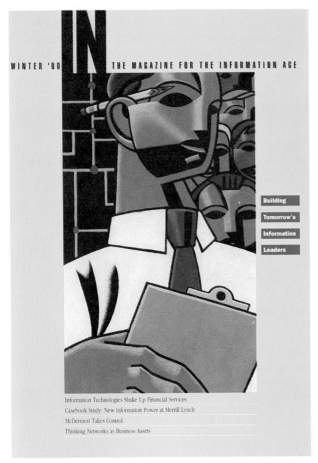

The design for **IN: The Magazine for the Information Age** was also created for MCI Communications. Danielle Joffe of Frankfurt Gips Balkind used Adobe Illustrator and QuarkXPress to balance photography and four-color art in an elegant and understated layout.

Emigré Graphics

Rudy VanderLans is a graphic designer based in Berkeley, California and is also publisher of Emigré *magazine. Zuzana Licko is a font designer whose Emigré electronic fonts are used worldwide. John Weber is a freelance illustrator specializing in electronic art tools.*

In this spread from *Emigré 11* magazine, the left page was designed by Rudy VanderLans in Ready,Set, Go 4.0. All typefaces used on the page were created in Fontographer by Zuzana Licko. The right page was designed by John Weber in FreeHand.

The cover of *Emigré 14* was designed by Rudy VanderLans. The "heritage" bitmapped type treatment was produced with FullPaint.

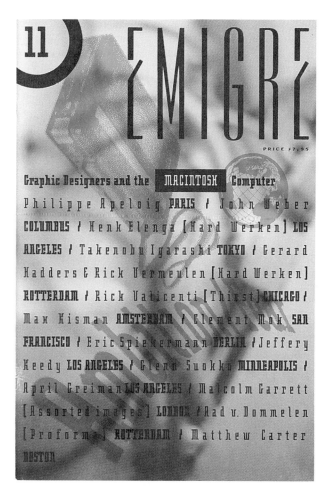

This **spread from Verbum 3.2,** produced with PageMaker 3.01, was designed with low-resolution color scans of the images, which were separated traditionally. The "4D Gallery" mark and the folio marks were produced with Aldus FreeHand by John Odam.

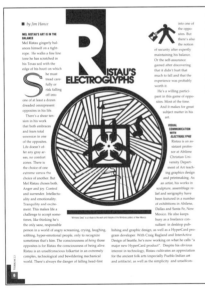

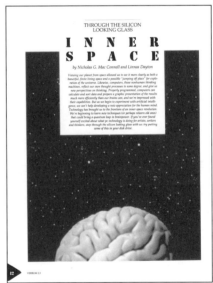

The **Ristau's Electro-glyphs title page** from *Verbum 2.2,* developed in Page-Maker, includes several elements rendered with Adobe Illustrator, including the folio mark, the large "R" and the iconic forms.

The **cover of Verbum 2.2** was produced on a Mac II with Adobe Illustrator 88 by Jack Davis and fashion designer Lisa King, who contributed the cut-out clothes. The photograph of the model was scanned on a Sharp JX450 scanner and re-touched in ImageStudio. The cover was separated through Illustrator, with a only a few problems, primarily caused by the halftone element.

The **Inner Space title page** from *Verbum 2.3* was produced with PageMaker and a grayscale video scan of a brain model. The space background and stars were created with ImageStudio and the finished illustration was placed as a TIFF file in PageMaker.

Verbum *magazine*

Verbum has been a showcase of desktop design and production since its first Macintosh/LaserWriter/PageMaker edition in the fall of 1986. Art director John Odam, artist/graphics editor Jack Davis and publisher Michael Gosney work to make each newly designed issue of the quarterly "Journal of Personal Computer Aesthetics" a kind of litmus test for cutting-edge dektop publishing technology, showing subscribers what is possible with each new generation of software.

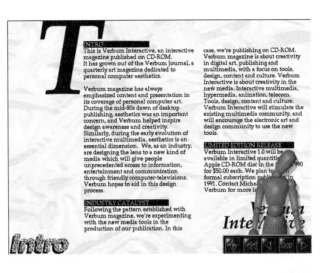

Designing interactive media has many parallels to print design. **Verbum Interactive,** a CD-ROM-based multimedia magazine, was developed with Macro-Mind Director 2.0 on a Mac II with 5 MB of RAM. This Intro screen includes the use of Adobe PostScript patterns and elements created with Studio 8 and LetraStudio. The puppet was rendered in Swivel 3D and animated in Director. Art directed by Jack Davis.

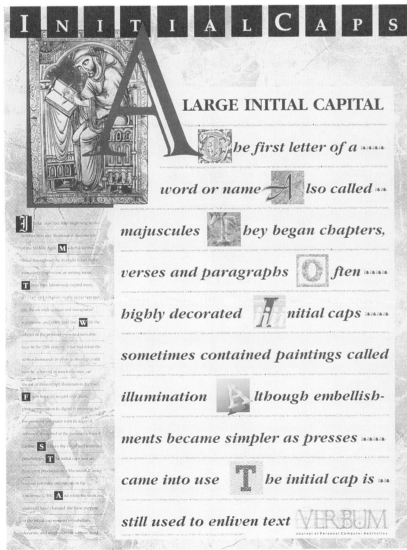

The **Initial Caps poster** by Jack Davis and Susan Merritt, vice president and senior designer at CWA, Inc. in San Diego, used scanned images and textures manipulated with ImageStudio in combination with PostScript letterforms created in Illustrator. The poster itself was laid out and typeset in PageMaker, and spot color separations were generated from within the program. Resin-coated paper output from the Linotronic L-300 was enlarged with a process camera to make final poster-size negatives.

This **Verbum flyer** by Jack Davis was assembled and printed in PageMaker 4.0. The color montage was designed in Adobe Photoshop by excerpting parts from various bitmapped illustrations. The curved lines dividing the various pieces are bitmapped also, but have been anti-aliased in Photoshop for a higher-resolution appearance. The three blocks of type were created in Adobe Illustrator and placed in PageMaker as EPS files. The finished page was separated through Aldus PrePrint software on the Linotronic L-300.

Team Design

of Seattle, Washington provides a range of creative services for corporate identity and image programs, marketing and corporate communications, annual reports and catalogs. They extensively use scanned images, QMS ColorScript output and laser output to create mock-ups used to sell concepts to clients.

These spreads from the **Ackerley Communications, Inc. 1989 Annual Report** was created entirely in PageMaker and FreeHand. Headlines were set in FreeHand and placed into position in PageMaker. All of the financial information was supplied by Ackerley's accountants on disk, which substantially reduced the time required for both layout and revision. In this center spread, all headlines initial caps, maps and illustrations were placed for size and position from FreeHand. The map and illustrations were created in Free-Hand process color, output at 150 lines per inch at 2540 dots per inch resolution as negatives, and supplied to the printer for stripping. The fill for the map was a scanned texture that was colored and inserted into the outline of the United States as a Paste Inside image. The stair illustration was created using the Blend command, which not only provided the appropriate number of stair steps but created the graduated color as well.

SU Today was a fundraising newsletter that targeted alumni of Seattle Pacific University. It was created in PageMaker. The graphs that appear throughout were created in FreeHand from pencil sketches that were scanned in and redrawn. The newsletter was output as paper positives and pasted up on boards. The graphs were output as separated negatives and stripped in by the printer.

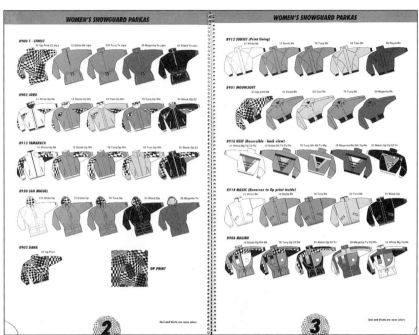

The **1990 Raven Sales Brochure** was created in FreeHand and PageMaker. Clothing was scanned from pencil sketches supplied by the client and redrawn in Free-Hand, where each item was cloned and moved a specified distance with the Move command. Each set was then placed in PageMaker, where headlines were added. Lino output was scanned into a Scitex system, where the clothing was colored and pattens were inserted.

The **Metropolitan Federal Savings and Loan Association of Seattle Annual Report** layout was created in PageMaker. The borders for the color photographs were created in FreeHand, rotated, exported and then placed in position.

The **U.S. Bank Financial Fitness** program was designed to generate enthusiasm among clients and employees for a new banking product. A scan of the illustration was used for size and position. In color versions the background color gradation was done in FreeHand and stripped in by the Printer. To make the gradation, two overlapping boxes with opposing yellow and magenta gradations were produced and then Overprint was selected for each ink color.

Team Design

The **Weyerhaeuser Forest Products 1989 Annual Report** was designed primarily as a communication vehicle to Weyerhaeuser's employees. It was laid out entirely in PageMaker. Keylines were used to show printer placement of background areas of ink.

The **Weyerhaeuser Paper Company 1989 Annual Report** was a long-run, high-visibility piece designed to relay information about the company and to showcase its various paper products. All illustrations were created by hand. To maintain a timely schedule and still allow the illustrators maximum time to complete their illustrations, their roughs were scanned in and placed in the PageMaker layout, allowing the designer to work independently. The scanned-in illustrations were output as a separate overlay (by assigning a different color to them) and used as size and position elements in the final pasteup.

The graphs shown in this spread were created in Persuasion and placed in FreeHand, where they were altered. The designer specified process colors that were appropriate to the color palette for the overall piece. They were output as film negatives and stripped in by the printer.

Beach Culture *magazine*

Beach Culture *magazine was launched in 1989, bringing beach, fashion, design and cultural trends to a national audience, primarily on the two coasts. Art director/designer David Carson oversees the Macintosh-based design and production of the magazine, working closely with a small staff. Beach Culture is produced with PageMaker, and most design elements are created with Adobe Illustrator.*

On this page, scanned photos were used in the design process and as position guides for traditionally stripped halftones and color separations. Carson combines computer-generated graphics and type output on the laser printer with traditional cut-and-paste mockups: He feels that the computer can be limiting when it comes to thinking in terms of overlaid imagery. But once he has developed the design, his production artists execute it totally on the Macintosh.

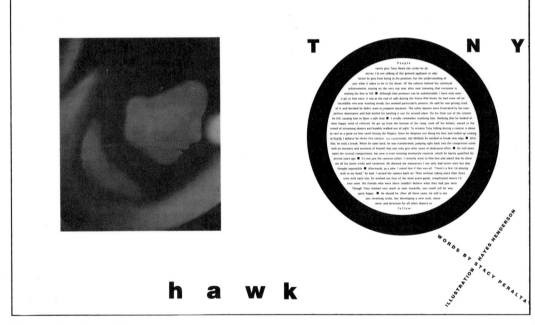

The cover logotype for *Beach Culture* is an Emigré font that has been modified to make it bolder. In the process of stretching the type in Adobe Illustrator, certain irregularities in the thick and thin elements occurred, which Carson liked and so retained for the final treatment. He sees the mistakes and unexpected results brought about by the computer as quite stimulating in the design process.

This spread is evidence of Carson's recent design direction for *Beach Culture*. Whereas early issues used contemporary fonts from sources such as Emigré along with other trendy elements, he now tries to work more imaginatively with basic fonts and simpler forms.

The **Robert Duvall cover** of the March-April 1990 issue of *SMART* magazine was designed by Roger Black. The photo was scanned and the color image brought onto the cover layout for design and comping. The fashion sticker at the bottom right, designed in Illustrator 88 and imported into Quark-XPress, provided a way to keep the cover bold and simple, but still announce another interesting story. From the beginning the page was designed in color and the options for various sizes of image and colors of type could be seen quickly. A QMS Color-Script print gave the editor a good idea of what the final cover would look like.

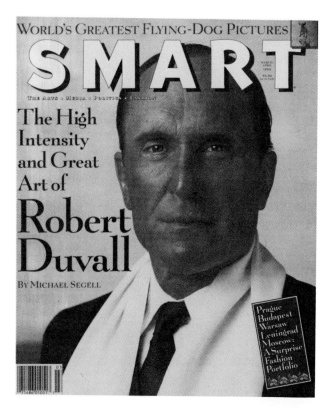

SMART *magazine*

Design director Roger Black originated SMART magazine, including its cover, as a desktop publication. The logotype was set in a special typeface redrawn from the Lucian face; by David Berlow of The Font Bureau used Fontographer to make the conversion. Art director Rhonda Rubinstein uses Black's QuarkXPress templates to lay out each issue.

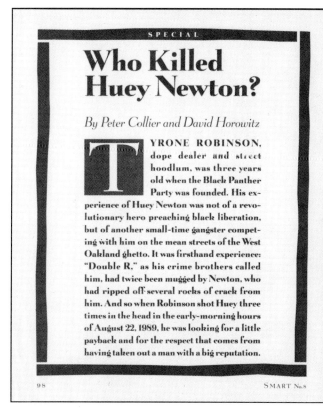

The title page for the **Who Killed Huey Newton?** article was designed in QuarkXPress. The rough border rules were created to look as though they were cheaply and quickly hand-cut (which they were initially going to be), but were easier to do in FreeHand on the Mac.

GALLERY

Skolos/Wedell, Inc.

Nancy Skolos received her B.F.A. degree from the Cranbrook Academy of Art in 1977 and her MFA from Yale University's School of Art and Architecture in 1979. Thomas Wedell received a B.F.A. from the University of Michigan in 1973 and studied photography at Cranbrook. They established their design and photography practice in Boston in 1980. they integrate techniques of graphic collage, multiple exposures and graduated papers to create three-dimensional, often surreal images. The studio's posters are in the graphic design collections of the Museum of Modern Art and the Metropolitan Museum of Art. Clients include Digital Equipment Corporation, James River Corporation and others.

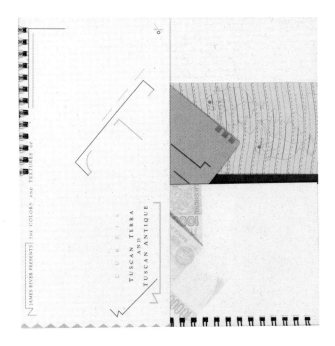

The **Curtis Tuscan Terra and Tuscan Antique** paper samples brochure includes a diversity of page sizes and shapes and wire-o binding in several directions, to engage the viewer both visually and mechanically. FreeHand's ability to manipulate type freely, clone images and layer objects made it the ideal for page layout for this project.

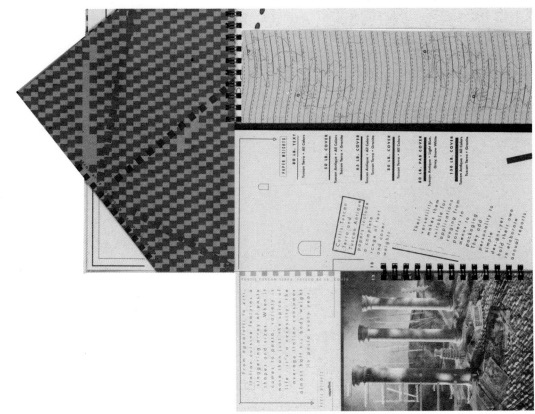

The Skolos/Wedell **holiday card** was created in FreeHand on a Mac IIcx to serve as a both a greeting and a promotional piece to current and potential clients. FreeHand's ability to draw and place rules precisely, provide gradations and arrange objects in layers made the piece much less expensive than it would have been with traditional typesetting and production methods.

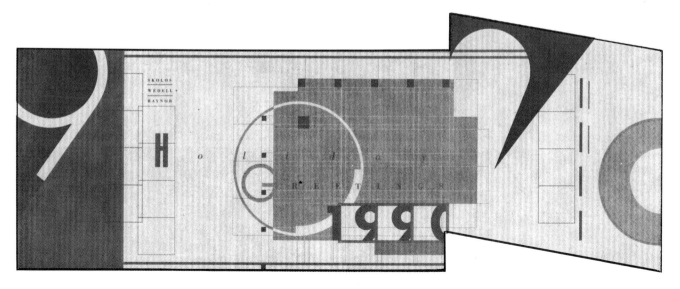

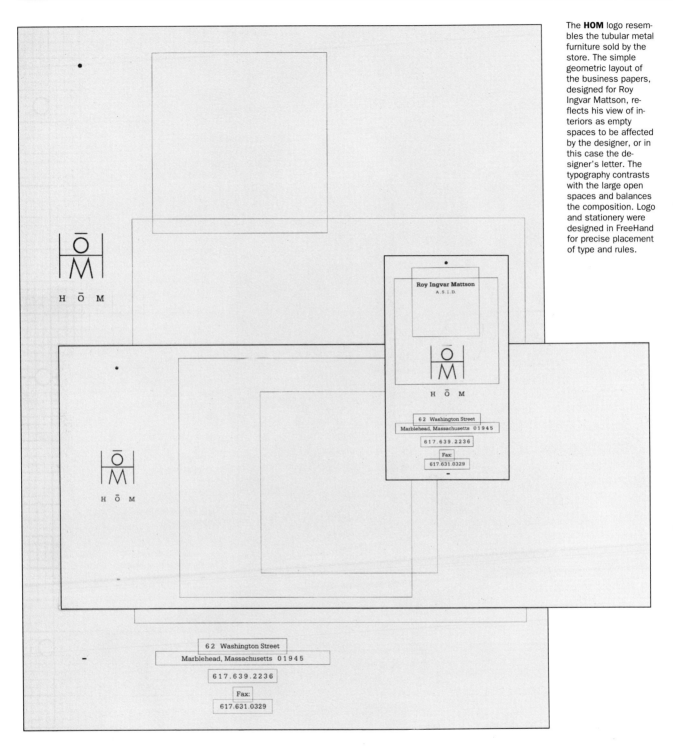

The **HOM** logo resembles the tubular metal furniture sold by the store. The simple geometric layout of the business papers, designed for Roy Ingvar Mattson, reflects his view of interiors as empty spaces to be affected by the designer, or in this case the designer's letter. The typography contrasts with the large open spaces and balances the composition. Logo and stationery were designed in FreeHand for precise placement of type and rules.

Skolos/Wedell, Inc.

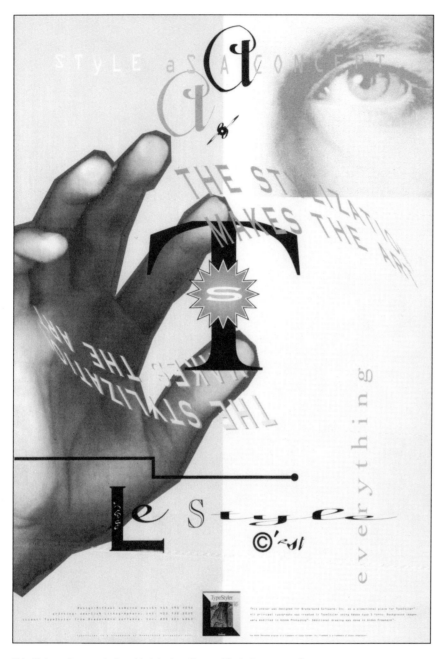

Michael Osborne Design, Inc.
_Michael Osborne graduated with honors
from Art Center College of Design in 1978.
In addition to being President and Creative
Director of San Francisco–based Michael
Osborne Design, Inc., which he established
in 1981, he is on the faculty at University of
California, Berkeley and lectures at other
California universities. His design firm, with
a staff of 12, specializes in package de-
sign, corporate identity and print collateral
materials for such clients as the Ansel
Adams Gallery, Bank of America, Dreyer's
Grand Ice Cream, Hiram Walker Inc., Levi
Strauss & Co., Porsche Cars North America,
Inc. and Stanford University._

This **Style** poster was designed to introduce the graphic design community
to TypeStyler by Brøderbund Software, Inc. — to show off the program's
type-handling abilities to an audience that possibly wasn't aware of the
program's existence. All of the typography except the copy along the bottom,
was done in TypeStyler, and the page was saved as an EPS file. The eye in
the upper right corner was scanned from a photo as a 300 dpi dithered
halftone. The hand was scanned directly (by placing one hand on the
scanner and using fill light) as a grayscale TIFF file. Both images were
touched up and colored in Photoshop and saved as EPS files. The green left
half of the poster, which was used as a mask to block out some of the
rough edges of the hand image, along with the type along the bottom was
done in FreeHand. The TypeStyler EPS file was placed in this FreeHand file,
and the whole thing was saved as an EPS. All of the EPS files were then
combined and scaled as necessary in QuarkXPress 2.12 and separated
directly to negative film on a Linotronic L-500.

Juan Thomassie

is a freelance artist and designer who uses FreeHand for most of his work. Formerly an informational graphics specialist for USA Today, *where he helped established the Macintosh-based computer graphics department, he now works for the* Los Angeles Times. *He graduated from Louisiana State University's School of Art and is a visiting faculty member at the Poynter Institute for Media Studies in St. Petersburg, Florida, where he teaches workshops for news artists using the Macintosh.*

The entire five-column layout for **Keeping 987 in Flying Condition** for *USA Today* was done with Free-Hand 2.02 on a Macintosh IIx with a 19-inch SuperMac color monitor. The three illustrations, arrows and position windows for the three photos were drawn with the combination tool. Illustrations, arrows and background box have graduated fills. Details of the plane's interior were Pasted Inside of the jagged, cutaway shapes provided by clipping paths.

Keeping 987 in flying condition

Jet No. 987, a 24-year-old Boeing 727-100, is completing five weeks of routine "heavy maintenance" at an American Airlines base in Tulsa. Some of the work is the result of FAA orders to modify aging aircraft. The work, at a cost of $4 million, includes:

STRUCTURE
- Landing gear inspected, new seals installed, reassembled. Jet has had four complete landing gear changes over its life.
- Corroded steel frame around the nose wheel well replaced.
- Complete internal inspection of wings. Flaps and ailerons removed.
- Jet has been through five structural life improvement programs, involving 88 modifications, since 1972 to prevent fatigue, fix corrosion and extend aircraft life.

SYSTEMS
- Navigation equipment, radios and other avionics pulled from cockpit, inspected and repaired, replaced.
- Autopilot in tail system rewired.
- Worn pivot bushings and metal sleeves for moving parts replaced.
- Fuel bladders in wings removed, inspected and overhauled if needed.
- All hydraulic systems checked for wear.

CABIN
- Interior removed, 115 seats overhauled and then reinstalled.
- Previous modifications include emergency lighting, fire-resistant fabric, new and improved galleys, ovens and coffee makers.

ENGINES
- No. 2 engine over the tail, due for overhaul, is replaced. Engine will be taken apart, components repaired or replaced, tested, then installed on another airplane.
- Other two engines on sides of jet serviced and remounted. 987 has had 40 Pratt & Whitney JT8D engines over its life.

SKIN
- Paint stripped and skin inspected for cracks visually and with sound waves and electric current.
- Aluminum doublers, or patches, placed over small cracks. Ends of cracks drilled to prevent growth.
- Belly skin under cockpit replaced, using about 1,500 fasteners. Belly skin under cargo bay, subject to corrosion from leaks, replaced about four years ago.

Many lap joints on older 727s must be repaired to prevent separation of cold-bonded skin, a discontinued manufacturing process.
- All three rows of flat, countersunk rivets removed.
- Lap joint pulled apart, cleaned, inspected and resealed.
- Top row of rivets replaced with button-head rivets which are less aerodynamic but also less likely to cause skin cracks.

Aluminum skin

Aircraft frame

Button-head rivet

Countersunk rivet

Lap joint

Photo by Steve Jennings

Douglas Demofsky
is a freelance graphic artist and art director in Vancouver, Canada. He uses the Macintosh to produce high-profile promotional materials for clients, including the Vancouver Symphony and Opera.

The **Vancouver Opera posters** were created in FreeHand for Studio Carré-Vert in celebration of its 30th anniversary. Linework was scanned and autotraced to produce closed-path elements that were used as clipping paths to contain various color blends. The large size of the process separations (10.5 x 21 inches) proved a test of the separation capabilities of the Linotronic L-300 imagesetter.

The **invitation** to a Vancouver arts organization party was created by Douglas Demofsky using Illustrator 88. Each panel has a background pattern created from different CMYK elements that were duplicated and tiled. The subtle colors would have been difficult and expensive to reproduce with traditional methods.

Pepe Moreno

Innovative visual storyteller Pepe Moreno gained his early reputation as a designer, animator and punk rock musician. He was one of the first comics artists to realize the enormous potential of the Macintosh computer for illustration and color separation.

©1990 DC Comics Inc.

Batman: Digital Justice is a computer-generated graphic novel for DC Comics. It was put together using QuarkXPress, FreeHand, Illustrator 88, Pro3D, Super 3D, ImageStudio, Studio 8, Photoshop and a custom comic book font by David Cody on a Mac II with 8 MB of RAM and a 19-inch Radius monitor with a 24-bit color card. The page separations were printed on positive film at 135 lines per inch on an Agfa Compugraphic imagesetter.

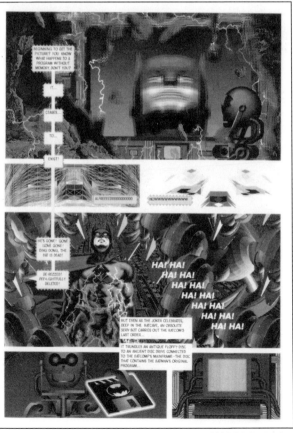

©1990 DC Comics Inc.

WhaleSong, Inc.

The underlying philosophy of WhaleSong's publications is "high tech, soft touch" — the higher the technology, the greater the need for the human touch. Computers used to produce the landmark WhaleSong coffee table book were Mac IIs. The Barneyscan V-3 was used to scan 35mm color images. Color manipulation and separation were done with Photoshop. Comps of the PageMaker 3.02CE layout were done on the QMS ColorScript 100 printer. Proofing of the Linotronic L-300 separations at 2540 dpi and 150 lpi was done on DuPont's Cromacheck overlay proofing materials using a NuArc printer.

The photo for the **Whales of the Pacific** spread from the book *WhaleSong* was reproduced as a Crosfield drum scan of an 8 x 10-inch Ektachrome transparency of the original painting. The technician at the color house repeatedly "stumbled" on this image — even after three tries he couldn't get it right. But deadlines forced using the best of the three, and some compensation was done during printing. Photoshop would have allowed the necessary brightening and gamma correction to be done easily, but a scanner was lacking. When this edition of *WhaleSong* was in preparation in late 1989, the Sharp JX-450 couldn't handle transparencies well. But the newer JX-600 at 600 dpi could create a beautiful scan of this large transparency. The RGB file would be huge, however, and would require compression of about 20 to 1 to be workable. The image in the lower right corner of the spread was created by tracing from the original painting with Adobe's Streamline, then assembling type and radial fills in FreeHand and finally creating L-300 CMYK separations for the printer to strip in.

Whales of the Pacific

Blue (1): rorqual; baleen; closely related to the Fin whale; largest living thing ever to exist on earth, bigger than 30 elephants, far larger than even the Brotosaurus; hunted only in the 20th century; the future for blue whales is questionable as there may not be enough breeding stock left.

Sperm (2): toothed; hunted extensively in both the 19th and 20th centuries for fine oil, spermaceti and ambergris; can dive to a depth of at least two miles and hold its breath for over an hour; ivory teeth used for scrimshaw; has the largest, most complex brain in the world; may hunt using sonic booms to stun its prey, which are primarily giant squid; the population numbers are relatively safe.

Right (3): baleen; named by whalers because it was the 'right' whale to hunt; the population has been almost exterminated and the future is uncertain; an Arctic cousin, the Bowhead, has baleen up to 14' long and is still legally hunted by the Eskimos.

Humpback (4): baleen; most-studied great whale; one Pacific population migrates annually from Alaskan feeding grounds to warm Hawaiian waters for mating and calving; famous for both acrobatic leaps and extremely complex songs.

Narwhal (5): toothed; twisted 'unicorn horn' on male is really a tooth which is extremely valuable; lives in cold waters around the North Pole.

Pilot (6): toothed; supposedly named because it guided mariners to safe anchorages; occasionally demonstrates still-unexplained mass beachings.

Beluga (7): toothed; its name means "white one" in Russian because of its unique cream-white skin color.

Gray (8): baleen; often hunted from shore stations along the West Coast; called Devil Fish by whalers because of ferocity, these are actually quite gentle whales (unless harpooned); their numbers have been rising.

Orca (9): toothed; common name Killer Whale; will attack, kill and eat great whales and polar bears, however it is gentle with human beings.

This **cover** of the first issue of the *Publish* redesign helps to establish a unique personality for the magazine and to set it apart from other computer magazines by using a conceptual photo and featuring the new bold logo design.

Publish *magazine*

At the time these pages were produced, Publish was being designed and produced on various Macintosh computers, from the Plus to the IIcx, as well as a Compaq DeskPro 386, IBM PC ATs and a PS/2. Sharp and Hewlett-Packard scanners were also used. Software included PageMaker 3.02 Color Extension for design and layout, Microsoft Word for word processing, Adobe Illustrator 88 and Smart Art III for illustration and special type treatments, Free-Hand for headlines, Microphone and Desktop Express for telecommunications, MacLink Plus Translators for file transfer and format conversion, DiskTop for file transfer, Capture for Mac screen capture, and Adobe Separator for color separation.

The design challenge for **Building Your Mac Business** was to tie together a special section of the magazine with several articles on that topic. Related type treatments, formats and tinted backgrounds were used throughout the section. Headline type was Agency Gothic Outline, and initial caps were digitized with Fontographer.

Under the Hood was the cover story for the first redesign issue (see cover above), so a portion of the cover art was silhouetted on the opening page of the feature. The headline, closely tied in with the art, was Trio, digitized with Fontographer.

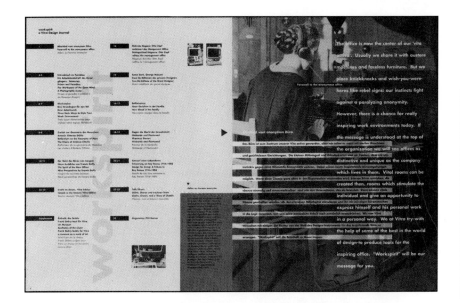

The **Workspirit brochure** was produced for Vitra International, a contract furniture manufacutrer based in Europe. The piece was used as an international marketing tool, communicating the Vitra philosophy on work environments and promoting the firm's ergonomic chairs and other furniture. The text of the brochure is printed in three languages — German, French and English.

The brochure was produced on a Macintosh II using Page-Maker, Adobe Illustrator, ImageStudio and MacPaint. All of the innovative text design was done in Page-Maker. Scanned images, some high- and some low-resolution, were used throughout as design elements.

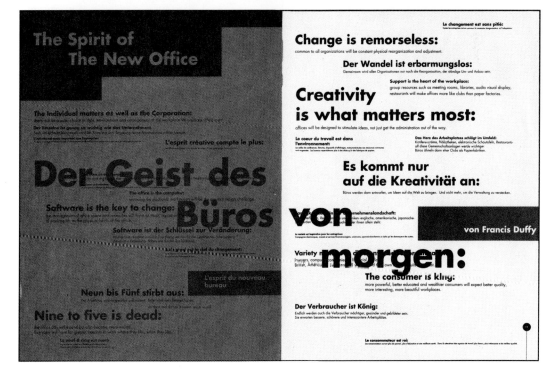

April Greiman

A Los Angeles–based designer whose work in the 1970s and '80s helped to define the West coast "New Wave" style in graphics, architecture and interiors, April Greiman has received many honors for her work for numerous international corporations. She has experimented continously with technology in the design process, working extensively with the Quantel Paintbox and Apple Macintosh.

Resources

This appendix lists hardware, software and other resources of use to artists using electronic page layout programs. The resources are grouped in categories in the following order:

Page Layout Programs

Templates

PostScript Illustration Software

PostScript Clip Art

Paint Programs

Draw Programs

Image-Processing Software

Fonts

Prepress Systems

Utilities, Desk Accessories and INITs

Scanners and Digitizers

Monitors

Color Calibration

Storage Systems

Printers and Imagesetters

Film Recorders

Periodicals

Books

Bulletin Board Services

Communication Software

Page Layout Programs

DesignStudio
Letraset USA
40 Eisenhower Drive
Paramus, NJ 07653
201-845-6100

FrameMaker
Frame Technology Corporation
1010 Rincon Circle
San Jose, CA 95131
408-433-1928

PageMaker
Aldus Corporation
411 First Avenue S.
Seattle, WA 98104
206-622-5500

Personal Press
Silicon Beach Software
9770 Carroll Center Drive
San Diego, CA 92126
619-695-6956

QuarkXPress
Quark, Inc.
300 S. Jackson Street, Suite 100
Denver, CO 80209
800-543-7711

Ready,Set,Go!
Letraset USA
40 Eisenhower Drive
Paramus, NJ 07653
201-845-6100

Ventura Publisher
Xerox Product Support
1301 Ridgeview Drive
Lewisville, TX 75067
800-822-8221

Templates

Desktop Manager Style Sheets
New Riders Publishing
31125 Via Colinas, Suite 902
Westlake Village, CA 91362
818-991-5392

Document Gallery Style Sheets
Micro Publishing
21150 Hawthorne Boulevard, Suite104
Torrance, CA 90503
213-371-5787

Layouts
Starburst Designs
1973 N. Nellis Boulevard, Suite 315
Las Vegas, NV 89115
702-453-3371

PageMaker Portfolio Series
Aldus Corporation
411 First Avenue S.
Seattle, WA 98104
206-622-5500

Page Designs Quick
Par Publishing Company
6355 Topanga Canyon Boulevard
Suite 307
Woodland Hills, CA 91367
818-340-8165

QuarkStyle
Quark, Inc.
300 S. Jackson Street, Suite100
Denver, CO 80209
800-356-9363

Will-Harris Designer Disks
Daniel Will-Harris, Dept. M
PO Box 480265
Los Angeles, CA 90048

PostScript Illustration Software

Adobe Illustrator
Adobe Systems, Inc.
PO Box 7900
Mountain View, CA 94039-7900
800-344-8335

Aldus FreeHand
Aldus Corporation
411 First Avenue S.
Seattle, WA 98104
206-622-5500

Arts & Letters
Computer Support Corporation
15926 Midway Road
Dallas, TX 75244
214-661-8960

Corel Draw
Corel Systems Corporation
1600 Carling Avenue
Ottawa, ON K1Z 8R7 Canada
613-728-8200

GEM Artline
Digital Research, Inc.
70 Garden Court
Monterey, CA 93940
408-649-3896

APPENDIX

Micrografx Designer
Micrografx, Inc.
1303 Arapaho Road
Richardson, TX 75081-1769
800-272-3729

Smart Art, Volumes I, II, III
Emerald City Software
1040 Marsh Road, Suite 110
Menlo Park, CA 94025
415-324-8080

Streamline
Adobe Systems, Inc.
PO Box 7900
Mountain View, CA 94039-7900
800-344-8335

PostScript Clip Art

Adobe Illustrator Collector's Edition
Adobe Systems, Inc.
PO Box 7900
Mountain View, CA 94039-7900
800-344-8335

Artagenix
Devonian International Software
Company
PO Box 2351
Montclair, CA 91763
714-621-0973

ArtRoom
Image Club Graphics, Inc.
1902 11th Street S.E.
Calgary, AB T2G 3G2 Canada
403-262-8008

Arts & Letters
Computer Support Corporation
15926 Midway Road
Dallas, TX 75244
214-661-8960

ClickArt EPS Illustrations
T/Maker Company
1390 Villa Street
Mountain View, CA 94041
415-962-0195

Clip Art Libraries
Stephen & Associates
5205 Kearny Villa Way, Suite 104
San Diego, CA 92123
619-591-5624

Clip Charts
MacroMind, Inc.
410 Townsend Avenue, Suite 408
San Francisco, CA 94107
415-442-0200

Cliptures
Dream Maker Software
4020 Paige Street
Los Angeles, CA 90031
213-221-6436

Designer ClipArt
Micrografx, Inc.
1303 Arapaho Road
Richardson, TX 75081
800-272-3729

DeskTop Art
Dynamic Graphics
6000 N. Forest Park Drive
Peoria, IL 61614
800-255-8800

Digiclips
U-Design, Inc.
201 Ann Street
Hartford, CT 06102
203-278-3648

Digit-Art
Image Club Graphics, Inc.
1902 11th Street S.E.
Calgary, AB T2G 3G2 Canada
403-262-8008

Illustrated Art Backgrounds
ARTfactory
414 Tennessee Plaza, Suite A
Redlands, CA 92373
714-793-7346

Images with Impact
3G Graphics
11410 N.E. 124th Street, Suite 6155
Kirkland, WA 98034
206-823-8198

**Pro-Art Professional
Art Library Trilogy 1**
Multi-Ad Services, Inc.
1720 West Detweiller Drive
Peoria, IL 61615
309-692-11530

PS Portfolio, Spellbinder Art Library
Lexisoft, Inc.
PO Box 5000
Davis, CA 95617-5000
916-758-3630

TextArt
Stone Design Corporation
2425 Teodoro N.W.
Albuquerque, NM 87107
505-345-4800

Totem Graphics
Totem Graphics
5109-A Capitol Boulevard
Tumwater, WA 98501
206-352-1851

Type Foundry
U-Design, Inc.
201 Ann Street
Hartford, CT 06102
203-278-3648

Vivid Impressions
Casady & Greene, Inc.
26080 Carmel Rancho Boulevard
Suite 202
Carmel, CA 93923
800-359-4920

Works of Art
Springboard Software
7808 Creekridge Circle
Minneapolis, MN 55435
612-944-3915

Paint Programs

MacPaint
Claris Corporation
440 Clyde Avenue
Mountain View, CA 94043
415-962-8946

SuperPaint 2.0
Silicon Beach Software
9770 Carroll Center Road, Suite J
San Diego, CA 92126
619-695-6956

Draw Programs

Canvas 2.0
Deneba Software
7855 N.W. 12th Street
Miami, FL 33126
800-622-6827

MacDraw
Claris Corporation
440 Clyde Avenue
Mountain View, CA 94043
415-962-8946

Swivel 3D
Paracomp, Inc.
1725 Montgomery Street, Second Floor
San Francisco, CA 94111
415-956-4091

Image-Processing Software

Digital Darkroom
Silicon Beach Software
9770 Carroll Center Road, Suite J
San Diego, CA 92126
619-695-6956

ImageStudio
Letraset USA
40 Eisenhower Drive
Paramus, NJ 07653
201-845-6100

PhotoShop
Adobe Systems, Inc.
PO Box 7900
Mountain View, CA 94039-7900
800-344-8335

Picture Publisher
Astral Development Corporation
Londonderry Square, Suite 112
Londonderry, NH 03053
603-432-6800

ColorStudio
Letraset USA
40 Eisenhower Drive
Paramus, NJ 07653
201-845-6100

Fonts

18+ Fonts
18+ Fonts
337 White Hall Terrace
Bloomingdale, IL 60108
312-980-0887

Adobe Type Library
Adobe Systems, Inc.
PO Box 7900
Mountain View, CA 94039-7900
800-344-8335

**Bitstream fonts and
Fontware Installation Kit**
Bitstream, Inc.
215 First Street
Cambridge, MA 02142
800-522-3668

CG Type
Agfa Compugraphic Division
90 Industrial Way
Wilmington, MA 01887
800-622-8973

**Corel Headline, Corel Loader,
Corel Newfont**
Corel Systems Corporation
1600 Carling Avenue, Suite 190
Ottawa, ON K1Z 8R7 Canada
613-728-8200

Em Dash fonts
Em Dash
PO Box 8256
Northfield, IL 60093
312-441-6699

Fluent Laser Fonts
Casady & Greene, Inc.
26080 Carmel Rancho Boulevard
Suite 202
Carmel, CA 93923
800-359-4920

**Font Factory Fonts
(for LaserJet)**
The Font Factory
13601 Preston Road, Suite 500-W
Dallas, TX 75240
214-239-6085

Font Solution Pack
SoftCraft, Inc.
16 N. Carroll Street, Suite 500
Madison, WI 53073
608-257-3300

FontGen IV Plus
VS Software
PO Box 165920
Little Rock, AR 72216
501-376-2083

**Hewlett-Packard Soft Fonts
(for LaserJet)**
Hewlett-Packard Company
PO Box 60008
Sunnyvale, CA 94088-60008
800-538-8787

Hot Type
Image Club Graphics Inc.
1902 11th Street S.E.
Calgary, AB T2G 3G2 Canada
800-661-9410

**Kingsley/ATF typefaces
(ATF Classic type)**
Type Corporation
2559-2 E. Broadway
Tucson, AZ 85716
800-289-8973

Laser fonts and font utilities
SoftCraft, Inc.
16 N. Carroll Street, Suite 500
Madison, WI 53703
800-351-0500

Laserfonts
Century Software/MacTography
326-D N. Stonestreet Avenue
Rockville, MD 20850
301-424-1357

Monotype fonts
Monotype Typography
53 W. Jackson Boulevard, Suite 504
Chicago, IL 60604
800-666-6897

Ornate Typefaces
Ingrimayne Software
PO Box 404
Rensselaer, IN 47978
219-866-6241

Typographic Ornaments
The Underground Grammarian
PO Box 203
Glassboro, NJ 08028
609-589-6477

URW fonts
The Font Company
12629 N. Tatum Boulevard, Suite 210
Phoenix, AZ 85032
800-442-3668

Varityper fonts
Tegra/Varityper
11 Mt. Pleasant Avenue
East Hanover, NJ 07936
201-884-6277

VS Library of Fonts
VS Software
PO Box 165920
Little Rock, AR 72216
501-376-2083

APPENDIX

Prepress Systems

Aldus PrePrint
Aldus Corporation
411 First Avenue S.
Seattle, WA 98104
206-622-5500

Crosfield
Crosfield Systems, Marketing Division
65 Harristown Road
Glen Rock, NJ 07452
201-447-5800, ext. 5310

Freedom of Press
Custom Applications, Inc.
900 Technology Park Drive, Bldg 8
Billerica, MA 01821
508-667-8585

Lightspeed Color Layout System
Lightspeed
47 Farnsworth Street
Boston, MA 02210
617-338-2173

Printware 720 IQ Laser Imager
Printware, Inc.
1385 Mendota Heights Road
Saint Paul, MN 55120
612-456-1400

SpectreSeps PM
Pre-Press Technologies, Inc.
2441 Impala Drive
Carlsbad, CA 92008
619-931-2695

Visionary
Scitex America Corporation
8 Oak Park Drive
Bedford, MA 01730
617-275-5150

Utilities, Desk Accessories and INITs

Adobe Type Manager
Adobe Systems, Inc.
PO Box 7900
Mountain View, CA 94039-7900
800-344-8335

DiskTools Plus
Electronic Arts
1820 Gateway Drive
San Mateo, CA 94404
800-245-4525

Exposure
Preferred Publishers, Inc.
5100 Poplar Avenue, Suite 706
Memphis, TN 38137
901-683-3383

Font/DA Juggler Plus
Alsoft, Inc.
PO Box 927
Spring, TX 77383-0929
713-353-4090

New Fountain
David Blatner, Parallax Productions
5001 Ravenna Avenue N.E., Suite 13
Seattle, WA 98105

On Cue
Icom Simulations, Inc.
648 S. Wheeling Road
Wheeling, IL 60090
708-520-4440

Overwood 2.0, shareware
Jim Donnelly, College of Education
University of Maryland
College Park, MD 20742

QuicKeys
CE Software
PO Box 65580
W. Des Moines, IA 50265
515-224-1995

Screen-to-PICT, public domain
Educorp
531 Stevens Avenue, Suite B
Solana Beach, CA 92075
800-843-9497

SmartScrap
Solutions International
30 Commerce Street
Williston, VT 05495
802-658-5506

Suitcase II
Fifth Generation Systems
10049 N. Reiger Road
Baton Rouge, LA 70809
800-873-4384

Scanners and Digitizers

Abaton Scan 300/FB and 300/S
Abaton Technology Corporation
48431 Milmont Drive
Fremont, CA 94538
415-683-2226

Apple Scanner
Apple Computer, Inc.
20525 Mariani Avenue
Cupertino, CA 95014
408-996-1010

Dest PC Scan 1000 and 2000 series
Dest Corporation
1201 Cadillac Court
Milpitas, CA 95035
408-946-7100

Howtek ScanMaster II
Howtek
21 Park Avenue
Hudson, NH 03051
603-882-5200

HP ScanJet Plus
Hewlett-Packard Company
700 71st Avenue
Greeley, CO 80634
303-845-4045

JX-300 and JX-450 Color Scanners
Sharp Electronics
Sharp Plaza, Box C Systems
Mahwah, NJ 07430
201-529-8200

MacVision 2.0
Koala Technologies
70 N. Second Street
San Jose, CA 95113
408-438-0946

Microtek Scanners
Microtek Lab, Inc.
16901 S. Western Avenue
Gardena, CA 90247
213-321-2121

ProViz Digitizers
Pixelogic, Inc.
800 W. Cummings Park, Suite 2900
Woburn, MA 01801
617-938-7711

ThunderScan
Thunderware, Inc.
21 Orinda Way
Orinda, CA 94563
415-254-6581

Monitors

Amdek Corporation
3471 N. First Street
San Jose, CA 95134
800-722-6335

Apple Computer, Inc.
20525 Mariani Avenue
Cupertino, CA 95014
408-996-1010

E-Machines, Inc.
9305 S.W. Gemini Drive
Beaverton, OR 97005
503-646-6699

MegaGraphics, Inc.
439 Calle San Pablo
Camarillo, CA 93010
805-484-3799

Mitsubishi Electronics
991 Knox Street
Torrance, CA 90502
213-217-5732

Moniterm Corporation
5740 Green Circle Drive
Minnetonka, MN 55343
612-935-4151

Nutmeg Systems, Inc.
25 South Avenue
New Canaan, CT 06840
800-777-8439

Radius, Inc.
1710 Fortune Drive
San Jose, CA 95131
408-434-1010

RasterOps Corporation
2500 Walsh Avenue
Santa Clara, CA 95051
408-562-4200

SuperMac Technology
485 Portrero Avenue
Sunnyvale, CA 94086
408-245-2202

Color Calibration

The Calibrator
Barco, Inc.
1500 Wilson Way, Suite 250
Smyrna, GA 30082
404-432-2346

PrecisionColor Calibrator
Radius, Inc.
1710 Fortune Drive
San Jose, CA 95131
408-434-1010

TekColor
Visual Systems Group
5770 Ruffin Road
San Diego, CA 92123
619-292-7330

Storage Systems

Jasmine Technology, Inc.
1740 Army Street
San Francisco, CA 94124
415-282-1111

Mass Micro Systems
550 Del Ray Avenue
Sunnyvale, CA 94086
800-522-7979

SuperMac Technology
485 Portrero Avenue
Sunnyvale, CA 94086
408-245-2202

Printers and Imagesetters

4693D Color Image Printer
Tektronix, Inc., Graphics Printing &
Imaging Division
PO Box 500, M/S 50-662
Beaverton, OR 97077
503-627-1497

4CAST
Du Pont Electronic Imaging Systems
300 Bellevue Parkway, Suite 390
Wilmington, DE 19809
800-654-4567

BirmySetter 300 & 400 Imagesetters
Birmy Graphics Corporation
PO Box 42-0591
Miami, FL 33142
305-633-3321

CG 9600/9700-PS Imagesetters
Agfa Compugraphic Corporation
90 Industrial Way
Wilmington, MA 01887
800-622-8973

Chelgraph A3 Imageprinter
Electra Products, Inc.
1 Survey Circle
N. Billerica, MA 01862
508-663-4366

Chelgraph IBX Imagesetter
Electra Products, Inc.
1 Survey Circle
N. Billerica, MA 01862
508-663-4366

ColorQuick
Tektronix, Inc.
Graphics Printing & Imaging Division
PO Box 500, M/S 50-662
Beaverton, OR 97077
503-627-1497

Colorsetter 2000
Optronics, An Intergraph Division
7 Stuart Road
Chelmsford, MA 01824
508-256-4511

Compugraphic Imagesetters
Agfa Compugraphic Corporation
200 Ballardvale Street
Wilmington, MA 01887
508-658-5600

CrystalPrint Publisher laser printer
Qume Corporation
500 Yosemite Drive
Milpitas, CA 95035
800-223-2479

DeskWriter
Hewlett-Packard Company
PO Box 60008
Sunnyvale, CA 94088-60008
800-538-8787

Fujitsu RX7100PS laser printer
Fujitsu America, Inc.
3055 Orchard Drive
San Jose, CA 95134
408-432-1300

GoScript
LaserGo
9235 Trade Place, Suite A
San Diego, CA 92121
619-530-2400

APPENDIX

HP LaserJet Series II
Hewlett-Packard Company
PO Box 60008
Sunnyvale, CA 94088-60008
800-538-8787

HP PaintJet
Hewlett-Packard Company
PO Box 60008
Sunnyvale, CA 94088-60008
800-538-8787

ImageWriter II
Apple Computer, Inc.
20525 Mariani Avenue
Cupertino, CA 95014
408-996-1010

JLaser CR1
Tall Tree Systems
2585 Bayshore Road
Palo Alto, CA 94303
415-493-1980

LaserColor
LaserColor
3875 Nautical Drive
Carlsbad, CA 92008
619-434-7718

Lasersmith PS-415 Laser Printers
Lasersmith, Inc.
430 Martin Avenue
Santa Clara, CA 95050
408-727-7700

LaserWriter II family of printers
Apple Computer, Inc.
20525 Mariani Avenue
Cupertino, CA 95014
408-996-1010

Linotronic imagesetters
Linotype Company
425 Oser Avenue
Hauppauge, NY 11788
516-434-2000

LZR Series Laser Printers
Dataproducts
6200 Canoga Avenue
Woodland Hills, CA 91365
818-887-8000

**Mitsubishi G330-70
color thermal printer**
Mitsubishi Electronics America
Computer Peripherals Products
991 Knox Street
Torrance, CA 90502
213-515-3993

Omnilaser Series 2000
Texas Instruments Inc.
12501 Research
Austin, TX 78769
512-250-7111

**Pacific Page
(PostScript emulation cartridge)**
Golden Eagle Micro, Inc.
8515 Zionsville Road
Indianapolis, IN 46268
317-879-9696

QMS ColorScript printers
QMS, Inc.
1 Magnum Pass
Mobile, AL 36618
800-631-2693

QMS-PS Series Laser Printers
QMS, Inc.
1 Magnum Pass
Mobile, AL 36618
800-631-2693

Series 1000 Imagesetters
Linotype Company
4215 Oser Avenue
Hauppauge, NY 11788
516-434-2014

Tektronix printers
Tektronix, Inc.
PO Box 1000 M/S 63583
Wilsonville, OR 97070-1000
800-835-6100

Turbo PS Series Laser Printer
NewGen Systems Corporation
17580 Newhope Street
Fountain Valley, CA 92708
714-641-2800

UltreSetter
Ultre Corporation
145 Pinelawn Road
Melville, NY 11747
516-753-4800

Varityper printers
Varityper, A Tegra Company
11 Mt. Pleasant Avenue
East Hanover, NJ 07936
201-884-6277

Film Recorders

Agfa-Matrix Film Recorder
Agfa
1 Ramland Road
Orangeburg, NY 10962
914-365-0190

Periodicals

Aldus magazine
Aldus Corporation
411 First Avenue S.
Seattle, WA 98104
206-622-5500

Colophon
Adobe Systems, Inc.
PO Box 7900
Mountain View, CA 94039-7900
800-344-8335

Font & Function
Font & Function
1584 Charleston Road
Mountain View, CA 94039-7900
800-833-6687

MacUser
Ziff-Davis Publishing Company
1 Park Avenue
New York, NY 10016
800-627-2247

Macworld
IDG Communications, Inc.
501 Second Street
San Francisco, CA 94107
800-234-1038

PC magazine
Ziff-Davis Publishing
1 Park Avenue
New York, NY 10016
800-289-0429

Personal Publishing
Hitchcock Publishing Company
191 S. Gary Avenue
Carol Stream, IL 60188
800-727-6937

Publish
PCW Communications, Inc.
501 Second Street
San Francisco, CA 94107
800-222-2990

Step-by-Step Electronic Design
Dynamic Graphics, Inc.
6000 N. Forest Park Drive
Peoria, IL 61614-3592
800-255-8800

U&lc
International Typeface Corporation
2 Hammarskjold Place
New York, NY 10017
212-371-0699

Verbum magazine
Verbum, Inc.
PO Box 15439
San Diego, CA 92115
619-233-9977

Books

Desktop Publishing by Design
(editions for Ventura Publisher and
PageMaker for IBM and Macintosh)
Microsoft Press
16011 N.E. 36th Way, PO Box 97017
Redmond, WA 98073-9717
206-882-8088

Expert Advisor: Adobe Illustrator
Addison-Wesley Publishing
Jacob Way
Reading, MA 01867
215-779-5525

The Gray Book
Ventana Press
PO Box 2468
Chapel Hill, NC 27515
919-942-0220

Inside Xerox Ventura Publisher
Micro Publishing
21150 Hawthorne Boulevard, Suite104
Torrance, CA 90503
213-371-5787

Looking Good in Print
Ventana Press
PO Box 2468
Chapel Hill, NC 27515
919-942-0220

Making Art on the Macintosh II
Scott, Foresman and Company
1900 E. Lake Avenue
Glenview, IL 60025
312-729-3000

PostScript Language Reference Manual
Addison-Wesley Publishing
Jacob Way
Reading, MA 01867
215-779-5525

PostScript Type Sampler
MacTography
326D N. Stonestreet Avenue
Rockville, MD 20850
301-424-1357

Real World PageMaker 4
Bantam Books
666 Fifth Avenue
New York, NY 10103
800-223-6834

Ventura Tips and Tricks, 2nd Edition
Peachpit Press
1085 Keith Avenue
Berkeley, CA 94708
415-527-8555

Bulletin Board Services

Compuserve Information Services, Inc.
5000 Arlington Center Boulevard
Columbus, OH 43260
800-848-8199

**Connect Professional
Information Network**
Connect, Inc.
10161 Bubb Road
Cupertino, CA 95014
408-973-0110

Desktop Express
Dow Jones & Company
Princeton, NJ 08543
609-520-4000

Genie
GE Information Services
401 N. Washington Street
Rockville, MD 20850
800-638-9636

MCI Mail
MCI Mail
1150 17th Street N.W., Suite 800
Washington, DC 20036
800-444-6245

Communication Software

Microphone II
Software Ventures
2907 Claremont Avenue, Suite 220
Berkeley, CA 94705
800-336-6477

Red Ryder
Free Soft
150 Hickory Drive
Beaver Falls, PA 15010
412-846-2700

This book was designed and produced primarily on Macintoshes, although several other kinds of computer systems were used. Text was input primarily in Microsoft Word on a Macintosh IIci and a Mac Plus. Other computers used in design and production of the book included two Mac IIs, a second Macintosh IIci, a IIcx, an SE and a Plus.

Text files supplied by artists were converted, if necessary, to Microsoft Word format on the Mac. Files were checked with Word's Spelling function; the Change (search-and-replace) function was used to find and eliminate extra spaces and to insert *fi* and *fl* ligatures.

Pages were laid out and styled using PageMaker 3.02 Color Extension and PageMaker 4.0. Body text was set in Adobe's Galliard (10/14.5), and captions in Franklin Gothic (8/11). A Zapf Dingbats "z" was used for the "hint" symbol.

Illustrations for the project chapters and gallery were created as described in the text and in most cases were supplied by the artist as application files. Most artwork was saved in TIFF, EPS or PICT format and placed in the PageMaker files. Screen shots to show software interfaces were made on a Mac II using FKeys such as Command-Shift-6 (color screen clip), Command-Shift-7 (screen-to-PICT) or the Camera desk accessory on a Mac Plus.

An Apple Scanner and a Microtek grayscale scanner were used to scan non-electronic artwork, such as printed page design samples, as low-resolution TIFFs and PICTs to indicate position for artwork to be stripped in. Some non-electronic line art was scanned and saved as high-resolution TIFFs to provide final art that could be permanently placed in the electronic pages.

During final layout and production, files were stored on 45 MB removable hard disk drives. Two Apple IINTX laser printers and a Tektronix Phaser color PostScript printer were used for proofing pages. Pages were output by Central Graphics of San Diego on a Linotronic L-300 imagesetter with a RIP 30. Pages with type and line art only were output as negatives at 1270 dpi; pages with screen tints or grayscale images were output as negatives at 2540 dpi. Pages with embedded four-color graphics were separated using SpectreSeps PM and output as negatives at 2540 dpi.

In some cases artwork was provided to the printer as Linotronic negatives or as original laser or Tektronix color prints, or as 35mm transparencies or as final printed pieces (such as magazine pages, stationery items and brochures), which were shot as halftones or color separated and stripped into the page negatives. Most of the Portfolio and Gallery works were handled in this manner by Applied Graphics Technologies of Foster City, California.

The cover (including the spine and back cover) was developed in FreeHand 2.03 on a Macintosh IIcx. Color separations, generated by the program, were output on a Linotronic L-300 imagesetter as negatives at 2540 dpi.

INDEX

INDEX

SUBSCRIBE!

KEEP YOUR EDGE!

"The emergence of good taste... these guys are very serious about doing things right." – John Dvorak, PC Industry Analyst

CHANGE THE WORLD!

"If I were stranded on a desert island, this is the magazine I'd want with me" – Bob Roberts, *MIPS Journal*

"Artists are grabbing the cursor and spawning a distinct design sense, which this classy journal explores." – *Whole Earth Review*

GET RICH!

PUSH THE ENVELOPE!

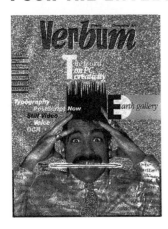

"I love your inspiring use of media...what should we call this? 'Magazine' hardly seems appropriate." – Chuck Pratt, subscriber, University of Texas

MULTI YOUR MEDIA!

THE JOURNAL OF PERSONAL COMPUTER AESTHETICS

Join the inner circle of electronic art, design and multimedia professionals who've counted on *Verbum* since 1986 to deliver the cutting edge: the Verbum Gallery, regular columns, feature stories, new products, ideas, insights — *synergy. Verbum* is both substance *and* style — each issue uses the latest tools and programs to push the limits of desktop publishing.

Verbum Stack 2.0 1990 version of the famous Verbum Stack with usable start-up screens and icons, as well as tons of great bitmap art, sounds, animations and surprises. Shipped on two 800k floppies.

Verbum **Digital Type Poster** Designed by Jack Davis and Susan Merritt, this deluxe 5-color, 17 x 22-inch poster showcases the variety of digital type effects possible on the Macintosh. Produced on a Mac II with Page-Maker 3.0, output on a Linotronic L-300 and printed on a 100 lb. coated sheet. Text explains the history of initial caps in publishing, and how each sample letter was created. A framable "illuminated manuscript" for every electronic design studio! Limited edition of 2000. Shipped in capped tube.

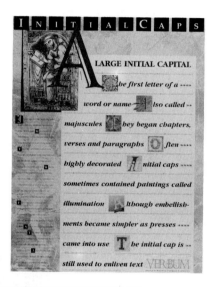